Across the Waves

First published in 2019 by Nick Bailey
Copyright © Nick Bailey 2019
Foreword © Paul Gambaccini 2019

9 8 7 6 5 4 3 2 1

A CIP catalogue record for this book is
available from the British Library.

ISBN 978-1-9999222-1-4

Picture credits Every effort has been made to credit the copyright holders
of the images used in this book. Please advise of any ommissions or errors,
and we will rectify these in subsequent reprints.

p79 (photos only) and p83 Martin Keeley; p126 (third from top) Peter
Forster/Creative Commons; p135 (top) Ogwen/Creative Commons;
p146 (top) Department of Immigration and Multicultural and Indigenous
Affairs, Australia; p178 (top) Moshi Anahory/Creative Commons;
p257 (both pictures) and p267 (top right) PA Images; p283 (top)
Alexey Kalganov and Alina Palto; p295 (centre) Bob Jones

Produced for Nick Bailey by Otherwise
otherwise-publishing.co.uk
Editing and design: Simon Daley
Project co-ordination and production: Angela Young
Proofreader: Siobhán O'Connor
Printed in China

NICK BAILEY

Across the Waves

From Radio Caroline to Classic FM

A

OFFICE OF THE HIGH COMMISSIONER FOR AUSTRALIA

Telephone: TEMple Bar 2435.

Telegraphic Address:
"CROTONATE, LONDON, W.C.2."

PLEASE REPLY TO—
THE CHIEF MIGRATION OFFICER,
AND QUOTE

CHIEF MIGRATION OFFICER,
CANBERRA HOUSE,
10-16 MALTRAVERS STREET,
STRAND,
W.C.2

15th January, 1968

Dear Sir or Madam,

I am now able to let you know that your passages are being arranged as shown below:—

FAIRSTAR From S'HAMPTON To: SYDNEY Date: 18th February, 1968

NAME	AGE	BIRTH DATE	SEX	M/S	SERIAL NO. 777
NOM: 2/6/376 CG.500 NSW.					OCC: Radio Announcer.
777 BAILEY, Nicolas	20	30. 4.47	M	S	52 South Hill Park, Hampstead, London, N.W.3.
					AGENT

It is very important that if for any reason whatsoever you are unable to accept this Booking, you should advise this Office immediately. Please furnish Medical Certificates in the event of illness preventing you from travelling.

Yours faithfully,

[signature]

(W. G. KIDDLE)
CHIEF MIGRATION OFFICER.

Contents

To Pat and Robin, who encouraged me to follow my dreams, and to Sally, Lucy and Edward, in the hope that they will continue to follow theirs

Foreword

One of the highlights of my career was my stint at Classic FM during its early years. It was there that I met Nick Bailey and identified him as a 'lifer' – my favourite kind of broadcaster, one who has dedicated their entire career to radio, from teenager to pensioner. A 'lifer' has to match their abilities to the available opportunities in an ever-changing broadcasting world. In doing so, they might be fortunate enough to be part of history (as Nick was on the pirate ships), to witness history (as Nick did with the British Forces Broadcasting Service) or to make history (as Nick did at Classic FM). 'Lifer' Nick has intrepidly worked his way around the world in places such as Australia, Gibraltar, Germany and Hong Kong, as a newsreader, a disc jockey and a presenter. Informing and entertaining listeners across the globe, he has always been professional, always calm and collected, even with a station in turmoil around him, and his personal life …

Ah yes, the personal life: listeners may never think about it, but the 'lifer' does have an existence off-microphone and it's not always an easy thing to balance. *Across the Waves* tells this side of Nick's story too – the moves, the changes of circumstance and the inevitable ups-and-downs. It chronicles his life, loves, travels and his contributions to the various radio stations he has worked at, with characteristic modesty. What is unmistakeable, though, is Nick's unwavering enthusiasm and dedication.

Paul Gambaccini, London, 2019

14 January 2008

I think I must have been at just about my lowest ebb as I set out for work on that cold, grey Monday evening in early 2008. I was presenting *The Evening Concert* at 9pm, and liked to be at the Classic FM studios in Leicester Square by 6pm, to give myself enough time to write the script before going on-air. It was just a half-hour walk to the studios from where I was staying in Marylebone, and I trudged along, huddled in my coat and lost in gloomy thoughts, totally unaware that life was about to take a turn for the better.

Things at that point were not going well for me. My marriage of twenty-five years had broken up eight years earlier, but I was still desperately missing family life. Because of this, my current relationship wasn't really working: Marcie and I had actually split up two years before and sold our flat in Hampstead, but then had somehow drifted back together. I was now living in a tiny studio flat that belonged to my brother, with most of my possessions in storage, and although I saw my three children regularly the flat was too small for us to have a meal together, let alone to have them stay the night. In an attempt to resolve this I'd just bought a flat, but it was proving to be a headache: it needed far more work than I'd initially thought, and I was going to have to extend the mortgage to cover the costs.

Things weren't much better at work. The growing financial crisis was biting into the radio market, sending the Classic FM share price plummeting, and as a result my afternoon show, *Relaxing Classics at Two*, had been axed. Following government cutbacks I was also about to present my last programme with the British Forces Broadcasting Service. I would often stay after my shift ended at the Classic FM studios and pour out my troubles to the overnight presenter Mark Griffiths, who became one of my greatest confidants.

The routine of work was at least some distraction from my woes: once at the studios, I was soon absorbed in my preparations. *The Evening Concert* was a prestigious show with a healthy audience, and quite demanding to present. My other programmes were mostly ad-libbed, but this had to be carefully scripted around the evening's playlist. Writing the links would often take up most of the time before I went on-air. I frequently wouldn't have a chance to get myself something to eat – I would just grab a cup of tea, go to my office and get to work, keeping my head down until it was time to take my place in the studio and start the broadcast.

Demanding as the programme was to present, one of the advantages of *The Evening Concert* was the lengthier pieces that were played. The longer gaps between links gave me time to sift through any listeners' emails that might have come in, looking for anything relevant that might be incorporated into the show.

14 January 2008

Once I'd opened the programme and introduced the first piece, I swivelled in my chair and logged into the email system on the computer that sat beside the control desk. Among the list of unread mails that evening was one from a Frances Hilton, a name I didn't recognise and assumed was simply another listener, until I'd worked my way down the list and opened the email.

To my surprise the message turned out to be from someone I had once known very well. Frances (Duckenfield, as she was then) had been my first girlfriend. We'd met when I was working at the Athenaeum Theatre in Plymouth when we were both sixteen, but we hadn't seen each other for forty years. Frances was the last person I spoke to in England before emigrating to Australia in February 1968 – she'd actually rather impressed me by managing to reach me by telephone when I was on the ship, to wish me luck. The call hadn't been tearful or heart-rending, but I remembered it as a lovely gesture, and it was the first thought that came to mind as I read her email, which began:

> *Hi Nicholas, whilst listening to you last night I had an overwhelming desire to say hello …*

London, 1949

My earliest memory is confused and impressionistic: of being in a dark, enclosed space, lit by flashing light. I remember a vague feeling of being comforted, but also a persistent clamour of noise and the sensation of travelling at great speed. And then, after just a few minutes, it all suddenly stopped. This was the night I was rushed by ambulance to St Mary's Hospital in Paddington, just around the corner from where we lived in Westbourne Terrace. I was two and a half years old, and I had contracted polio in the most recent epidemic.

I was paralysed in my left arm and right leg, and was in and out of hospital for six months. Compared to others I got off lightly: my right leg recovered completely, but it wasn't until I was five that, after continued physiotherapy, I was able to raise the arm above my head. The muscles had wasted – my left arm and shoulder have remained weak throughout my life and were made far worse when, years later, I broke my left shoulder. Since then I haven't been able to raise my arm beyond waist height. Luckily this has never affected my job, but my children always laugh whenever I need to be searched for security purposes in airports.

Westbourne Terrace

I was born on the 30th of April, 1947 at a nursing home in Kensington. My father, Robin, was an actor, at that time mostly on stage but starting to make a name in films. He'd met my mother, Patricia, in Nottingham in 1939 when they were both in an amateur production of *Night Must Fall* by Emlyn Williams. He was nineteen and my mother was two years younger. She always said the attraction for her was that my father looked like the actor Lesley Howard, who had starred in *Gone with the Wind* that year. My mother was very beautiful, so it's not surprising my father fell for her; they were soon engaged, and married in 1941.

Until I was nine we lived on Westbourne Terrace in Paddington, in a rented maisonette that had central heating, a rarity for the time. I can remember visiting the caretaker and his wife in the basement: in their living room they appeared to have a furnace that had to be continuously fed with coal.

According to my mother, the ground floor of the house was occupied by a White Russian princess who'd managed to escape the Bolshevik revolution – though I never actually encountered her. Our family occupied the three floors above, with me, my mother and father on the first, and the upper two rented out to lodgers, including the actor Harold Lang, who was rather like a second father figure to me. We all shared the kitchen and there was only one bathroom, but somehow we managed.

The first floor had a magnificent balcony: as a four-year-old I remember seeing the funeral procession of George VI pass by on its way to Paddington Station. The following year I witnessed the funeral of Queen Mary travelling the same route. Other than the

Pat and Robin's wedding, 1941

With my mother, aged
about nine months

At home with my father after six
months in hospital, 1949

Aged five

balcony there was no outside space, but we used Hyde Park, only minutes away, as our garden. Westbourne Terrace also had off-street parking and there were relatively few cars around at the time, so it was a great area for me to learn to ride my bike.

One of my most vivid memories is of being taken around London as a five-year-old in complete darkness in the middle of the day. This was the famous Great Smog of December 1952, which engulfed the city for five days.

Pat and Robin

I grew up calling my parents 'Mummy' and 'Daddy' but at a certain age this seemed too sissified. 'Mum' and 'Dad' felt too matey, so from about the age of twelve I called them 'Pat' and 'Robin'. I didn't realise how much this bothered them until years later when I read a letter left by my mother, to be opened after her death. In it she joked about me not calling her 'Mum', but I think she would have loved me to have done so. It hadn't seemed to be an issue for my father until one day, after my mother died, he berated me about it. I called him 'Dad' from then on.

It's only looking back that I realise my parents didn't really spend much time with me as a youngster. I was mostly looked after by the au pair girls my parents employed, and in the holidays I'd go to visit my grandparents. Neither of my parents took me to school on the first day – my father was working and my mother was at RADA, where her fellow students were Joan Collins, Paul Eddington and Gerald Harper. It was left to my mother's brother-in-law to take me instead. Uncle Goosh, who'd escaped from his native Poland during the war, was a lovely man and particularly good with children, though he never had any of his own. He also dropped me off in Lyon when I was eight, where I spent the summer with the family of one of our au pairs. As I didn't know any different, the lack of parental contact seemed perfectly normal and certainly taught me independence.

I was always close to my mother, and I do remember some wonderful holidays with her: two on a horse-drawn canal barge, and one (in 1955, while my father was away working in Australia) in a gypsy caravan. She made me the most extraordinary birthday cakes, including one shaped like a train. She couldn't find the right food colouring for the icing, so she used ink – but I survived.

My relationship with my father was more distant and troubled. When my mother was there it was usually fine, and he could be great fun, particularly at Christmas. It was from him I acquired my love of cricket, and he taught me to play chess when I was six and I was soon beating him. But he could be impatient, and as a result I rather dreaded being alone with him.

This wasn't helped by my acute shyness and the fact that I felt I was a slow learner. It was only many years later, when my second daughter Lucy was diagnosed with dyspraxia (a lack of physical coordination and spatial awareness) that I realised I was the same way. Not that it's held either of us back: Lucy got a good degree and is now a primary school teacher. But my clumsiness and hesitancy were like a red rag to a bull with my father – he couldn't understand why I was unable to grasp certain things, and I would be in tears over my homework.

I remember that often when I wanted to play a game with him he would say he was too busy. To be fair, he was working very hard in those years to establish himself as an actor. The schedules

London, 1949

of theatre work can be very punishing, and he was frequently away for long stretches. In the period we were at Westbourne Terrace, my father seemed to be on the brink of stardom. While his reputation in the theatre was growing, he was offered his first film role in 1946, in *School for Secrets* directed by Peter Ustinov. This led to Ustinov (who was to become a lifelong friend) casting him in a starring role in *Private Angelo* in 1948. That year, my father also won the Clarence Derwent Award for Best Supporting Performance, but it wouldn't be until the mid 1970s that he would really become a household name, following the success of the BBC sitcom *I Didn't Know You Cared*.

Harold and Charles

The living arrangements in our part of the house were quite informal: our lodgers shared the three floors with us, rather like an extended family. I would move about freely, finding a place to play by myself or seeking out adult company as I wished. Outside Harold's room there was a frosted window, and I would sometimes see shadows and hear the voices of people walking up to the flat on the fifth floor. One shadow, longer than the others, was accompanied by a deep female voice, and this terrified me. I named this apparition 'Mrs Speak'.

Despite my fears, I would often gravitate towards Harold's room. He was always happy to talk or play, to make up stories or to read to me. He loved verbal games, getting me to repeat some seemingly nonsensical phrase such as 'pull-ap' quickly enough for the word 'apple' to magically emerge. Once he asked me to prod him with a match, at which point he collapsed on the floor

Across the waves

Some of my father's roles

'Private Angelo', 1948

'My Fair Lady', 1960

'I Didn't Know You Cared', 1975

'Black Snow', 1991

and played dead. I really did think I'd killed him, until after what seemed like an age he suddenly jumped up and startled me. He and I would often play hide-and-seek – one day he managed to climb up on top of a cupboard, watching in amusement from on high as I wandered about below.

Harold was a marvellous man: witty, ebullient, full of mischief and intellectually really ahead of his time. Later, whilst we were in Australia, he became well known for a one-off BBC television film directed by John Schlesinger called *The Class,* in which he was seen teaching the Stanislavsky method of acting to a group of students from RADA. He was probably best known as a director, with a production of *As You Like It* at the Open Air Theatre in Regent's Park and numerous engagements overseas. He died in Cairo in 1970, tragically young at the age of forty-seven, having suffered a heart attack. Theatre critic Kenneth Tynan bemoaned his loss in a glowing obituary in *The Times*, and when I got news of Harold's death some months later, it hit me really hard.

At some point Harold, who was gay, acquired a live-in lover, an actor called Charles Laurence. In the privacy of our home, they were relaxed and open, and I grew up thinking it was quite normal for two men to share a bed. Homosexuality would not be decriminalised, however, for another fifteen years.

Charles had a mischievous sense of humour that appealed to me enormously, and an interesting past. Born Carlos Felipes in Tangier in 1931, he grew up speaking French and Spanish, learning English only when the family moved to the UK when he was seven. Later in life he became a playwright, achieving great success in the West End with *My Fat Friend*, starring Kenneth Williams. Sadly, I never saw the play, but my parents did and they told me the main character had a lot of Harold's characteristics. Charles continued to write plays until 1999, and died in 2013 at the age of eighty-two. Charles's mother, a lady of Swiss-Scottish descent, came to visit sometimes. She more than anyone treated me like an adult; for some reason our conversations always ended with her saying, 'You're very sensible, Nicholas!' I realise now that for this part of my childhood I really did get on better with adults.

French lessons

My penchant for adult company was particularly reflected in the relationships I formed with the various au pair girls employed by my parents, starting with Mimi when I was two. I seemed to fall in love with each one – or perhaps it was something more like hero worship, as it certainly was with Marie-Thérèse who was an expert at mending any broken toys. We had French au pairs because it had been decided that I would be sent to the French Lycée in South Kensington and grow up bilingual. This was very much the done thing at that time, particularly with the artistic fraternity, and so from the age of five most of my lessons were in French, including French history, and I learnt how to read in French before I did so in English.

I was certainly fluent in French by the time I was eight and sent to France for six weeks to stay with a previous au pair, Chantal, whose family had a run-down chateau in the Loire Valley. It was a glorious summer of boating, tennis, and bike riding, and it was there that I learnt to swim. I also developed a taste for *menthe à l'eau*, which I still sometimes drink as a nostalgic reminder of that holiday. This minty, syrupy concoction isn't as popular in France

London, 1949

as it used to be and is mostly consumed by the older generation.

Another adult I became friendly with was their gardener, who seemed incredibly wise to me and taught me all about plants and trees. But my hero quickly became a villain when, one day in his shed, he slit the throat of a rabbit in front of me and hung it on a hook to drain away the blood. It was served for dinner that night, and I couldn't bring myself to eat it.

Another eye-opening experience took place the next morning, when I entered the wrong door and walked in on Chantal's fifteen-year-old sister Piou. She was completely naked and in her panic hid under the bed. I was just as embarrassed and we didn't refer to the incident at breakfast. Several years later Piou followed in her sister's footsteps and became an au pair with us. By this time I was in the throes of puberty and couldn't look at her without imagining her in the nude.

When I was ten I had another French holiday at the charming village of Saint-Marceau, near Le Mans. Here was another run-down chateau, with another au pair, Rosalyn. She introduced me to *café au lait* in a bowl and bars of chocolate on French bread, so much nicer than the *pain au chocolat* you can buy now. I also had my first taste of alcohol: red wine with lots of water.

But my abiding memory from this trip is of the room I was allocated to sleep in. Upon my arrival I was greeted by the patriarch of the house and led up many flights of stairs to the very top of the chateau. A door was swung open to reveal a room with dingy black walls. As I stood hesitantly in the doorway thinking what a depressing colour they had chosen for the decor, I noticed the walls were seething: every inch of them was completely covered with flies. The family hadn't used the chateau since the previous summer, which meant the shutters had all been closed and there had obviously been a breeding frenzy since the family was last in residence. Without a word my host threw open the window and began sweeping at the walls with a broom. He was so laissez-faire and adept that I thought this must be an annual occurrence. As the flies swarmed out it was like watching a miniature murmuration.

Visiting Nanny

I was quite used to travelling without my parents, so I was never homesick on these trips away. From the age of seven I travelled to school by myself, taking the tube from Paddington to South Kensington. It was a different time: a child would automatically give up their seat for an adult, and smoking ruled the roost. Only two compartments were designated non-smoking and, to alienate the non-smokers even more, these were at either end of the train. By the time I got to school my nostrils would be black.

Even before that I was regularly put on the train to Nottingham to stay with my maternal grandmother. For the two-hour journey I would be looked after by the guard, and my grandmother – 'Nanny' – would meet me at the other end.

Nanny was a wonderful lady, and I loved my visits to Harrington Drive. She was a brilliant cook, especially pastry, and a keen gardener. Her strawberries were luscious, and I relished cleaning out the bowl after she'd made a cake. The house had been bought in 1933 when my grandfather was transferred by Barclays Bank from Leicester, where his grandfather had been the station master. I called grandfather 'Poppa' but I was the only grandchild he got

London, 1949

to know: he died when I was seven, just after my brother Simon was born. Poppa was ten years older than my grandmother and they'd met during World War I. He'd actually begun by courting Nanny's sister, before inexplicably switching his attention to her younger sibling. The sisters never spoke to each other again.

Nanny's house was a haven, particularly from my father's verbal bullying. But it did have a downside: while I was in Nottingham I would be expected to visit my paternal grandmother in the nearby town of Hucknall, where she and her late husband had owned what was known as Bailey's Pot Shop. Officially described as a china dealer, my father's father had travelled the region attending auctions and acting as an auctioneer himself.

I never knew him, but I mostly couldn't stand her. Everything I did always seemed to be wrong. Things became bearable only at weekends, when my Auntie Renie, a studio manager at the BBC in Birmingham, would come home, and Granny would redeem herself by making the best rice pudding I've ever tasted. Strangely, the holidays I had with Granny and Renie in Bournemouth for several consecutive years were a joy, with Granny changing personality completely and becoming quite fun to be with.

Childhood pleasures

A big event for the children of Britain took place in February 1953, when sweet rationing finally came to an end. I soon became addicted to fruit pastilles and fruit gums, and devised the ingenious scheme of using the train fare to buy sweets, then going to the ticket counter to say I'd lost my money. This worked brilliantly until I tried it once too often and was recognised.

Across the waves

On holiday in
Bournemouth, aged six

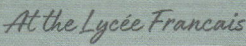
At the Lycée Francais

With Granny and Auntie Renie

Poppa and Nanny circa 1952

Much as I was happy in the company of adults, I was beginning to gather a circle of friends my own age. One was George Kingston, whose father ran a chauffeur business and who lived in a mews around the corner from the Lycée. I spent many a happy afternoon there after school, plied with orange juice and tomato sandwiches by his mother. There was also Yuri, whose father ran a fireworks factory, leading to some very exciting fireworks parties in their back garden. Another friend was Michael Anthony, whose mother became very famous whilst we were in Australia. Her name was Esma Cannon: she played 'Brother' Lil in *The Rag Trade* and appeared in four *Carry On* films.

And then there was Matthew Carrington, who became a conservative MP and was made a life peer in 2013 with the title of Baron Carrington of Fulham. As ten-year-olds, Matthew and I had a ritual every Wednesday afternoon of having baked beans on toast at our local Lyons tea shop and then visiting the Natural History Museum. We weren't playing truant; the Lycée had a very liberal attitude towards sports, and you could choose whether you wanted to take part in the mid-week activities or have free time instead. We took full advantage of this – and of South Kensington's proximity to most of London's museums.

In 1956 we moved from Paddington to Ewell in Surrey, as my father had always wanted a garden. But after six months we were all fed up with the daily commute – my father to the West End, my mother to her job at the National Buildings Record in central London, and I to the Lycée in South Kensington.

We moved to the City, where we lived in a house in Devereux Court around the corner from the Inner Temple. It was a quirky but rather dingy place, with a kitchen that wasn't just the size of a broom cupboard, but actually was *in* the broom cupboard. The soft furnishings had certainly seen better days, and I was fascinated by the plume of dust that shot up every time I sat in the sitting-room armchair. But the house did have two redeeming features: a grandfather clock that required a man to come once a week to wind it up and a four-poster bed in which my parents slept. I had to share a single bed with my brother Simon, but at least by being at the top of the house we got some light.

I think my parents had imagined that living in the City of London would be exciting, but in reality it was lifeless after 5pm and totally dead at weekends. However, I managed to amuse myself: some friends and I discovered a trapdoor in the Inns of Court that led to the most amazing sewer system, a set of tunnels that opened up a wonderful subterranean world reminiscent of *Les Misérables*. We would often play down there and were never found out. But I did come a cropper with my use of water pistols. I loved squirting the bowler-hatted lawyers from my bedroom on the top floor, until the day one of them came to complain.

Chelsea residents

Eventually my parents found the ideal location in Chelsea, just off the King's Road in Oakley Street, which was centrally located and had a garden. We rented the flat from a Mrs Kennedy, who lived on the first floor. I don't remember much about her, except that her son had been killed by a cricket ball. I didn't think about it at the time, but it must have been rather painful for her to have us blithely playing cricket in her garden, which she could see from her bedroom window.

London, 1949

While in Chelsea we reacquainted ourselves with Benjamin and Peggy Creme and their son Julian, with whom I'd been to nursery school just around the corner in Glebe Place. (My only memory of the school is that following our lunchtime nap we were fed dripping sandwiches. This would have been in 1950 – meat rationing didn't end until 1954.)

Benjamin, known to us as Benny, was an artist and also vice president of the Aetherius Society, a 'UFO religion'. At its centre was the 'Master from Mars', with whom Benny was said to be in direct contact. Every time I had a meal at their place, I was required to run my fingers around the rim of any glass or bowl to get rid of evil forces. Benny later asserted that the Second Coming would be in the form of Maitreya, the 'World Teacher', and in 1982 he placed ads around the world saying that Maitreya was already here, working in the Asian community in Brick Lane in London. Benny and I shared the same dentist and, although I lost touch with him and Julian, I was kept informed of his latest prophecies and numerous lecture tours, for which he had a huge following. Benny died in 2016, aged ninety-three, still waiting for Maitreya to emerge.

My Fair Lady

We were in Chelsea when my father was offered the part of Professor Higgins in the Australian debut production of *My Fair Lady*. The musical had been a great success on Broadway, where it had opened in 1956, with Rex Harrison and Julie Andrews in the starring roles. After two years – the longest run on Broadway up to that time – it came with the same cast to Drury Lane, where I remember going to see it. My father auditioned for the part and the fact that he had a passing resemblance to Rex Harrison must have helped. He started taking singing lessons – we would hear him singing the English folk song 'Foggy, Foggy Dew' as part of his practice routine, round the house.

In early December 1958 my father flew to Australia to start rehearsals, with the rest of the family to follow him by ship later in the month. I was excited by the prospect of life Down Under, fuelled no doubt by the exciting stories my father had told me after his visit to Australia in 1955.

He had toured for six months with the Old Vic company, performing Shakespeare with Katharine Hepburn and Robert Helpmann. I remember the day he returned to Westbourne Terrace with a suitcase full of presents, including a boomerang for me. But it was the tales he told that left a lasting impression. He'd visited North Queensland in some of his time off, and he told me about the cane cutters he had seen there. He said that if they were unlucky enough to get bitten by the world's most dangerous snake, the taipan, they would have to resort to cutting off their finger before the venom reached the rest of their body, bringing certain death. Heady stuff to feed a young boy's imagination.

London, 1949

To Australia, 1958

I had my first taste of international travel on the voyage out to Melbourne in 1958. The *Iberia* set sail from London on the 17th of December, and we spent Christmas on the ship. Gibraltar was our first port of call: we anchored only briefly and it was night time, but I remember seeing the silhouette of the Rock.

At the next stop, Port Said, the bumboat men rowed out to the ship to sell their wares. They had a clever system of throwing a rope up to the promenade deck and rigging up a pulley with a basket attached. This was used to transfer the goods to the purchaser, who in return would put their money in the basket. Of course bargaining was all part of the fun.

These were the dying days of empire, but Port Said was still known for its famous department store, Simon Arzt, a kind of Harrods of the East. It was just the place to stock up on mosquito nets, sola topis and tropical suits. My mother knew it from some time she had spent in Egypt just after the war, in a company of actors entertaining the troops. Despite the relatively recent debacle over Suez, the store was still there in all its art deco splendour overlooking the harbour, with staff dressed in white suits and red fez. The building survives to this day, but the customers are long gone – a rather sad monument to what was once a world-famous institution. At night on the ship we were entertained by a 'gully gully man' (a term unique to Egypt, referring to magicians who would visit ships with other traders selling souvenirs). Resplendent in fez, he performed magic tricks with cards, ropes and a final flourish with cups and balls. As an eleven-year-old I was fascinated, spending days trying to mimic the trick in my cabin afterwards.

We passed through the Suez Canal and on to Aden, which at the time was still a British colony. The main district of the city, around the harbour, was in the crater of an ancient volcano and I found it rather bleak – what I imagined the moon to be like – but that didn't matter much to me because I'd heard it was famous for its cheap toys. My mother bought me a precursor to the radio-controlled car, with a control console and a long wire that allowed me to make it go backwards and forwards. This was a bargain, but my mother didn't fare so well with other purchases. She found some jewellery at a knock-down price, but didn't have any change. The Arab trader told her not to worry, as he could easily change a pound (worth £20 now); we never saw him again.

We then traversed the Indian Ocean. I remember stopping in Colombo in what was then Ceylon, and spending the day at Mount Lavinia. Next was Singapore, which I recall as being charming but stiflingly hot, with lots of colonial-style buildings – totally unlike the futuristic city it has now become.

Eventually we reached the continent of Australia. Our first port of call was Fremantle on the western coast. From there we sailed on to Adelaide, and finally, after five weeks on the ship, to our destination, Melbourne.

To Australia, 1958

Melbourne

We arrived in Melbourne in the middle of a heatwave so severe that I found it hard to breathe. This was the first time I'd experienced air conditioning, which was a lifesaver.

I loved Melbourne, though, and my time at South Yarra Grammar School, despite having to go to chapel every morning. I could never remember when to say 'amen', but one morning I was so confident that I shouted it out with gusto at what I thought was the end of a particular prayer. My solitary 'amen' seemed to echo around the chapel for ever. It was almost as if I'd farted.

The school had extensive grounds with its own cricket pitch, and I used the lunch hour to put in some bowling practice. I once even made the school team when a batsman dropped out at the last moment. I received a Norm O'Neill cricket bat for Christmas 1959, which for years I lovingly oiled with linseed. O'Neill was the leading Australian batsman of the time, and I was thrilled when, thirty years later in Hong Kong, I played in a charity match with him and two other heroes of the same era, Alan Davidson and Neil Harvey. The rubber from the handle may have long gone, but my treasured Norm O'Neill bat is still proudly displayed in my umbrella stand.

On my first day at school I was asked whether I was Melbourne or Collingwood. I didn't have a clue what they were talking about – it turned out they were referring to Aussie Rules football, which as I discovered is almost a religion in Victoria. Melbourne and Collingwood were then the two top teams, rather like Scotland's Rangers and Celtic. I became a fanatical follower myself, but decided to be different and support Essendon instead.

Across the waves

My best friend was Ernie Poke, whose father ran the public baths in the nearby suburb of Richmond. We had many an out-of-hours swim, and once held a birthday party there.

Our rented house was in Toorak, a very attractive village type of place, close to the city and convenient for my school, where I thrived academically. I hadn't done well at the Lycée and had repeated twice, but now that everything was in English I found lessons so easy that I was pushed up a class and ended up being one of the youngest in my form.

Melbourne was, and still is, seen as the cultural capital of Australia, and that's why *My Fair Lady* went there for its initial eighteen-month run. The show opened to great reviews, and my father was the toast of the town. Even my mother was asked to make guest appearances on television panel shows.

Whereas my father had people keen to know him because of his fame, my mother had the uncanny knack of seeking out some very interesting characters who weren't connected with show business. One such person was Irene Newton-John, a divorcee living in a small flat nearby with her youngest daughter, Olivia, who was a year younger than me. We saw each other quite often and sometimes I'd stay overnight at their flat, sleeping in the same room as Olivia. She had a knack for memorising the lyrics of current pop songs, in particular 'Beep Beep' by the Playmates, a popular novelty song of the time. When I remarked on her ability, she replied that it was something that came naturally and that she enjoyed singing. After leaving Melbourne I didn't see Olivia again until she came to England with her mother in 1966, after winning a singing contest of which the first prize was a trip to the UK. They rented an apartment in Hampstead, and I invited her to a

To Australia, 1958

party in my flat which must have been successful because she was still there the next morning, along with quite a few others nursing hangovers. The next time I came across her was on the radio in Australia in 1971, when she had her first big hit 'If Not for You'. I've often told my children – in particular Lucy, my middle daughter, who was a fan of *Grease* – that I once slept in the same room as Olivia Newton-John.

Sydney

Upon arrival in Australia, my father had been given a Rover car and an unlimited supply of Rembrandt cigarettes, free of charge, as some kind of publicity deal. It was in the Rover that we drove in May 1960 from Melbourne to Sydney, where *My Fair Lady* would continue its run. The drive didn't go too well: the fuel tank sprang a leak and had to be patched with chewing gum.

When we first arrived in Sydney from Melbourne we set up home in Point Piper, a very posh part of the city. Though the area lacked character, we did have access to a private beach. I went to the local state school, Vaucluse High, and for the first time in my life it was all boys. Although the classes had more than forty pupils I did well, particularly in history, where I came top in my year after submitting a project on ancient Greece. But it felt rather unnatural without girls around, so I was glad when we moved in early 1961 to the atmospheric and historic suburb of Hunters Hill, where I went to the local co-ed. It was at this school that I was caned, for the first and only time. My crime was that I had been singing out of tune; the teacher thought I was doing it deliberately, but the sad truth is I really can't sing at all.

Across the waves

Misplaced as that punishment was, I was clearly going through a slightly rebellious phase. I started smoking, and it was during this period that I decided to become vegetarian. I said it was because I hated the idea of eating something that had been killed, but really it was more of an aversion to the standard meat-and-two-veg type of meal. Meat itself wasn't the issue at all – if I could have just eaten bacon sandwiches, sausages and hamburgers I'd have been quite happy.

My dislike was such that whenever my mother's back was turned I would scrape my entire plateful into the bin. I remember a doctor, a guest at one of my parents' dinner parties, warning me my bones wouldn't grow. He didn't manage to change my mind, and I stuck to my guns for about a year. But on a school skiing trip I thought it would be a bit wet to make a fuss and say I needed a special diet, so I accepted whatever I was given, and haven't looked back since.

Now aged fourteen, I'd developed a full-blown Aussie accent and was loving every minute of my sun-drenched childhood. At the weekends I'd hitch-hike with my school friend Allan Broadhead to the nearest surf beach. Following an invigorating swim riding the waves we'd refresh ourselves with a malt milkshake, which was always served in a large metal container. We smoked Alpine cigarettes with the strapline 'cool as a mountain stream'. At this time, whenever cancer was mentioned in relation to tobacco, people were accused of scaremongering, but a boy in my class said that every cigarette you smoked would take five minutes off your life. My maths was never that good, but even I could work out that my fourteen years could be very quickly reduced to zero. Nevertheless, I continued to smoke.

To Australia, 1958

Island mentality

Although I had been doing well at school since coming to Australia, my mother worried that I wasn't reading enough. To encourage me, she borrowed James Norman Hall and Charles Nordhoff's books about the mutiny on the *Bounty* from the local library. The trilogy begins with the mutiny itself, then follows Bligh's epic open-boat voyage, and finishes with the story of Pitcairn Island, where the mutineers ended up.

I was instantly hooked and couldn't read the books quickly enough. The stories sparked an appetite for adventure and a fascination with islands, Pitcairn in particular, that remain with me today. For my seventieth birthday I achieved a lifetime ambition of landing on the island and meeting some of the mutineers' descendants. I took my original copies to read on the voyage and realised they'd never been returned to the library in Sydney – they were overdue by about fifty-five years.

Since starting his run in *My Fair Lady* almost two years earlier my father hadn't taken any time off, so it was decided we would take our first-ever holiday as a complete family.

We went by flying boat to Lord Howe Island, almost 400 miles east of Sydney. The population of the island was about 360, and the philosophy then (and it remains so to this day) was to have only 400 guests at any one time. There are no high rises and no hotels, just attractive lodges; and there are no snakes, no dangerous spiders, and even the sharks stay away from the reef. Lord Howe is only 6 miles long and 2 miles wide, and in parts is so narrow that you can see right across the island. As there were no cars we all had bikes, including my brother Simon, who by

With my father and Simon in Melbourne, 1959

Lord Howe Island, 1961

this time was six. We'd spend our time at the surf beach on one side of the island or over at the lagoon on the other. The lagoon leads out to the planet's southernmost coral reef, where I had my first experience of snorkelling. The underwater world was just breathtaking, although I was scared when I came across a giant stingray. I swam quickly back to the boat, only to be told stingrays were nothing to worry about. We'd booked for only a week, but we enjoyed it so much we ended up staying another seven days.

Having just read the *Bounty* books, I was thrilled when one day we met Mrs Christian, a lady visiting from Norfolk Island almost 600 miles away, whose husband was a direct descendant of Fletcher Christian, the ringleader of the mutiny (in 1856, many of the mutineers' descendants were relocated to Norfolk Island).

Our final act was to bury some treasure – some money in a tin box – vowing to come back and retrieve it in years to come. At the time of writing this is still to be done, but my mother did make a wonderful model of the island out of plasticine, which we kept in the family for years.

Social blossoming

Back in Sydney we settled down to life in Hunters Hill, which had a wonderful village atmosphere. I was able to walk to school, where I had an eclectic mix of friends, including my best friend Allan and a bubbly girl called Sue Howard whom I took a shine to. It appeared to be a classless society, and I revelled in it. I had a great time, with parties and scavenger hunts and after-school dips on the Lane Cove River at Mooney's Mud Hole, so-called because of Mr Mooney's kiosk, which sold sherbets.

Across the waves

Hunters Hill was where I had my first job, washing cars in the local neighbourhood. I went into business with Paul, the local vicar's son, and although I don't think either of us was any good the local housewives seemed to take pity on us. Soon I had enough money to buy Buddy Holly's *Greatest Hits* and the latest fashion at the time, a car coat, which I loved so much that I continued to wear it into my late twenties.

Because of my shyness on first arrival in Australia, I'd thrown myself into schoolwork, but now this suffered accordingly. For the first time in my life I blossomed socially, thanks in no small part to having girls in the class. I'd been at a co-ed school in Melbourne when we first arrived in Australia, but had been too shy to take full advantage. I did fall in love, though, with a girl in my class called Kristina Froiland – but it was totally unrequited. Falling in love from afar was becoming a habit.

It happened with another girl, Jane Hamilton, this time in Sydney. Ballroom dancing was part of the school curriculum, and my heart skipped a few beats every time it was my turn to dance with her, but that's the closest I got.

As for sex, I'll always blame my brother Simon for thwarting my first encounter. I'd just turned thirteen and we were spending the day with some friends of my parents who had a daughter the same age. After lunch all the adults went out, leaving the three of us alone. The girl was quite precocious and suggested we play Strip Jack Naked. The only problem was that Simon was with us. I tried my utmost to persuade him to go and play by himself in another room, but to no avail. So the opportunity passed, but not before my love interest had declared, 'There's no point in taking your socks off because it doesn't show anything!'

To Australia, 1958

It was left to Vicky, a voluptuous blonde, to give me my first kiss during a session of spin-the-bottle on a school skiing trip the following year. You might find it odd to hear that Australia, land of beaches and drought-stricken outback, actually experiences more snow than Switzerland. Australia's ski culture is all centred on the Snowy Mountains in New South Wales and Victoria.

Us boys didn't stand a chance of having a real relationship with the girls in our year, the Second: they were all going out with older boys in Fifth and Sixth. And if they weren't, that's what they wanted. The girls in any case were much more advanced and spent the journey to and from the ski resort boasting about their 'Richter scale of sex'. I can't remember anyone scoring a ten, but there were certainly a few sevens and even a seven and a half. If number one was holding hands, and two a peck on the cheek, then by my reckoning Vicky had got me to number three.

A family secret

In the midst of this blissfully happy time came the discovery that my father had been bipolar since his early twenties, but until now he and my mother had kept it from us. In his manic phases (it was still called 'manic depression' then), my father would go off with other women and spend money recklessly. For example, he had enough shoes to make Imelda Marcos jealous, but I'd always put this down to his star status. The final straw for my mother was when my father returned from the chemist's having bought their entire stock of sunglasses. She broke down and told me the whole story, explaining that although my father was the highest paid actor in Australia we were absolutely broke.

Across the waves

'French Night' with Pat,
Hunters Hill, 1961

With best friend Allan,
Hunters Hill, 1962

Hunters Hill High School, 1961 (top row, second from left)

My father's battle with depression stretched back to his time in the war. He'd been a driver with the 211th Field Ambulance, Royal Army Medical Corps. He was invalided out in 1944, after gaining the rank of lieutenant, because of his first manic episode. There was a history of depression in my father's family: he was only six when his father, my grandfather, hung himself, and his uncle had also committed suicide. Something that may have contributed to the strain on him was my mother's infidelities: my parents weren't allowed to live together until my father left the army, and that same year she'd had a lesbian affair with a girl called Fran (as well as, according to family folklore, one with an American airman). My father was transferred to a psychiatric hospital near Birmingham, but only a month later was acting on stage at the city's Alexandra Theatre. My parents separated soon after – Robin remained at the Alexandra until the end of the war, while Pat toured with Donald Wolfit's Shakespeare company in England and Scotland in 1944, and in Egypt for a spell the following year. In September of 1945 she returned to Cairo with ENSA, a company of actors sent to entertain the troops overseas (the initials stood for Entertainments National Service Association, but it was better known as 'Every Night Something Awful'.) My mother came back to the UK in June 1946 and went to join my father in weekly rep in Worthing. By that time, they'd patched things up. Robin suffered periodic bouts of mania over the years, but my parents had until now always managed to keep them a secret. But my mother was now at her wit's end: very little was known about manic depression then, and doctors could easily be bamboozled into thinking their patient was quite well. This left my mother feeling betrayed and unsupported.

Across the waves

Everything came to a head when my father collapsed during a performance of *My Fair Lady*, which had finished a successful run in Sydney and moved to Brisbane. When he came round, he seemed to have lost a lot of his memory and had forgotten that he and my mother had told me they were getting a divorce. He'd been having an affair with an actress he'd known for years, but following this episode that relationship fizzled out and divorce proceedings were halted. In a letter to Granny and Renie in December 1961, my mother wrote that my father was recovering from the 'effects of sedation and shock treatment and now he is much better except for the fact that he cannot remember anything that has been happening for about the last four months'. Despite numerous affairs between them, my mother and father remained married for fifty-two years.

Parties

Until my mother explained my father's condition to me I'd never suspected anything, but had certainly revelled in the glamour of his extravagance, particularly when he threw parties. In 1959 he'd invited the entire England cricket team to our house in Melbourne. As an avid cricket fan myself it was a thrill to meet the likes of Freddie Trueman, Godfrey Evans and Brian Johnston.

My father loved to tell the story of the night Maurice Chevalier came for dinner. Brandy glasses had been bought specially for the occasion, along with some very expensive cognac. My mother served a delicious meal and the time finally came for coffee and the chance to show off the new glasses – only for Chevalier to announce he didn't drink brandy.

To Australia, 1958

Back in Hunters Hill at another party I met Vivien Leigh and her partner John Merivale, who were on a tour of Australia. I remember her as being quite imperious but at forty-eight she certainly still had her looks – although I would describe her more as handsome than pretty. I'm sure it wasn't lost on my father that she was one of the most famous manic depressives.

Falling for radio

As an escape from the worries of those times, at night in my room I would listen to the radio in the dark. Initially I listened solely for the music; mostly American pop, but Cliff Richard and the Shadows were also making steady inroads into the Australian charts. Soon, though, I was more interested in the presentation, in particular the gravelly-voiced John Laws on 2UE (now in his eighties, but still on air). He'd recently introduced the use of an echo chamber to make his voice sound even deeper than it naturally was. I was lulled into an imaginary world where one person could hold court for three hours and play their favourite music at the same time. It seemed to me to be a job made in heaven, and I wanted to be part of it.

I think much of my attraction was to do with the fact that I had always been so painfully shy. I remember being so nervous at my first school in Sydney that, when I was asked to appear at assembly along with other non-Australian pupils, I could barely speak, and all I was supposed to say was my name and where I was from. Even my school reports from the French Lycée had always said, '*Il est trop timide.*' I had never wanted to follow my father onto the stage, but somehow radio didn't hold the same fear. It was almost as if you could hide behind the microphone – throughout my radio career I've noticed how many introverts are attracted to the industry.

Full of enthusiasm for my new 'career', I set about creating my own radio station in my parents' living room, called Radio XYZ, following the Australian tradition of using letters as a call sign. I used my father's tape recorder to make programmes which included comedy clips from the George Martin–produced album *Songs for Swingin' Sellers*. Great fun, but I never expected for a moment it could become reality.

Back to Blighty

My father's collapse on stage in Brisbane brought an end to his run in *My Fair Lady*, which meant we would all be returning to England rather sooner than expected. By this time I'd become so Australian that I dreaded the prospect. England was a distant memory, and not a very good one at that: I remembered crying at school in London because it had been so cold.

My mother, too, would have been happy to stay in Australia permanently. She had suffered with bronchial problems since childhood, and it was only in dry heat that she felt truly well. But she was always supportive of my father's career, and he felt he'd been in Australia too long and it would take some time to resurrect his acting career in the UK. He would indeed take a little time to find his feet again, but manic depression never really affected his acting, apart from at the very end of his life. For more than two decades he performed regular leading roles at the National Theatre, garnering three Olivier award nominations.

To Australia, 1958

In April 1962, just before my fifteenth birthday, we began our journey home by sea, but not before all my friends came aboard to my cabin to say goodbye. For the first time I gave Sue Howard a proper kiss, and wished I'd been brave enough to act on my attractions a little sooner: this poignant moment finally brought us together, and we snogged in one of the bunks while my friends chatted away. When my mother came to the cabin I think she could tell we'd all been smoking, but she defused the situation by simply saying, 'What a fug!' I had made so many friends and was dreading what England was going to be like, but the journey ahead promised to be exciting.

England, 1962

We travelled back to England first class, on board P&O's *Orsova*. Although this was before the days of regular cruising, we followed a circuitous route to the UK, via New Zealand and the Panama Canal. It was exciting that our six-week return journey would not simply take us back along the route we had followed on the *Iberia* four years before, but would go in the opposite direction instead, meaning that by the time we reached England we'd have completed a full circumnavigation of the globe.

The journey back

After the first stop in New Zealand we went on to Fiji and then Honolulu, where I saw colour television for the first time. Next was Vancouver, where it rained non-stop. At the end of the nineteenth century a great-aunt had emigrated to Canada, and we now had relatives scattered across the country, many concentrated in Regina (home of the Royal Canadian Mounted Police). Some had moved further west, including to Vancouver, and we spent our day ashore with a group of distant cousins. Apart from the weather, what I remember most was my younger brother Simon having an almighty tantrum. The lady of the house was very forgiving and said, 'Never mind, that's what happens to five-year-olds.' He was eight at the time.

I also have a vivid musical memory from the Vancouver visit. Upon our arrival in the harbour, a military band came aboard and played Gershwin's 'The Man I Love' with a trumpet solo, which I found profoundly moving. The trip opened my ears to all kinds of music – from the frenetic trumpets of Mexican mariachi to the exotic steel drums we heard on arrival in Jamaica – and I've had a liking for so-called 'world music' ever since.

We docked in San Francisco for three days, staying with friends who showed us the sights, including the giant Californian redwoods. I loved the city and found Americans so friendly and welcoming. I celebrated my fifteenth birthday there in style, in a revolving restaurant overlooking the bay. The weather was lovely, too, in stark contrast to Vancouver.

The next port of call was Los Angeles, which held no charm for me: I even found Disneyland rather boring. On the other hand, Acapulco in Mexico was very exciting with its cliff divers, made famous by the Elvis Presley film *Fun in Acapulco,* which came out the following year. I realised the risks of diving off precipices over 100 feet high into water that at times was only 6 feet deep when I saw some poor wretch being dragged out of the waves. It was the first time I'd seen a dead body. At night we went to a restaurant where some of the customers were carrying guns in holsters – it was what I imagined the American Wild West to have been like.

We then sailed to Panama City, where I noticed that, although most of the population lived in very basic conditions in huts in shanty towns, they all seemed to have a television. We transited the Panama Canal and sailed on to Kingston in Jamaica. But the highlight of the trip for me was Haiti, which at that time still had the ruthless Papa Doc as dictator. We hired a taxi for a tour around the capital, Port-au-Prince, and stopped to see a cockfight, which was incredibly cruel but very exciting to my teenage eyes, with hundreds of dollars being staked on the outcome. The opulence of the royal palace contrasted starkly with the poverty in the streets. In Haiti I learnt how to bargain in the market: I still have the two masks I bought more than fifty years ago.

What I remember most of all was a voodoo ceremony that took place on board ship. The 'performance' involved a live chicken, climaxing with the chicken's head being pulled off and its blood being drunk. The passengers didn't know whether to clap or run. In the end there was just stunned silence. Suffice to say it was the first and last time P&O visited Port-au-Prince.

After that Bermuda was an anticlimax, although I remember it fondly as being very genteel and British, but with a pleasant climate. Our journey back was coming to an end and I was dreading returning to what had become an unknown country.

Fish out of water

When we arrived back in the UK my parents rented a flat in Chartfield Avene in Putney in South London, and I attended the local comprehensive school, Elliott, where in a lower class was a future James Bond, Pierce Brosnan.

I hated my time there partly because I felt like a fish out of water, not helped by my strong Australian accent. On my first day the form teacher said to me, 'Close the door, lad, you're not

England, 1962

in the outback now – and bring your boomerang with you!' I befriended the one black boy in the class and, although we weren't bullied, we both felt we were very much outsiders. I also didn't do well academically. I might have blamed my parents – this was my fifth school after all – but in truth it was more to do with laziness. I didn't revise for my O-levels at all and managed to pass only two subjects, English Language and French.

In despair, my mother took me out of school and enrolled me in the local secretarial college, where I was one of two boys in a class of twenty girls. I learnt to touch-type listening to Leroy Anderson's *The Typewriter*, a skill that has been so useful throughout my career.

Music for pleasure

Although I was interested in pop music, it was classical that always gave me the most pleasure. I joined the local library and instead of books I would take out classical LPs, listening to Mendelssohn's Violin Concerto over and over again as well as both the Schumann and Ravel piano concertos. Neither of my parents was particularly musical, but they did have a handful of Music for Pleasure albums which I listened to avidly; we also had an Austrian au pair who introduced me to Smetana's *Má Vlast*. Mind you, she could have introduced me to anything: I was more than a little in love with her.

When I started at Classic FM the girl I had sat next to in typing class got in touch. She was working in the music business herself and said she remembered me saying that I wanted to get to know all the composers from A to Z.

Across the waves

Arrival at Waterloo Station, June 1962

Our garden

*Chartfield Avenue, Putney, 1964,
with new arrival Justin*

Plymouth

I took more O-levels at the secretarial college, but when I failed these as well my parents decided enough was enough. My father found me a job with the Margate Stage Company, which had a residency at the Athenaeum Theatre in Plymouth. It was run by Sally and her husband, Gerald. He had previously headed the publicity department at London's Mermaid Theatre, which had been founded by Sally's father, the well-known actor Bernard Miles, who shared an agent with my father. Although I had an interview with Bernard, it was a foregone conclusion, and I duly arrived in Plymouth a month before my seventeenth birthday.

I loved working for the theatre company. I had the grand title of 'Assistant to the Directors', but in reality I was the general gofer. Playing to my two strengths – I could type and I seemed to have the knack of being able to get something for nothing – I became the prop man and I even managed to get free servicing for the company bus. I was also front-of-house manager, complete with a battery-powered flashing bow tie.

I shared a house in Plymstock with Graham d'Albert, an actor, and Mick Hughes, who was the theatre electrician. He was a colourful character with a view on most things – including a hatred of curtains, which he declared were 'bourgeois'. He also slept with half the female members of the company – or so he said. I also became very friendly with the assistant stage manager David Dundas, who was a real-life lord and whose father was the Marquess of Zetland. He had the looks and charm of Hugh Grant and, even though he'd had no formal training, he was a very talented musician. He was with us before going off to the Central

School of Speech and Drama, where in his final year he was talent-spotted and landed a big part in the film *Prudence and the Pill* which starred David Niven and Deborah Kerr. But his dilettantish approach to acting led him eventually to give it up and turn to music, and he became very successful writing jingles. He composed the inaugural jingle for Channel 4 and for a while was a pop star following the release of 'Jeans On', which he'd written originally as a commercial. I had one rather *Downton Abbey* moment when I tried to ring David at the family seat of Aske Hall, in Yorkshire. The butler answered and said, 'I'm afraid Lord David is not in residence at the moment.'

Theatre policy was that everyone should earn the same – £10 a week, although somehow as the most junior member of the team I was only on £8. But this proved to be plenty – I even had money left over at the end of the week. With memories of Australia still fresh in my mind, it was lovely to be near the sea again and, although it must have rained at times, my recollection of that summer in 1964 was that the sun shone constantly.

My rose-tinted memories might have something to do with my infatuation with an usherette called Frances who was still at school and studying for her O-levels. With my fear of the stage I was very impressed that she had many amateur productions under her belt, including playing the part of Viola in *Twelfth Night* when she was thirteen, which had received a rave review from the local drama critic. It was she who introduced me to Cornwall, as there was a little ferry that travelled from Plymouth to Cawsand, a tiny fishing village with a pleasant beach, where we would go swimming. I think I must have come across as far too keen and after a few months Frances began to lose interest.

England, 1962

Although I was hurt, I tried to be philosophical and was soon going out with a waitress I'd met at a waterfront café on the Hoe. I'd actually had my eye on her for ages, and when I eventually plucked up the courage to ask her out I was shocked to find she was four years older than me. This new relationship came to an end when she went to teacher training college in Reading.

Northern exposure

In order to secure funding from the Arts Council, the Margate Stage Company had agreed to undertake a tour of northeast England in October 1964. This was my first experience of the North and I loved it – everyone was so friendly. As someone said to me at the time, 'If you approach another man in the pub in the South they think you're a poof, whereas in the North it's taken for granted that you'll chat to the person next to you.' I also caught up with Lord David Dundas, whose family seat in Richmond was close to Darlington.

I got used to having high tea at five o'clock, followed by supper (a pie) at about nine. The eldest son of the family I lodged with in Middlesbrough was a member of a rock band called the Denmen, and I acted as an unofficial roadie when they went out on gigs. There was one in Redcar where they supported Long John Baldry and a group called Steam Packet whose lead singer was an unknown named Rod Stewart. The sister of one of the Denmen was a gorgeous blonde with a great sense of humour. We were really getting on when Rod came over and attempted to muscle in. She clearly wasn't impressed, but thanks to Rod's interruption neither of us got anywhere.

Across the waves

Aged seventeen, with David Dundas outside the Athenaeum Theatre, 1964

Frances, aged sixteen, at the house in Plymstock, summer 1964

With Lyn Hardy-Smith London, 1965

The Mermaid

At the end of 1964 the finances of the Margate Stage Company were in such a parlous state that it was decided to wind up the company. Gerald returned to the Mermaid Theatre in London to run the publicity department, and I went with him to become his assistant. There I fell for another usherette, this time one named Liz, whose father was the chairman of the Ilford Photo company. They lived in a Georgian house close to where Tony Blair now lives in Connaught Square. The Mermaid Theatre was a kind of repository for the sons and daughters of either rich parents or people already in the theatre. Liz's connection was that her brother-in-law was the theatre manager. Another girl, Sandra, was the daughter of the Academy Award–winning film composer John Addison. One of the assistant stage managers was an aspiring actress called Georgina Simpson, heiress to Simpsons in Piccadilly. It was through her work in the theatre that she met her husband, the actor Anthony Andrews.

During my time at the Mermaid I met Lyn Hardy-Smith, a very good-looking playboy type who worked in the bar. He was about four years older than me, could also speak fluent French as well as German, and could drive. We shared a similar sense of humour, and I rather hero-worshipped him as he certainly had a way with the ladies. He was the boyfriend of Jan, one of the usherettes at the Mermaid, whose parents had a B&B in St Ives. Over the Easter of 1965, just before my eighteenth birthday, Lyn, Jan, Liz and I piled into an old post-office van that Lyn had bought and drove down to Cornwall. It was during that weekend that I lost my virginity to Liz.

Across the waves

Liz and I would spend weekends together at her parent's place in Connaught Square while they were away at their second home in Oxford. We even slept in her parents' bed and I don't know how we got away with it. One weekend I left my washbag behind, which raised suspicions, but Liz somehow managed to bluff her way out of it.

We had some trips away, including a holiday in Ilfracombe where we'd booked in as Mr and Mrs Bailey. A lot of places then wouldn't allow unmarried couples to share a room, and our cover was blown when a letter arrived with Liz's maiden name; she'd told her parents she was on holiday with a friend. Our relationship lasted for almost a year, but what broke us up was my increasingly roving eye, spurred on by a growing confidence with the opposite sex. But Liz and I remained very good friends and kept in touch until she got married some years later. There was no shortage of girls at the Mermaid, as the Guildhall School of Music and Drama was close by and many of the female students were employed as waitresses or to serve behind the bar. There were three Guildhall girls in particular, Elaine, Patsy and Sheila, who shared a flat in Tulse Hill, and they became very much part of my social circle.

A reunion

Although the Margate Stage Company was no longer performing in Plymouth, I still had to go down there from time to time to deal with props in storage and other business. One night at the Marquee Club in London I happened to bump into a girl I'd known vaguely whilst working at the Athenaeum. She was a student, but worked part-time at a restaurant on the Barbican in

England, 1962

Plymouth called the Green Lanterns. We went out in London several times, and I promised I would look her up at the restaurant next time I was down in Plymouth. This I did, but the girl hadn't started her shift when I arrived, and as I turned to leave someone suddenly called, 'Nicholas!' It was Frances, the girl I'd fallen for eighteen months earlier. As we chatted, the girl I'd originally come to see walked in. Without knowing Frances's circumstances I had to make a split-second decision, but I thought I could feel a mutual attraction and Frances had been the girl of my dreams after all, so of course I chose her. She was there on a tea break from rehearsals with her drama group and had to get back, but I managed to steal a kiss before we said goodbye. And so we began an open-ended relationship (it was the Swinging Sixties, after all) that would continue until I emigrated to Australia two years later.

Mermaid or pirate?

At the Mermaid, part of my job was to field press enquiries, and my trickiest assignment was when I was asked by a student magazine to arrange an interview with Sir Donald Wolfit, who was appearing as Long John Silver in a production of *Treasure Island*. By reputation Wolfit was a terrifying character, so I tentatively knocked on his dressing-room door and was shouted at for daring to mention this 'student rag'. They never did get their interview. Years later, when I saw both the play and film of *The Dresser* by Ronald Harwood, 'Sir' came across exactly as I remember Wolfit, and also confirmed the stories my mother had told me about him from her time playing Ophelia to his Hamlet when she was touring with Wolfit's company in Egypt. Despite this failure I was awarded a bursary, sponsored by the Leverhulme Trust, to study theatre management. I should have been excited – before me the bursaries had only ever gone to Oxbridge graduates – but, although I was enjoying the social scene, I didn't think the work was playing to my strengths. To be honest, though, I wasn't really sure what I wanted to do.

In June 1966 Lyn had left the Mermaid and was managing a club in Nice, which played the hits of the day for couples to dance to. He made periodic journeys back to the UK to stock up on the latest new releases, and on one of these trips it was agreed I'd take my two weeks of annual leave and go back with him and stay at his place in Nice.

I fell in love with the place – the weather, language, food, sun and sea. I also revelled in the café life as opposed to the pub culture of the UK (I've never been a great drinker). Such was the glamour of the Swinging Sixties that just being English was an attraction to the opposite sex. Buying some groceries one day, we were overheard talking by two French girls, who shouted, '*Les Anglais!*' The next thing we knew, we were being driven around in their 2CV. Lyn's work kept him busy at night, but by day he would chat up girls on the beach. He met three students studying English at Nice University, and as it turned out one of them was looking for someone to read to her in English and so Lyn suggested me. Her name was Caroline, and it was love at first sight. She had been born in Algeria where her father had been head of customs in Oran. The family was caught up in the Algerian war and Caroline saw her uncle shot dead in front of her. That was the final straw and the family had retreated to Nice.

England, 1962

By her own admission she modelled herself on Brigitte Bardot, and there was certainly a strong resemblance. Caroline introduced me to her university friends, and I met a few English people who were so in love with France that they were willing to work at anything, no matter how menial, just to be able to stay there. I began to picture myself living that sort of bohemian life, picking grapes with Caroline, and when I returned to the Mermaid at the end of my leave my heart just wasn't in it any more.

Within a short space of time I resigned, but I quickly realised this was rather a stupid move as I had no money and no other job to go to. But then Sally Miles phoned to ask whether I could come back temporarily to sort out the press tickets for the next production, as Gerald had taken rather ill. This would allow me to return without losing face, so I went back to the Mermaid as a strictly temporary measure. During this time, Caroline made the first of several visits to England to work as a French teaching assistant, which enabled us to meet up and express our unspoken feelings for each other.

I befriended Bob Larkins, a Tasmanian actor working in the Mermaid box office. Like me, Bob was searching for something more challenging, and in the summer of 1966 he landed a job as a newsreader on Radio Caroline, the original 'pirate' radio ship. I'd inherited my father's strong, deep voice, which had led to me being asked to pre-record the interval announcements at the Mermaid. Maybe it was this that prompted Bob to suggest I apply for a job on Radio Caroline. Having had a great interest in radio since childhood, I jumped at the chance.

Radio Caroline, 1966

Prior to 1964, the only radio stations playing pop music were Radio Luxembourg and the BBC Light Programme. Luxembourg broadcast only at night, with a signal that would fade in and out (although this was seen to add to its allure), and its programmes were pre-recorded in London in fifteen-minute segments. They were sponsored by certain record companies so you'd hear only the records they'd released, and you wouldn't even get to hear the whole song – the fear was that if a record were played in its entirety nobody would bother to go out and buy it. Meanwhile, the BBC Light Programme was in thrall to the Musicians' Union, with restrictions on what was called 'needle time'. By law, only a few hours a day could be devoted to actual record play, so the BBC broadcast 'cover' versions instead, performed by various in-house orchestras.

Neither station was satisfying public demand, particularly with the emergence of the Beatles and Rolling Stones, and the Swinging Sixties scene. Many new groups were on independent labels which didn't get a look-in. This sorry state of affairs was what eventually inspired Irish businessman Ronan O'Rahilly to set up Radio Caroline. As manager of the group Georgie Fame and the

Blue Flames, Ronan was finding it hard to get them any radio play. He thought the best way around this was to have his very own radio station.

His father owned a shipyard in Ireland, where they converted an old Danish ferry, the MV *Federicia*, into a radio ship complete with a 10-kilowatt transmitter. Provided they remained outside the 3-mile limit of British territorial waters, they could flout British law. This got round the needle-time restrictions, and gave the station the flexibility to play records on their merit.

Anchored 3 miles off the coast of Felixstowe, Radio Caroline started broadcasting at the end of March 1964, with an opening announcement by Simon Dee. Operating from on board a ship and outside the law, the broadcasters were dubbed 'pirates', and their success was such that O'Rahilly soon decided to have two ships, one for the north and one for the south. In July of that year the original ship sailed from Felixstowe to the Isle of Man, where it anchored 3 miles off Ramsey. In the south a new ship called *Mi Amigo* took over. At its height Caroline had an audience of 12 million, split between the two ships. Caroline was so successful that other radio stations soon followed suit, in particular Caroline's main rival, Radio London, along with some based in abandoned forts in the Thames Estuary.

Auditions

I badly wanted to be part of the buzz and excitement that surrounded Radio Caroline. I was quietly confident when I went to the audition at Caroline House in Mayfair, but was immediately put in my place about my delivery by the news director, Graham

'Spider' Webb, a stalwart of Australian radio and who would go on to become the voice at the Australian end of *Family Favourites*. I failed miserably but, whether it was to humour me or simply to fob me off, Graham sent me away saying I should practise and come back in a few weeks to try again.

My flatmate lent me a tape recorder and I practised for hours with the single page of script I'd been given. Although Graham didn't really remember me when I applied again, the position amazingly was still open. I read my sheet once more – and this time I passed. I was asked to join Radio Caroline South the following week, and would be paid £25 a week all found, tax-free, including a cigarette and beer ration. This was triple what I'd been earning at the Mermaid, and in practice worth even more due to the shift pattern. I would work two weeks on the ship, then have one week off, and for the fortnight aboard there would be nothing to spend it on. I haven't felt as rich since.

Welcome aboard

Funnily enough, I was with Caroline the night before I started at Radio Caroline. Next morning I overslept despite an alarm call, and missed the train to Felixstowe. I had to go home and try again the next morning, and this time I made it. On the train I travelled with Ed Stewart and Tony Blackburn from Radio London, the rival pirate ship moored alongside ours.

On Mondays the offshore tender – a boat ferrying personnel and supplies to the radio ships – served Caroline but on this day, a Tuesday, it was the turn of Radio London. The tender dropped off Ed and Tony at Radio London, then kindly took me to the

Radio Caroline, 1966

Radio Caroline ship. It turned out that one of my heroes, Emperor Rosko, was leaving the ship that day, and we met briefly as he boarded the tender. With his zany, larger-than-life persona and slick American-style delivery, he was perhaps the station's best-known DJ and I was thrilled to meet him. He appeared to lead the ultimate glamorous lifestyle: following my first audition at Caroline House I'd overheard the receptionist trying to get a message to the ship to say that Rosko's helicopter was waiting. Whether his chopper was waiting for him on the day I joined the ship I don't know: although everyone seemed to think he was going on his week's leave, to my disappointment he never came back. He resurfaced the following year on Radio 1.

The other disc jockeys on board were Mike Ahern, Dave Lee Travis, Robbie Dale, Rick Dane and a couple of Canadians – Keith Hampshire, who would later become a successful pop singer, and Steve Young. Tom Lodge hosted the breakfast show alongside his duties as chief disc jockey. My fellow newsreaders were my friend Bob Larkins, who'd told me about the job in the first place, and Mark Sloane, who was just about to leave Caroline to run a radio station in the West Indies.

My job involved writing and reading the news. We would shamelessly record the BBC's bulletins, rewriting them slightly and inserting station jingles. I was incredibly nervous and daren't even begin to think of the 6 million people listening to me. To make matters worse I was put through an initiation ceremony during my first week. I was chased up the radio mast by Dave Lee Travis and Robbie Dale. They timed this so that my ascent coincided with the arrival of the regular tourist boat, and as soon as it came alongside they pulled my trousers down.

The hitmakers

Without the pirates, many of the hit records of the 1960s might never have happened. The Musicians' Union had such a stranglehold on the BBC, and it was no substitute to hear the week's new releases played by an in-house, easy-listening-style orchestra such as Bob Miller and his Millermen. I would often refer to them when complaining about the awfulness of the Light Programme, the precursor to Radio 2 (Radio 1 at this stage didn't exist). I remember ranting about this when trying to chat up a girl at a party one evening, only for it to be followed by embarrassed silence before she told me her father was one of the Millermen.

Radio Caroline and the other pirate stations subsequently became the soundtrack to the Swinging Sixties with such hits as 'A Whiter Shade of Pale' and 'San Francisco (Be Sure to Wear Flowers in Your Hair)'. Record companies vied for our attention, sending their latest releases over on the tender on its weekly run, along with our food supplies and mail. We couldn't possibly play all of the records, so a listening meeting would be held to weed out those we didn't want. We would listen to only about thirty seconds of each one and I'm sure quite a few potential hits slipped through the net, but the decision was democratic – even the engineers had their say.

It was thanks to an Australian engineer that Australian rock band the Easybeats had their first international hit with 'Friday on my Mind'. The disc was about to go on the reject pile when he remarked that they were huge Down Under and that we should give them a fair go – which we did. As a result, the record was soon in the top ten.

Radio Caroline, 1966

Going north

I was just getting into my stride when the newsreaders were cut from three per ship to two. As part of the reshuffle of staff, the news director sent me to the north ship. I felt I was lucky to escape with my job, as I'd been the last to be employed.

The transfer turned out to be a blessing. Not only was Caroline North a lot bigger, but it had a much better working atmosphere as well. There wasn't nearly the same pressure as we couldn't be heard by Ronan and the bosses in London. We also had 6 million listeners covering the north-west of England, including Manchester and Liverpool, the South of Scotland, Belfast and Dublin. Though we only had a 10-kilowatt transmitter (as opposed to 50 kilowatts for Caroline South) our position meant that the radio waves were able to bounce across the water and we could be heard in Cornwall. (I even picked up Radio Caroline North when I visited Tangier in 1967).

On the south ship I'd had to share a cabin with three others, but here I had my own cabin complete with sink. The communal shower was much bigger, and as opposed to one cramped table we had an enormous dining-cum-sitting room with a table-tennis table. I used to play Dave Lee Travis (who by this time had joined the North ship) at 10 shillings a game.

I was welcomed by the chief disc jockey, Jerry Leighton, a former antiques dealer who, along with Kenny Everett, had covered the Beatles final tour in America for the *New Musical Express* earlier that year. The other disc jockeys were 'Baby Bob' Stewart, a club DJ from Liverpool who was in love with everything American and indeed sounded as if he were from deepest Texas,

My first day on
Caroline South, 1966
(taken by Bob Larkins)

Caroline
North

The offshore
tender battling
stormy seas
(photographed
by engineer
Carl Thomson)

and Tony Prince, who dubbed himself the Royal Ruler and had the distinction of being the only real-life jockey to become a disc jockey. As with the South ship, there were also several Canadians: the improbably named Mick Luvzit, who'd recently married his girlfriend Jan on board the ship and who delighted in setting fire to my news; 'Daffy' Don Allen, who hosted the morning programme; Jerry King, who went on to become a foreign correspondent with the ABC network in the US; and Gordy Cruse, who moved from newsreading to DJ duties and with whom I'm still in touch. With the cutbacks, my hours were from 5am to 6pm during the first week. During my second week I was joined by Dave Williams, a seasoned newshound, and I finished my shift at midday. This suited Dave and me: he liked a lie-in, whereas I wanted a kick-start to my day.

Life on the waves

I didn't get seasick, which was just as well – it could get incredibly rough sometimes. These were the days of vinyl, and in stormy weather the stylus could be thrown off a record mid song. Sometimes when reading the news I'd see sky through the studio window during one story and sea the next.

One morning the captain woke everybody up at 2am and ordered us to put on life jackets. The storm eventually blew over, but the crew weren't taking any chances following the incident on Radio Caroline South in early 1966 when the ship ran aground. The captain had been so engrossed in a television programme he hadn't realised the ship had broken anchor. Nobody had to be rescued from the ship because of the weather during my time, but getting on or off the tender in rough weather could be perilous. You had to judge exactly the right moment and then jump to a rope ladder. If you missed you would fall into the water with a very high risk of being squashed to death.

At other times the Irish Sea was like a millpond and during the summer we'd jump off the side of the ship and swim, trying to avoid the jellyfish in the process. For his party piece Tony Prince would dive from the top deck whilst the rest of us sunbathed. On occasion a lifeboat would be lowered into the water for a fishing expedition and we'd have fresh fish for dinner that night.

The crew on both ships were Dutch, which was not reflected in the meals except that we were served the Indonesian dish of nasi goreng at regular intervals. We kept chickens on board, so there were always fresh eggs, and bread ovens were dotted around the deck. We also had an endless supply of Manx kippers. We were all given a beer and cigarette ration, and most of us smoked, though I did have to give up temporarily following a severe case of laryngitis. Some would swap their beer for more cigarettes, and the odd crew member would sacrifice their cigarettes for drink. As the cigarettes were duty-free we weren't supposed to bring them ashore, but many of us did.

For a nineteen-year-old this was an ideal existence. The pattern of two weeks on/one week off suited me very well, and I've loved shift work ever since – I've always hated the idea of working nine to five. As we came off the ship we would be paid in cash. In my case it was £75, and with everything all found it was very easy to save. Our laundry and dry cleaning was free and my airfare to London was provided. But on one occasion I did learn a salutary lesson. Sometimes the tides would prevent us getting off

Radio Caroline, 1966

the ship in time for the flight to London, which would mean an overnight stay in Douglas before flying home the next day. The Isle of Man's semi-autonomous status meant that it was the only place in the UK to allow gambling, and Douglas had the country's sole casino. I was partial to roulette, but soon came to my senses after I lost £20 in one spin of the wheel: that was most of one week's wages gone.

Broadcasting from the middle of the Irish Sea did have its challenges. Sometimes it felt like the transmitters were held together by bits of string, and we'd go off air for no apparent reason. We were all partial to late-night snacks and on one occasion someone using the toaster tripped the transmitter.

Although the engineers didn't get the audience recognition, they were vital to the whole set-up, and sometimes they were desperate to have a go at the microphone. Whereas Caroline South was on air for twenty-four hours, Caroline North would stop broadcasting at 8.30pm every night for maintenance. Tony Prince was last to broadcast and one night, after finishing his shift, he was having a beer with the rest of the team when we heard the engineer's voice over the loudspeakers. Aping the radio programme *Animal, Vegetable, Mineral* he announced, 'And the next object is – a dozy cunt.' He then repeated this with gusto, not realising that we were still on air.

Pirate notoriety

What made Caroline so thrilling was that we were not only smashing the BBC's staid monopoly on pop music, but were also barely on the side of legality: if the ship breached the 3-mile limit

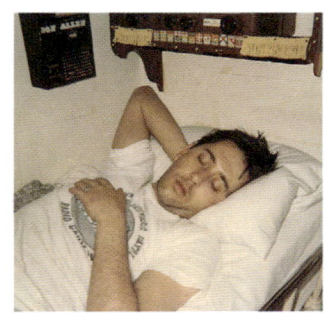

'Daffy' Don Allen

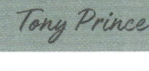

Tony Prince

Pretending to be a DJ

Me with engineer Phil Perkins (left) and Tony Prince (right), with one of the Dutch crewmen in the background

Left to right: Jerry Leighton, chief engineer Manfred Sommer, Mike Wright and Jerry King

Striking a pose

we could be boarded and arrested. The authorities had no power to take us into custody once ashore, however, and advertisers – the lifeblood of pirate radio – were also immune.

But things were beginning to change: the government of Harold Wilson proposed the introduction of the Marine Broadcasting Offences Act, which would make our broadcasts illegal. This would apply to advertisers too, who would be breaking the law by buying air time, though they couldn't touch the ship provided she remained in international waters. It's this aspect that the Richard Curtis film *The Boat that Rocked* concentrates on, including the twelve months prior to the act being passed – a period that exactly coincides with my time on board the two ships.

There's a scene in the film in which Philip Seymour Hoffman, playing a part based on Emperor Rosko, says, 'These are the best days of our lives.' This was true for many of us, and certainly for me: it was incredibly exciting and I was doing a job I'd always wanted. We weren't just living through the Swinging Sixties, we were part of it, with DJs being elevated to the status of pop stars. We broadened our audience when the Mandrake column in the *Sunday Telegraph* ran a long article with photos and quotes from all on board. I think in many people's eyes this mainstream coverage made what we were doing seem respectable.

My awareness of Caroline's popularity was reinforced by a story my father told me when he had a stint in hospital in Manchester, following a heart attack. He said the man in the bed next to him had looked over in awe and said, 'Are you really Nick Bailey's father?' And when I spent a week in Dublin at the invitation of Mike Wright, one of our Irish engineers, I realised how big Caroline was there too.

Across the waves

Even as a humble newsreader I became a household name and received fan mail from all over our broadcast area. To my shame I never replied to any of the more than 200 letters but I've kept them all as part of my social history. They make interesting reading more than fifty years later and what strikes me is how well written they were. Of course my ambition was to be a DJ, but in the meantime I was happy to bask in the fame and the notoriety of being a pirate and to take part in the fight against the impending Marine Broadcasting Offences Act. We were constantly in the news and the public knew that it wouldn't be long before we were silenced. It generated the kind of hysteria usually reserved for the break-up of a favourite pop group.

A seminal moment for me was at the end of May 1967, just over two months away from the law being passed, when the Beatles released their long-awaited album *Sgt. Pepper's Lonely Hearts Club Band*. Tony Prince and I were the first to listen to it on board, and we sat spellbound for the full duration of the two sides. I remember it as a lovely day with the sun streaming in as we revelled in each tune and realised that this was a moment in history. It would be through us that our 6 million listeners would hear it for the first time.

On dry land

On my weeks off I'd go back to London, where I shared a flat with Adrian Reynolds, a friend from the Mermaid Theatre who would later go on to become a successful director. Since 1965 we'd been living in a flat with the most magnificent view over the ponds of Hampstead Heath. We had to share the bathroom with

Radio Caroline, 1966

the flat below and to get enough hot water for a bath required twelve pennies in the gas meter. We also had what was called a 'party line', a quaint piece of history in that the landline was shared by a house further down the street. I was still seeing Caroline at this time, and she delighted in whistling down the phone whenever she heard the neighbours on the line.

The relationship with Caroline seemed typically French to me, in that it was really a ménage à trois. She had a boyfriend in Nice, Bernard, whom I'd met and liked – they'd both driven me to Villefranche and Saint-Paul de Vence the summer before. But on her visits to England, Caroline was totally devoted to me – or was she? Her love letters from France seemed heartfelt but, whilst in London, was she writing similar letters to Bernard? I suppose the guessing game was all part of it. Towards the end of the affair she admitted she was in love with both of us, and referred to a famous French film of the time, *Le Bonheur*, in which a man was in love with two women.

She was definitely tempestuous, but that only added to the attraction. Around June in 1967 I asked for some extra time off to take a holiday – I can't remember anybody else doing this so it must have been rather cheeky, but nevertheless it was granted. The plan was for us to go to Cornwall and the Scilly Isles in early July but, true to form, Caroline pulled out at the last moment and I decided I would go by myself and use the time to think.

Even though I knew Radio Caroline's days were numbered, I hadn't thought too much about plans for the future. Sitting alone on the beach in Newquay, seeing the surf rolling in, brought back happy memories of Australia. At that time there was an assisted passage scheme, offering British citizens the chance to emigrate to

Australia for just £10. Believing their country had narrowly escaped a Japanese invasion during World War II, the Australian government had launched its 'populate or perish' programme. I was aware of the scheme, as it was frequently on the news and there was an advertising recruitment campaign, and a plan to emigrate began to take root. This was July 1967, with the Marine Broadcasting Offences Act just six weeks away. With only newsreading experience behind me, I knew that getting a job in radio in the UK would be virtually impossible. There was no commercial radio and, as yet, no local BBC stations either. Australia had given me the radio bug in the first place, and it was only five years since I'd left the country I'd loved as a child.

End of an era

Everyone at Radio Caroline wanted life to continue as it was, but we knew this was unrealistic. Ronan O'Rahilly came to the North ship to rally the troops, saying that Caroline would fight on regardless, although to avoid prosecution we would not be able to live in the UK. I had no qualms about breaking the law – in fact, that side of it was appealing for me – but some of the others had families and were worried about their long-term futures and the negative impact of a police record. As our key talent departed and recruiting replacements became increasingly tricky, standards started to slip. The combination of this and the fact that I didn't really want to relocate to Ireland made me decide to leave.

On the 8th of August 1967, I read the news on Jerry Leighton's breakfast show for the last time. Jerry and I left later that day for Ramsey in the Isle of Man, never to return. The other DJs had

Radio Caroline, 1966

either left already or decided to jump ship before the deadline, which the Isle of Man's local parliament had extended to the end of August. The one exception was the Canadian Don Allen, who had the housewives slot of 9am to 12am. He remained with the ship and set up home in Ireland.

On Caroline South, Johnnie Walker and Robbie Dale had also decided to stay on, living in Amsterdam. I was visiting my Nanny in Nottingham when at 3pm on the 14th of August I heard Caroline's great rival Radio London close down. I immediately switched to Caroline to hear Johnnie welcome all the new listeners, followed by him playing 'We Shall Overcome'. So for the moment Caroline had put its fingers up to the government.

As part of the procedure for the 'assisted passage' scheme, I had an interview at Australia House, which went well: you had to have a medical, but it seemed that they would take anybody as long as you were white and could walk. The White Australia policy had been in force since 1901, and although successive governments had relaxed the rules slightly after World War II it was still extremely hard to enter the country if you weren't white. At this time, Australia had the draft for Vietnam and I was warned that I could be called up, but this was thought unlikely because I was in the second half of my twentieth year and the call-up was usually triggered by your twentieth birthday.

There was no points system then, luckily for me. What possible use would I be to the country when I was only an out-of-work newsreader? I'd managed to save £500 whilst on Caroline (worth £8500 now) and by the time of the interview I was down to £300, but that didn't seem to worry them. It should have done because, when I did emigrate, I was £19 overdrawn.

Across the waves

Left to right: Dave Lee Travis, Mike Wright, a member of the Dutch crew, Manfred Sommer, and Jerry Leighton

With Mick Luvzit (left) and Mike Wright (right)

Gordy Cruse on the tender in Ramsey, Isle of Man

Tony Prince looking at his fan mail

Typing up the news report

Reading the news

Soon a date was set for the 18th of February 1968, for me to travel on the *Fairstar*, a former troopship but by then part of the Italian Sitmar Line. This left me six months to sort things out and do some travelling, but first I had an invitation to spend the weekend with Tony Prince in Oldham, where he lived with his parents in a two-up-two-down with no bathroom and an outdoor loo. We even shared a bed, but I was a dab hand at this, having once shared a bed with Dave Lee Travis on the Isle of Man.

For the first and only time in my life I experienced the world of groupies. Whilst on Caroline North I'd always flown back to London, which was not within our broadcast area, but now I was right in the centre of the station's fan base. Even as a humble newsreader I was well known, whether it was in a club in Manchester or at a gig in Blackpool, where Tony Prince and I, with two girls, went swimming in the sea in our underwear. At a Flower Power party in Liverpool the police were called because of complaints about the noise, but one of them recognised my voice and they ended up joining the party themselves.

Back in London, Caroline and I got together again but understandably she took my decision to go to Australia badly. Still, as we knew the relationship couldn't last, we had a wonderfully romantic and poignant few weeks before she had to return to France. Although I knew she was coming to London one more time before I left, she refused any romantic involvement on that occasion and we just had one final uneasy meeting at a coffee bar where I played 'Out of Time' on the jukebox. I never saw her again, but there was a loving letter waiting for me in Australia with the sign off of '*Adieu*', which at least meant we had ended things on good terms.

Across the waves

Tangier, 1967

Through my friend Jan, an usherette from the Mermaid Theatre, I had an open invitation to stay in Tangier. Jan's new boyfriend Jon had been working as a graphic designer at an advertising agency in London, but he really wanted to be a painter and had hired a studio called the Camel Gallery on the Rue de la Plage in the centre of town, where Jan had joined him. With some time on my hands before I departed for Australia, I thought I'd take them up on the offer. Just before I left an old family friend, Martin Keeley, asked if he could join me. He stayed with us at the Camel Gallery for the first two weeks of my trip, taking some atmospheric photographs that captured the era brilliantly.

The cheapest way to get to Tangier was to fly BEA to Gibraltar, and then take the ferry. At the beginning of October, Martin and I flew to Gibraltar and spent one night there. The place was still festooned with flags, banners and graffiti from the referendum that had been held that summer, proclaiming the territory's allegiance to British sovereignty. Only forty-four had voted for Gibraltar to secede. It struck me as being a rather seedy outpost of empire, a little bit of Britain in the sun with red telephone boxes, bobbies on the beat, and pubs with fish and chips.

The ferry ride was only 36 miles across the Straits of Gibraltar to Tangier, but on arrival the contrast couldn't have been greater. This was Africa after all: the first thing to hit me was the smell of camel leather from the local tanneries. In 1967 there were very few tourists in Morocco, but Tangier was an exception due to the traffic of ships passing in and out of the Mediterranean.

Intriguing Tangier

Until 1956 Tangier had been designated an 'international zone' under the joint administration of France, Spain and the UK, but with Morocco gaining independence that year from France, the enclave was incorporated into the newly independent country. In 1967 there were still French officials running parts of the government, and Spaniards were also in evidence. Woolworths heiress Barbara Hutton, at one time married to Cary Grant, still had her villa in the city. Walking tours always pointed out her mansion, where drug-fuelled parties were held during the city's heyday. The Rolling Stones came to Tangier for the hash, and it was known as the gay capital of the world. Joe Orton and his lover Kenneth Halliwell had cruised for young Arab boys in the city, and I couldn't walk down the street without being propositioned by European gentlemen of a certain age.

I spent six weeks there on that first trip, living the local life and smoking marijuana for the first time. The cost of living was cheap. I loved the bohemian lifestyle and the sense of intrigue Tangier still had. Somehow the boys who followed you around everywhere wanting to be your guide only added to the mystique. The government was very encouraging to artists, in much the

Jon drawing

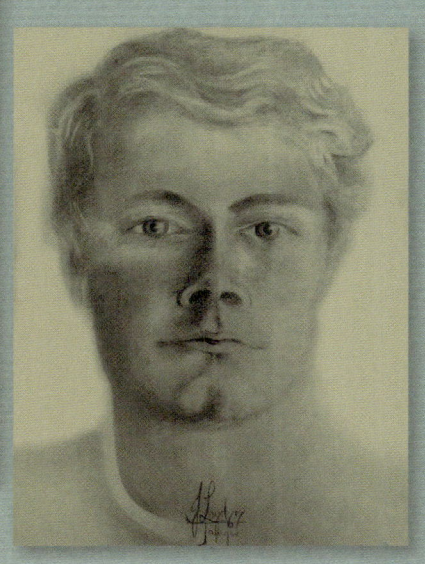

A portrait of me by Jon

Jan and a visitor at the Camel Gallery

same way that Ireland is to writers. If you could prove that you could draw or paint you would be granted the use of a studio in Marrakech for a month. To do this, though, you had to go to the capital, Rabat, with a portfolio. It helped if you could speak French, so this is where I came in. Jon and I took the local bus, via Fez, where we stayed in the kasbah. There was no harassment whatsoever and it was wonderful to see a real souk, so much better than the one in Tangier, which had become rather touristy.

Peddling pouffes

Once in Rabat I successfully negotiated the deal on Jon's behalf. On our return to Tangier I was joined by my friend Lyn, and between us we decided to have a go at importing certain handcrafted items for sale in London: beads, hats, bags and in particular cushioned leather footstools, or 'pouffes'. Initially we took everything through customs saying they were presents for friends, the intention being to gauge demand and take it from there. Back in London, we used old newspapers to stuff the pouffes and then approached boutiques offering our wares on a sale-or-return basis.

The pouffes were snapped up so quickly that we immediately planned another trip to Morocco, this time with the intention of buying in much bigger quantities. The pouffes had cost us £1 and we'd sold them for £3, with the shops marking up by at least 100 per cent. The woollen hats had cost us a shilling and were sold for five. So far so good – but on the second visit we'd have to take into account purchase tax, so it would end up working out as rather less profitable.

Across the waves

Nevertheless, we were learning all the time and decided to approach the big boys to see if we could get some sizeable orders and start a full-time business – if so, I would abandon my plans for Australia. We decided to start at the top and approach Harrods. Without even phoning for an appointment, we travelled to Knightsbridge on the bus with a couple of pouffes and asked for the buyer at the information desk. We were ushered into an office on the top floor and immediately won them over, to the extent that they ordered one gross (144) of pouffes on the spot to start with. They even thought they might run a Moroccan theme during the Christmas period. We couldn't believe our luck, but realised we needed one more big hitter to make the business viable: we badly needed funds to invest in a delivery van.

So our next stop was John Lewis, and we followed the same procedure, transporting ourselves and the pouffes by bus, and asking for the buyer once we arrived. Again, there was a lot of interest and we were just about to close on a sale when the buyer called in the head of soft furnishings. This proved to be our downfall: he took a white handkerchief from his pocket, licked it, then rubbed it on the leather of the pouffe. The dye came off – and our deal evaporated. He said John Lewis couldn't afford to have complaints from posh ladies having their white dresses stained, but he had the good grace to say that if we ever found a way of making the dye fast, they would reconsider.

That put an end to our grander business plans, but our orders from boutiques justified and paid for a second trip, and on this occasion my mother joined me. She loved an adventure and because she'd been an asthma sufferer all her life I thought the climate in Tangier in December would do her good.

Tangier, 1967

A spot of smuggling

One hurdle was the currency limit for overseas travel, brought in by Harold Wilson's government in 1964. Travellers were only allowed to take £50 out of the country, and would have their passports marked with the amount of foreign currency they had bought at the bank. This was an attempt to reduce huge deficits and revive the UK economy, but foreign companies and investors saw no point in pouring money into Britain if it was impossible to get profits out. As a result the economy suffered, but it wasn't until 1979 that the currency controls were abolished. People got round the restrictions by getting a doctor's note saying they needed to go to the South of France for a longer period of time for their health, giving them an excuse for taking more money with them, but that wasn't going to help me.

On my first trip, £50 (worth £700 now) had been sufficient, even for six weeks, as Morocco was so cheap, but as a trader in pouffes and handicrafts I needed a lot more, so I took £200, evenly distributed in my socks, hoping I wouldn't be searched as I passed through immigration. Luckily, I wasn't.

On the return from my first trip a rather camp customs official had checked the unstuffed pouffes for drugs. My father was really concerned and phoned to ask whether I was drug running. This is something I would never do, although many people were, and making easy money.

Although marijuana had been officially banned in Morocco since the country's independence in 1956, it was widely used and largely tolerated. Tobacco was actually the riskier prospect: it was prohibitively expensive because it was highly taxed, and many

A local drinking mint tea in a typical Tangier café

A guide leading tourists on a visit to Barbara Hutton's house

Traders in the souk

locals grew and sold their own. This was illegal because it avoided the tax: ironically, the police could get you for smoking a joint on a technicality, if you happened to have some untaxed tobacco mixed in with your marijuana.

Although we hadn't landed the John Lewis deal, Lyn and I were still selling well to boutiques, but running the business was costing more than we were bringing in. Our operation would need a big injection of cash to put it on a professional footing, and even if we'd honoured the Harrods order (which we didn't in the end) we wouldn't have seen any return on the investment until delivery. This would have meant a loan from the bank to tide us over, and we both felt this wasn't realistic. So I decided to continue with my plans for Australia, while Lyn stayed in England and eventually opened his own shop on the Portobello Road.

Return to Oz, 1968

Christmas 1967 was spent with my parents at their house in Wandsworth, along with Simon and my youngest brother Justin, who had been born in 1963 just before I left home. I was full of mixed emotions as I said my farewells to Frances, who was now living in London and training to be a science teacher. I cried the day I left my flat in Hampstead, as I'd been so happy there: I think it was also finally beginning to sink in that I would be leaving friends and family behind, in particular Nanny, whom I thought I might never see again.

On the 18th of February 1968 my father drove me, with the rest of the family and Adrian, my flatmate, to Southampton where the *Fairstar* was waiting. I had one suitcase and a duffel bag, and I was looking forward to a great adventure. It wasn't a total unknown of course: I'd spent part of my childhood in Australia, and I was going to stay initially with the parents of an actor friend of my father's. Though I had no idea when I'd see my family again, my mother said she was determined to come out for a visit.

I was allocated a cabin with five other berths and a washbasin, with a shared toilet and shower facilities along the corridor. Lunch had just started when there was an announcement from the purser's office to say there was a telephone call for me. It was Frances to wish me luck, which was a great morale boost. There were no tears or heartbreak, but we were both pretty sure we'd never see each other again.

Back on the seas

The ship set sail that afternoon with 'Land of Hope and Glory' blaring out over the loudspeakers, which seemed particularly tactless to me. It was bad enough for a single guy, but for a family it must have been a huge wrench to be leaving loved ones behind. Australia being over 10,000 miles away, the fare was beyond the reach of most people. Telephone calls in today's money cost £17 a minute, making letters the only realistic way for people to keep in touch.

As a migrant you had to stay two years; otherwise you had to repay the Australian government the going rate for the passage. Most of the single people on board were doing it for the adventure, but had every intention of returning after the two years had elapsed. But the Australian government wasn't stupid: they knew that in that period most people would put down roots, form relationships, and think twice about coming back.

Although it was officially a migrant ship, the *Fairstar* was fitted out like a passenger liner and also took fare-paying passengers. I was assigned a table at dinner with an Australian couple who were travelling back to Sydney with the husband's father. In contrast to the basic cabin conditions we ate extremely well – on the first night we even had oysters. I remember remarking that they were an aphrodisiac, a word the couple wasn't familiar with.

The Fairstar
at the quayside,
Southampton

Dinner aboard, with the Australian family

Megan (far right) sitting opposite her parents
with a fellow migrant, at dinner

When asked for an explanation I said it was something that makes you feel sexy, and at that point the subject quickly changed and the evening carried on as normal. The next day the husband cornered me in the corridor and asked whether I knew where I could get some of this 'aphro stuff'.

Maiden voyagers

More than three-quarters of the *Fairstar's* passengers were migrants, a mixture of families and singletons. The single females on board were mostly travelling with their parents, and a typical example was Megan, a very attractive, perky cockney from the East End, travelling with her mum and dad to Brisbane. Her brother Alan had emigrated in 1962, and they were going out to join him and his wife Irene in one of Brisbane's outer suburbs. Much as Megan was excited about her big adventure, she was sad to be leaving her four other siblings behind; however like most of us she intended to return after the required two years. We're still in touch fifty years later. Megan recalls the day we left:

'As the ship was pulling out I noticed an older woman on the dock holding tight to a streamer. On the other end was a young girl on the deck standing not far from me. I watched as the streamer broke, and as the ship pulled further and further away they just kept on looking at each other. It broke my heart and I thought, What on earth am I doing? I stayed on deck, with tears welling up, until England completely disappeared. When we got to our cabins, I was with my mum and two other ladies who constantly complained when I came into the cabin in the wee small hours. My dad was with three other men. Every day my mum complained to the captain about being separated from her husband, as they had never spent a day apart during their forty years of marriage. My dad on the other hand was very happy about the situation!'

One girl who wasn't with her parents was an attractive blonde named Abigail, whose looks caused quite a stir. She was an actress who'd been offered the female lead in the Perth production of *There's a Girl in My Soup*. The play had originally opened in 1966 in London, where it ran for more than six years in the West End, becoming the longest running comedy of the time. My father had actually been the original choice for leading man but he'd turned it down. The part had gone to Donald Sinden instead, prompting my mother to say that it was the worst professional mistake of my father's life. For Abigail, though, the play was to be the launchpad of a very successful acting career in Australia. During the 1970s she became the country's top sex symbol whilst playing the part of Bev Houghton in the soap *Number 96*, and later as the conniving Caroline Morrell in *Sons and Daughters*.

As a single guy I had a very sociable time, with dancing every night, and a bevy of single girls to choose from. The main drawback was that if I were to take a girl back to the cabin there would be five other blokes there – so that didn't happen. Being by myself was an advantage, as I could play the little-boy-lost card. This worked with a rather elegant and statuesque girl who was travelling with her family and getting off in Perth. We became an item, and I was very proud of the fact that later in the cruise she was voted Miss Fairstar. She turned out to have a pragmatic view of romance: when it was time to say goodbye and I suggested we exchange addresses, she quite rightly said it wouldn't work.

Return to Oz, 1968

Perth is more than 2,000 miles away from Sydney after all. To put that into context, it would be like living in London and having a relationship with someone in Cairo.

Fellow travellers

The single men on the ship, many of them in their twenties, were mostly without their families. Some, like me, were on their own, but most were travelling with a friend or as part of a bigger group. That was the case with Norman, Jeff and Bill, who'd met in Jersey the previous summer, where they'd been working during the holiday season. In the pub one night they'd decided to emigrate to Australia together, a decision helped in part by the fact that Norman's parents and his brother had already emigrated.

We all struck up an immediate rapport, and by the time we arrived at our first stop of Las Palmas we were the best of mates. We'd left England on a dull February day, and here we were a few days later in lovely sunshine. We hired a car and explored the island, going into the hills for lunch, where of course we had to taste the local wine. We liked it so much we lost track of time, and ended up leaving it rather late to get back for the 4pm sailing. We would have made it if we'd been able to remember where we'd hired the car from, but the more we tried to find the side street the worse it got. With only five minutes to go we found the place and pleaded with the owner to rush us to the quayside, only to discover to our horror that the gangplanks were up and the ship was already a couple of feet away from the dockside. No doubt word had got round that we were missing – the decks were full of people looking out for us and we all got a round of applause as we jumped onto the lower deck with our arms full of booze. If we'd been any later it would have meant us having to pay for the pilot boat to take us out.

Jeff was very quick to make a play for Megan, who went along with it because she really wanted Bill and hoped to make him jealous. By the end of the voyage her ploy succeeded; Bill and Megan later married and had two children.

Norman, who was from London, was one of those characters who always looked on the bright side of life and was a born leader. He organised a run around the decks at 7am that involved knocking on several cabin doors to rouse us. Enthusiasm waned after a while as our bedtimes grew progressively later, with hangovers to follow. On one occasion Jeff had such a heavy drinking bout that he didn't get to his cabin until 6am. Norman and Bill woke him an hour later and persuaded him it was dinner time. Jeff put on his best bib and tucker, and it was only when he reached the dining room that he realised it was breakfast instead.

All these shenanigans created a bond, and soon Chris, a former merchant seaman, was brought into our circle. Chris had come out with a friend who went round the ship saying, 'Come and get me girls, I'm full of babies!' I don't think this chat-up line ever succeeded and indeed it's all I remember of him, as he and Chris had a big falling-out.

Norman and I were almost identical in age, and had a handful of O-levels between us. Bill, on the other hand, had an A-level, so we considered him the intellectual one. But Jeff was in the most powerful position because he had a trade as an electrician, and would probably be one of the few of that intake of 1968 to be allowed into Australia now.

Return to Oz, 1968

Entertainments and diversions

The man in charge of entertainment was an Italian officer called Mario, who tried to bed every single woman on board. He'd already done so with a girl from the Mermaid Theatre who had emigrated before me. But one girl he didn't succeed with was Megan, and she takes up the story:

'He reminded me of Frank Sinatra, so I always referred to him as Frank. I caught his eye one day and, despite all the warnings from you boys, I took his invitation to drinks at face value. I was obviously very naive because as soon as I was in his cabin he locked the door with one hand and started to unzip my dress with the other. I said, "What are you doing?" trying to zip it up again. He replied, with his Italian accent, "Oh, come on, you know why you're here." I said, "I've come for a cup of tea." He pointed towards the door and said, "Get out!" As I was walking out my parting shot was, "So no tea, then?"'

To most people, though, Mario was a witty master of ceremonies who organised a variety of entertainment from horse racing to fancy dress. There was no such thing as a show company with a lavish theatre in those days – instead an instrumental trio ended each evening with 'Arrivederci Roma', and a trad-jazz group from Australia called the Red Onions sang for their supper with such tunes as 'Just a Gigolo'. This was in return for their free passage back to Melbourne.

The ship had a daily newspaper, and on March the 3rd I read that both Radio Carolines had been forced to close down because the tender operators had not been paid. Also, the Broadcasting (Offences) Act had been introduced in Ireland by this time and

On the deck of the
Fairstar, left to right:
Me, Chris, Megan,
Bill, Jeff and Barry,
another fellow migrant

The 'crossing
the line' ritual

Me as Lawrence of
Arabia, with Jeff, Bill
and Norman as the
camel, in the fancy
dress competition

had scared away most of the advertisers. The two ships were boarded and towed away: a sad end to a brave venture.

The *Fairstar* had all the accoutrements of a cruise ship, including a swimming pool which came in handy during the crossing-the-line ceremony, a centuries-old ritual to initiate equator-crossing 'virgins'. I'd done this a couple of times before when travelling with my parents, but for the majority of migrants this would have been their first time. The virgins, known as 'pollywogs' (another word for 'tadpole'), were paraded in front of King Neptune while his assistant read out the offences with which they were to be charged, including dancing without rhythm. I was one of Neptune's helpers and along with others we covered our victims with spaghetti before we all ended up in the pool.

Our next stop was Cape Town, which had been in the news just two months previously because of Dr Christiaan Barnard and the world's first heart transplant. On a taxi ride we were shown the Groote Schuur Hospital, where the operation had taken place. Cape Town reminded me of Sydney with its harbour, and had a similar climate, but beautiful as the setting was, apartheid cast an oppressive shadow. I witnessed this first-hand: when travelling on a bus I saw the absurd separation of white from black.

There was great excitement over the ship's fancy dress night: we decided to depict Lawrence of Arabia riding a camel. I was the lightest so I was chosen to act as Lawrence. Jeff was the head of the camel and poor Bill and Norman provided the legs and arse.

I had taken £20 with me to last the entire trip (equivalent to more than £300 today), but if it hadn't been for a substantial win during one of the ship's horse-racing nights I would have struggled. Thank goodness, also, that my parents had set up an insurance fund for me from birth which had matured when I was eighteen and amounted to £100 (almost £1700 now). This had been transferred to a bank in Sydney, so at least I had some funds to fall back on once we arrived.

Boomerang Poms

Those who took advantage of the assisted passage scheme were nicknamed '£10 Poms' ('Pom' being Australian slang for someone from England). When you consider everything that was laid on for us on board the ship, £10 for the journey was incredible value. But by the mid 1970s migrants were being encouraged to go by plane instead, as it was cheaper for the Australian government. By then the fare had gone up to £75, and gradually a points system was introduced. In under thirty years 1.5 million Britons took advantage of the scheme, but it's estimated that about a quarter of a million returned to England after the first few years. Of these returnees, about half eventually decided that returning home had been a mistake and ended up going to Australia after all. They were known as 'boomerang Poms'.

This scenario played itself out with almost all my friends on the ship. Norman, Bill and Megan (who was by then married to Bill) all came back to the UK after several years, but decided life was better in Australia and went back. Only Jeff decided to stay in England, in part because his wife Cath understandably didn't want to leave her extended family in Newcastle.

For a couple of families on the ship the separation from their families became too much even before they arrived in their adopted country. One family got off in Las Palmas and another in

Return to Oz, 1968

Cape Town, having to repay the Australian government thousands of pounds in today's money as well as their fares home.

None of the single people on the ship had the same qualms, except maybe for Pat, a Brummie lad, whose father had died in England whilst he was on board. We all looked upon it as a great adventure and, even if it didn't work out, the journey alone was worth it. As it turned out, it was the best £10 I would ever spend.

A £10 Pom

We eventually arrived in Fremantle for the migrants wanting to settle in Western Australia, before sailing on to Adelaide, Melbourne and finally to Sydney. During the journey I'd written to all the school friends I'd left six years before and was looking forward to several reunions. My priorities were finding a job and somewhere to live. I stayed in Narrabeen on the Northern Beaches in a lovely house owned by the parents of Mark Edwards, an actor who had appeared with my father in the Australian production of *A Severed Head* in 1965. Mark's mother was a potter and his father a publisher, so it was a very laid-back environment.

Wiley Park

Back on the *Fairstar* before we went our separate ways, Norman, Jeff, Bill, Chris and I had decided that we would share a house in Sydney. Norman found us a large place with a garden in Wiley Park, in what was the Western Suburbs. Sydney has some beautiful residential areas, but this wasn't one of them – it was very much the working-class area, but within our budget. (I say 'our budget', but this was only theoretical – none of us had a job.) It was quite a change to leave the beaches and relaxed atmosphere of Narrabeen. Norman and Chris had already been called 'Pommie bastards' whilst playing pool at the local pub. I'd also had a brush with a boorish man who complained about migrants until I pointed out that his parents had emigrated from England – though it was true that many migrants didn't help matters by complaining, saying nothing was the same as 'home'. This had become a cultural stereotype known as the 'whingeing Pom' – the ones that would invariably return to the UK.

As expected, Jeff found work as an electrician straight away, while Chris had managed to save enough money for him not to bother for the time being. For our first jobs, Norman and I sold ice creams at the Moscow State Circus, which was in Sydney for a short season. We didn't even get past the first day: we sold so few ice creams that we had more in our float than in our takings.

At the factory

We tried a more sensible route and applied for a job at Smiths Industries, a factory where Norman's brother Mick already had a job. There were three candidates for the two jobs, and we were given a maths test. I can't believe the third man failed this very simple test: maybe they just preferred the look of me and Norman. We were to start the next day on the minimum wage, which by UK standards seemed very generous – in the region of £30 a week – though Aussie living costs were admittedly higher. Bill had also applied for a job at Smiths, but with his A-level he was fast-tracked into management, presumably at a higher wage.

Across the waves

I never knew what he did, but he wore a tie and went about carrying a clipboard looking very important. I joined three others making up a team that kept the factory floor supplied with various nuts and bolts, and whatever else they needed.

One of my teammates was Kevin, whose standard reply to the question 'How are you going?' would be 'Up the shit.' And then there was Bill, a gentle man of about fifty-five, who came to work every day with his sandwiches neatly made by his wife. When I asked him how long he'd been in the job, he said, 'I've been in stores all my life, mate.' His words filled me with dread: I realised unless I did something about it, this could be my fate too.

My grand plan had always been to find work in radio, but this was proving to be not so easy. (When I mentioned my ambitions to a sweet woman on the production line, who became a kind of mother figure to me, she very kindly told me there was a radio factory close by I could try.) I went for various newsreading auditions, but it didn't help speaking with a Pommie accent. My old boss from Radio Caroline, Graham Webb, had returned to his homeland just before the station was shut down, and he very kindly invited me to appear as a guest on *Blind Date*, a primetime programme he was presenting. I had to choose from three girls behind a screen. With a girl chosen, a date was arranged, but it turned out to be a gathering whereby 'dates' from several programmes congregated at the same venue. Graham arrived with a gorgeous model called Margaret, but because he'd damaged his foot she asked if she could dance with me. I don't think I saw my original date all night: there was an obvious chemistry between us but I felt I couldn't take Graham's girl so I left with an innocent kiss on the cheek thinking I wouldn't see her again.

Several weeks later, however, I saw Margaret on the train and we started going out. It was a relief to hear that she wasn't Graham's girlfriend after all, but the downside was that she would soon be going to Canada to be a nanny in the wilds of the Yukon. We had a romantic couple of months, greatly helped by her living in the next suburb of Bankstown, walking distance from Wiley Park.

To be absolutely frank I was pretty useless at the factory job, leading to one of the management shouting at me one day. The foreman immediately came to me and said, 'If he treats you like that again, we're all out.' This was my first experience of Australia's strike mentality, which was known as the 'British disease'.

Our boss was a burly man called Jack Stoddart. He wasn't actual management but he had a lot of power, equating to a sergeant major, and we rather liked him. His brusque approach was deceptive because it hid a wicked sense of humour. It was from his mouth that I first heard the expression: 'Up here for thinking, down there for dancing.' This would be declared every time he thought he'd said something clever – pointing to his head first, but then pointing to *my* feet when it came to the second part of the phrase, insinuating that I had no brains.

Surfers Paradise

Norman and I had a joint twenty-first birthday party at Wiley Park, which was a chance for me to see many of my old school friends, including Allan and Sue, and her best friend, Penny. I was somewhat deflated when Penny said she couldn't understand why I'd come back to Australia when she and all her friends were desperate to get to England and be part of the Swinging Sixties.

Across the waves

Acrobatics with the gang in our garden in Wiley Park

Setting out on our hitch-hiking race, left to right: Jeff, me ,Bill, Chris, Norman

Celebrating our arrival in Surfers Paradise

The factory work may have been good money, but it was taking up too much time in terms of looking for other jobs. I pulled as many sickies as I could legally get away with, but eventually these ran out and it seemed there was no other option but to leave. After three months Norman and I clocked out for the last time, and Bill followed soon after.

We celebrated our new-found freedom with a hitch-hiking race to a pub in Surfers Paradise, a town on the Gold Coast. For some reason, rather than heading off individually, which would have made it easier to get lifts, we decided to split into two groups and drew lots to see who would go with whom. Chris and I got lucky, drawing to travel as a twosome, whereas Norman, Jeff and Bill had the unenviable task of hitch-hiking as a trio.

We left after work on a Friday afternoon, and it was dawn before we reached Taree, about halfway up the coast. Chris and I were just accepting a lift for the next leg of the journey when a police car screeched to a halt behind our car and ordered us out. I thought it was because hitching was officially illegal in Australia, but it wasn't that and they weren't interested in Chris – it was me they were after. They looked me up and down for a good sixty seconds, but then let me go. When I asked for an explanation they said they were looking for an escaped prisoner who was a half-cast Aboriginal with dyed red hair. Back in the car, I asked the driver why they'd picked on me, and without hesitation he said, 'It's your high cheekbones and snub nose, mate.'

Twenty-three hours and twelve lifts later, Chris and I made it to Surfers Paradise, only to find the pub had been demolished. By chance we saw the others also looking for the pub, so we headed to the nearest beer garden to celebrate. We decided to fly home.

Across the waves

Radio contacts

Every weekend Graham Webb would host a party at his house in Hornsby where a lot of radio people would gather. One of the guests was Ian MacRae, an Australian broadcaster who had worked on the pirate station Radio City. When that had closed he'd worked on Caroline South, and stayed at my place in Hampstead, before returning to Australia. He gave me some great advice and said if I wanted to be a presenter the best place to get experience was in the outback.

But first I needed some confidence, so I enrolled on a radio course run by another broadcaster, Max Rowley. It was exactly what I needed: in the studio in his back garden we had to do dummy programmes, which were then critiqued.

But what about work? The money I'd saved from the factory was rapidly running out, so I applied for a job delivering leaflets around Sydney. The ad had said it was part-time work that would suit a pensioner. Every morning I'd be picked up and join three old codgers, with each of us being dropped off in different areas. These were usually in the more affluent parts of Sydney and if the weather was nice, which it usually was, it could be a very pleasant job, and it certainly kept me fit. The main hazard was the dogs, who could be vicious and at one point blood was drawn. My fellow leafleteers debated as to whether this warranted a stand with our bosses, but the wound wasn't too serious so I didn't pursue it. The pay was very low and my funds were dwindling, so in the end I decided I'd have to look for full-time employment.

Graham Webb suggested I try modelling, so I got an agent and at great expense had a series of photos taken that led to a few interviews but not one commission. I then managed to get a job selling barbecues at Nock & Kirby, a famous hardware store in the centre of town.

I still had time to attend my announcing course, and this was starting to bear fruit. Max had already given my confidence a boost by saying my voice was suited to the Australian Broadcasting Corporation (ABC), and after about six weeks he said he'd found a job for me in Warwick in Queensland at 4WK. At the last moment this didn't materialise, but it did spur me on to apply for more jobs off my own back.

I borrowed my housemate Chris's tape recorder to practise and to make tapes, and I sent one off to Katoomba in the Blue Mountains. I was very excited when they phoned, but they said there was nothing on the tape! This was the problem of recording on a domestic recorder and sending it to a radio station: quite often the equipment wouldn't match, hence the silence. But when I saw an ad in the *Sydney Morning Herald* for a junior announcer at 2VM Moree I tried again, and this time I got it. It was just as well as I was now totally skint.

Moree, 1968

Bill very kindly lent me the train fare, and I travelled the 400 miles north-west of Sydney on the overnight sleeper. It was a bright October day when I arrived in Moree, a town of 10,000 people at that time, in the wheat-and-wool belt of New South Wales. I was greeted at the station by Mrs Reed, assistant manager of the radio station 2VM, who told me the manager had died suddenly a few months before and they were still looking for a replacement. This proved to be to my advantage: Mrs Reed took to mothering me, and in a less guarded moment said that if she had been a lot younger she'd have done other things too. I took this to be innocent banter – she appeared to be quite happily married – but I milked it as much as I could.

Moree's 2VM had started up in 1956, following catastrophic floods the year before when most of the central business district and 800 homes were flooded. The community realised they needed a form of instant communication, and with ten major floods since then the station has certainly proved its worth.

Once at the station I soon found out that when they'd placed the ad for a junior announcer they'd been hoping for someone under twenty-one, legally allowing them to pay substantially less than the minimum wage. They obviously hadn't had any takers, and so they'd decided to go with me and pay the standard rate. Since being in Australia I'd never been paid more than the minimum wage, but it seemed quite adequate to live on – and in small-town Moree even more so.

I was given the evening show, broadcasting from 7pm to 11pm, Monday to Friday, and a request programme in the same slot on Saturdays. But first I had to learn the desk, which was rather like learning how to drive while broadcasting at the same time. I also had to do copywriting and production, and I chose to do this work in the morning, giving me the afternoon off, and then coming back to broadcast in the evening.

I soon settled in with my fellow disc jockeys. Our chief announcer was Peter Crawford, who at the age of twenty-eight seemed ancient to me. Paul Dubois was only seventeen, but had such a deep voice that he sounded much older, and then there was Bob Murray, who became a good friend. He must have been slightly younger than me because he actually got called up to go to Vietnam. Australia had a system whereby one in ten men was conscripted, and employers at the time were obliged to hold your job open for you. I thought this seemed somewhat unfair because, while you were serving your country for two years, your peers could be leapfrogging you in terms of promotion.

Apart from learning the desk I had to master the pronunciation of Aboriginal place names. Our broadcast area extended just across the Queensland border to Goondiwindi, with names such as Pallamallawa and Yallaroi along the way, and the cotton-growing area of Wee Waa to the south. This name was surely an accident waiting to happen – but luckily one that never happened on air. It was left to the local newspaper, *The Moree Champion,* to refer to it one day as 'Wee Wee' – I suspect a naughty subeditor was the culprit. It was drilled into us to say *Gun*diwindi, but when I eventually visited the town I discovered the locals called it *Goon*diwindi: so much for the Moree pronunciation police.

On my first day I was taken to the local pub, only to find that because of a bush fire in the nearby town of Narrabri the electricity supply had been cut off to the fridges, and so there was no beer. Actually there was beer – but one thing Australians won't do is drink warm beer.

Social order

Moree has an average temperature of 26°C, and I took full advantage of its public swimming pool, little realising that it had been a scene of confrontation some years earlier.

The town had been one of the destinations on the famous 1965 Freedom Ride, an historic bus trip through the country towns of New South Wales led by the activist Charles Perkins in a campaign to expose the culture of discrimination against indigenous Australians. Most white Australians in the 1960s weren't aware of the problem: the Aboriginal population in the capital cities tended to be minimal, with maybe Redfern in Sydney being the exception. Meanwhile, in the outback, the problem was swept under the carpet, with the 'abbos', as they were referred to, relegated to the outskirts of the towns. Media coverage of the Freedom Ride brought racial segregation in rural areas to the attention of urban Australians, focusing on the pubs and theatres where Aborigines were refused entry, and in particular on the

Moree, 1968

Moree swimming pool. After a clash with the council and pool management, it was agreed that indigenous children could swim in the pool outside school hours. But I never saw any evidence of this – the only Aboriginals I ever saw lived in squalid conditions on the outskirts of Moree and rarely ventured into the town.

I'd always thought Australia to be a classless society but in Moree it was different, as I suspect it was in many country areas. Top of the heap were the landowners, known as 'cockies', an originally derogatory term given to settler farmers scratching their living in the outback. This certainly wasn't the case in Moree – the area is blessed with some of the world's most fertile black soil in what is known as the Golden Wheatbelt. With sheep and cattle farming going on alongside the grain production, it was one of the richest areas of New South Wales. A step down in the hierarchy were business owners, and below that were agricultural labourers or those serving in shops. Coming from England I was used to class divisions, but working in the media I found I could easily move between the classes.

Mrs Butterworth

I boarded with Mrs Vera Butterworth in a house within walking distance of the radio station. She was a widow in her late seventies, and I was provided with dinner, bed and breakfast, and could watch television in her cosy sitting room. She served the full Australian breakfast, which included chops and potatoes. At night there was more meat, usually with two veg. As for fruit, there was always delicious rock melon, which she kept cut up in a jar with liberal helpings of sugar. Bread was always available,

Outside the 2VM office with Norman

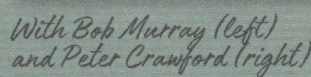

With Bob Murray (left) and Peter Crawford (right)

Jeff on a visit, camping out and making friends with some Aboriginal children

In the 2VM studio

but invariably full of ants and weevils. Without batting an eyelid Mrs B would simply put the loaf in the oven for a few minutes to get rid of the invaders.

At Christmas that year my mother came out for a visit, and Mrs Butterworth invited us to join her family for a jolly celebration – a favourite memory of my mother's that she would often recall. Later, Norman and Jeff stopped off on their way to Queensland, and Allan, my old school friend from Sydney, came to enjoy Mrs Butterworth's hospitality – ant-infested bread and all.

On the air

At work I was loving being on air and playing records I selected myself – there were no computerised playlists then. But I did get told off for playing too many tracks from the Beatles' *White Album,* which had just been released.

A new manager eventually arrived who was much stricter than Mrs Reed. He banned certain records, including 'The Boxer' by Simon and Garfunkel because it referred to the 'whores on Seventh Avenue' and Peter Sarstedt's 'Where Do You Go To My Lovely', simply because of the line 'when you're alone in your bed'. After a petition we persuaded him to change his mind.

There was great excitement one day, as we were expecting the leader of the labour opposition, Gough Whitlam, to visit. I was awestruck by this tall, charismatic man. In 1972 he would go on to become the twenty-first Prime Minister of Australia, leading the Labor Party to power for the first time in twenty-three years. Apart from abolishing the White Australia Policy, he also ended military conscription and instituted universal health care.

Across the waves

Moving on

I spent most of my free time at the pool, where I met a tall, attractive blonde. Her name was Zeeta: her parents were Polish, and like me she'd had polio as a child, although there was no way of knowing. One afternoon I snuck her back to Mrs Butterworth's place, where we made love in my bedroom. Just as we were *in flagrante* the door burst open. We both shot up expecting an irate Mrs B, but it was only the wind. After this scare, our trysts took place at Zeeta's parents' house, where she had a bedroom on the verandah. To avoid my footsteps being heard I would leave in my socks, then creep across the lawn praying that a light wouldn't go on in the rest of the house. I'm afraid I treated her rather badly, as I became infatuated with a new girl in town, a brunette called Janine, who was setting up her own hairdressing salon. Her parents were from Moree, but she'd lived in Sydney for some time and had a certain air of sophistication. It didn't last long, however, as I was soon dumped for a cockie.

I don't know whether this was the catalyst for moving on or whether I realised that to get on in radio I would need to gain as much experience as possible in the shortest period of time. The ambition of all country radio announcers was to get to capital city radio, and I was no exception. Since hearing my father's stories about North Queensland, I'd always had a romantic notion about the place. It sounded like a tropical paradise to me, so when a job came up in Townsville 900 miles to the north I eagerly applied and was very excited to be accepted.

Moree, 1968

Townsville, 1969

Townsville, then Queensland's second-biggest city, was quite a shock after laid-back Moree. As the main port for North Queensland's sugar exports, along with copper, lead and zinc from Mount Isa, it was nothing like I was expecting – no swaying palm trees, no golden sands – just a rather unattractive industrial town.

Townsville had two radio stations. One was 4TO, where my hero John Laws, whose broadcasts I had listened to when I lived in Australia as a boy, had worked for a while before starting his career in Sydney. The other was 4AY, where I was heading. It was officially based in Ayr, a small cane-growing town an hour's drive away, but its transmitters easily covered Townsville, so it had moved its main office to the city many years earlier.

I stayed overnight at a cheap hostel and started work the next day, where I met the station manager Graham Schmid, who was to prove a hard taskmaster but soon gained my respect. Although I can't say I really liked Townsville overall, my eighteen months at 4AY would turn out to be invaluable experience. For the first time since I'd been in Australia, I was earning more than the minimum wage and had a salary of $56 a week. Initially I was put on an evening show from 7pm to 10pm, five days a week, and an early evening programme on Saturday that included live coverage of the 'trots' (harness racing) where I had to act as anchor.

Luckily for me, one of 4AY's journalists, Murray Massey, was looking for a flatmate, so I joined him and his friend Archie Stevenson in a small modern house fairly close to the centre. I still hadn't learnt to drive and was hoping to get by on local transport, but because of my shifts this didn't work out, so I ended up getting a pushbike instead.

4AY

I soon got to know my colleagues. There was Russ Walkington, who'd been a big star on Sydney stations 2UE and 2UW in the 1950s and 1960s, with a character called Gerald the Grasshopper. He was programme director and we all looked up to him.

Jack Grant, a former Catholic priest with the joviality and looks of Friar Tuck, did what was known as the 'housewives slot'. Allan Porter, who'd trained as an actor in Sydney, presented *Drivetime*. Bob Raven, an easygoing American, was doing late nights, the shift after me. He interspersed his show with recordings he'd made of the sea, the sort of thing that some doctors' surgeries now use. He was ideal in this slot, as he had the sort of voice that would gently lull you to sleep. And there was a veteran journalist, John Sullivan, a very distinguished-looking gentleman with white hair and moustache to match, who hosted a phone-in programme during lunchtime. The backroom staff was headed by the assistant manager, a Dutchman called Jo Oost, who'd sailed to Townsville from the Dutch East Indies following independence after World War II. He later became manager of rival station 4TO. On

Townsville, 1969

reception was Roslyn, who was a bit of a man-eater, although I was never on the menu. She was quite brazen about her love life, but Pauline in the library was the complete opposite, wearing her girdle as a kind of chastity belt and guarding vinyl as if her life depended on it. Only the studio had air conditioning, so to stop the records warping they were placed on top of each other, which made it very awkward if you wanted to browse.

One advantage of presenting at night was that I could make the most of the weather during the day. I was also able to watch the moon landing on July 20th, which occurred at lunchtime in Townsville. After the first month I began to settle into the way of life, but my presentation style was rather forced: I was under the impression that to broadcast I would need to affect a certain type of voice, and it took me some time to realise that I just needed to be myself. Mr Schmid gave me quite a bit of guidance on this and, although I hated being called into his office, his coaching gradually started to pay off.

As with Moree I was heavily involved in production, voicing and producing many of the station's commercials, an aspect of the job I really enjoyed. The hours were quite long, but as I considered the job my hobby I didn't mind this at all.

Social life

Socially there was a world of difference from what I'd been used to. Even compared to Moree, Townsville seemed to be behind the times in every respect, from fashion to food to its views on life. The city itself was mostly ugly and dry: where was the lush greenery I was expecting? But at least there was the Strand, the

At the desk at 4AY

Allan Porter on-air

Doing an outside broadcast, 1970

esplanade by the sea with some heritage buildings, including the Queen's Hotel, which refreshingly had fans as opposed to air conditioning. From here one had a magnificent view of Magnetic Island, named for the 'magnetic' effect it seemed to have on Captain Cook's compass as he passed the island in 1770. Magnetic Island was the only reason tourists would come to Townsville, and it was certainly worth a visit or even a short stay.

I started to branch out socially and, following my shift on Saturdays, I would go to Lowth's Hotel, where they had a dance band and there was a chance to pick up some girls. I was getting fed up with short-term relationships and wanted something more meaningful. But this was tricky: whereas in England, Sydney and even Moree, a shy, sensitive Englishman had a certain attraction, in Townsville the girls wanted someone more macho – someone who ate cars for breakfast. The first girl I got to know seemed to be keen and we went swimming on Magnetic and attended parties, but she suddenly lost interest. I suspected it wasn't going to be the first Townsville romance to end this way.

Exploring

It was thanks to my flatmate Archie that I got a glimpse of the tropical world I'd been hoping for. He'd grown up in the area, knew the region well and offered to be my guide. One weekend we drove 30 miles north to a tiny outpost called Rollingstone, where the terrain had that lush, tropical look I had dreamt of.

From Rollingstone it was the same distance again to Ingham, which became one of my favourite destinations. This was sugar-cane country where before harvesting the cane was burned to remove the leaves from the stalks. Ingham had a population of under 5,000 but more people of Italian descent per head of population than anywhere else in Australia. Italian migrants had come in great numbers at the end of the nineteenth century to work as cane cutters. They laboured hard, many saving enough to buy land and grow sugar themselves, and by the 1960s most cane farms were owned by Italians. Archie told me his class at school had been full of Italians, and there had been none of the casual racism towards migrants that was prevalent elsewhere – but then the Italian community did own most of the town.

The burning cane, with its sweet smell, and the sight of cane trains carrying their cargo are among my most evocative memories. I think my fascination with these things stems from my father's stories about his visit to North Queensland in the mid 1950s. His tour of Australia had coincided with the premiere in Melbourne of a play by Ray Lawler called *Summer of the Seventeenth Doll*. It opened in London two years later, and also captured my mother's imagination. It was about a couple of cane cutters from Melbourne who earned big money labouring in Cairns and would then blow it all on women and booze in the off season, until it all went terribly wrong.

Driving further north we reached another sugar town, Innisfail. Slightly larger than Ingham, it has an attractive position on the wide Johnstone River and a variety of art deco architecture. It's also one of the wettest places in Australia, second only to Tully, where we also stopped, which has an annual average rainfall of 160 inches. You can't have lushness without rain, but this was warm rain that came in short bursts instead of the depressing drizzle that can carry on for days in Britain.

Townsville, 1969

From there we decided to take the scenic route to Cairns via the Atherton Tableland, a fertile plateau on the Great Dividing Range. This took us to Millaa Millaa and its famous waterfall, but with an area covering almost 65,000 square kilometres we could only get a brief glimpse of what the Tableland had to offer.

My first impression of Cairns was a town full of houses built on stilts, a style unique to Queensland that is both attractive and practical: it prevents termite attacks, keeps venomous snakes out of the house and is a good way to cope with periodic flooding. The space under the houses was often used as a garage and laundry. The city, with not a skyscraper in sight, had an air of sophistication that was lacking in Townsville. This could be the result of Melburnians, fed up with their climate, decamping en masse to the northernmost tropical city in Australia. The population was a quarter of Townsville's at 25,000, and there was no international airport (it didn't open until 1984). There were hardly any tourists, despite the town being the gateway to the Great Barrier Reef. Australians didn't come, due to the astronomical airfares from the capital cities – it was far cheaper to fly to Bali. Few foreign tourists visited North Queensland either, except for the occasional Japanese group on fishing trips.

We travelled on to Port Douglas, which was just a sleepy fishing village with a renowned fish restaurant and a wonderful beach that stretched for miles. It's now home to one of the most exclusive resorts in the world, the Sheraton Grand Mirage, and is the major jumping-off point for outings to the Reef.

Although the trip didn't change my opinion of Townsville, I was heartened to know these things were on my doorstep. But as I still had no transport, my explorations were mostly closer to home, and what better place than Magnetic Island. Every Sunday on my day off I would go there and explore more and more of the island. It was only twenty-five minutes by ferry from Townsville, and on my first visit I went in search of pineapples, having heard there was a plantation. But no one had told me that pineapples grow on low-growing plants, so I spent the whole day looking up and thought the pineapple-shaped fruit of the pandanus tree was what I was looking for.

Cars, cane toads, and crocodiles

Much as my bike helped me in the short term, I really needed to learn how to drive. I'd had lessons in London whilst on Radio Caroline, but because of my shift pattern these had been only every third week and I hadn't got anywhere. Aware that my aptitude for learning anything mechanical was limited, I thought my best hope would be to have a continuous stream of lessons until I cracked it. I would also need a teacher with infinite patience, and luckily my Dutch driving instructor had bags of it.

After the twentieth lesson he said I was ready for my test, which I passed first time. The sense of freedom this gave me was immense, as it opened up a whole new world. Allan at work had a sailing friend, Sid Ramsay, who was a second-hand car salesman and I bought my first car, a Mini, from him. On my first journey to work I couldn't understand the squelching sound my tyres were making: it was a combination of cane toads and mangoes being run over. The toads were everywhere despite the fact there was no sugar cane in Townsville. As for the mangoes, there were so many they were left to rot on the roadside.

Townsville, 1969

My first trip was to discover Dunk Island, which I'd heard was a tropical paradise, a couple of miles off Mission Beach, halfway between Townsville and Cairns. I wasn't disappointed: it was just what a desert island should look like, with a golden beach shaded by coconut palms and a rainforest interior. I would have loved to have bought land on the island, but most was designated national park, so I turned my attention instead to Magnetic, one of the few Great Barrier Reef islands where you could buy a plot. In Moree I'd managed to save quite a bit of money by working overtime – this wasn't normal practice in commercial radio, but thanks to Mrs Reed's soft spot for me I'd accrued $500 by the time I left. This was more than enough for a deposit on the quarter-acre plot in Horseshoe Bay I bought for $1200. When I shook hands with the vendor over the deal in a local pub, I noticed terrible scars on his hands. He explained he was a crocodile hunter (crocodiles weren't protected then). A croc he thought he'd killed with a shotgun had not been quite dead, and it had tried to get its own back when an attempt was made to retrieve the body.

Open Line

Russ Walkington left us to host the breakfast show at 4BH Brisbane, and Allan took over. I continued in the evenings, but was given the golden opportunity of presenting *Open Line*, whilst the regular host, John, was on leave. The show was a recent experiment that hadn't really taken off and callers were kept on for far too long. By law we had to have a seven-second delay system in case someone said something slanderous or profane. Callers would be be cut off at the point they said anything problematic, and the gap would be covered by a bright and breezy jingle. I remember one time I heard John dealing with a particularly obnoxious person at the end of the line. They said something rude about a local dignitary, but John pressed the button too late and what we heard instead was '… and he's a big fat turd,' followed by, 'You're listening to the brighter 4AY!'.

The real danger, though, was having monotonous conversations with boring callers, but on my first day there were some controversial comments made, including one from a Melbourne businessman berating Townsville for being such a scruffy city. This led to an avalanche of indignant responses, and it was only months later that I realised the calls had been set up by my friend Allan and Sid the car salesman. The boss couldn't believe the response, and was loving the fact that *Open Line*, which had been his idea in the first place, was finally taking off. He put it all down to my presentation.

The Italian girl

On the romantic front I was interested in a girl who was a sugar tester at the sugar mill in Home Hill about 50 miles to the south. One night I picked her up after work and then drove another 50 miles to where there was a barbecue party on the beach. I thought this could be it, but all I got was a chaste kiss.

I was in Home Hill again at Christmas when Archie kindly asked me to join in the festivities with his family. His father was the manager of a cane farm, and when I was offered a tour to see the elaborate irrigation systems I accepted at once. On the first night we went to a local hall, where I danced with two sensual

Italian sisters. There was immediate chemistry with the elder one, Rita, who teasingly played with the hair peeping out from my shirt. We subsequently set up a dinner date in Brandon, a small town nearby, where Rita knew the owner. A bottle of Asti Spumante was provided on the house, and the evening went extremely well, leading to a romantic rendezvous in my room. It was well worth the reprimand I got from her parents for getting her home too late. On another occasion we stopped in a cane field for a steamy encounter only for it to be interrupted by a mosquito that went for the most sensitive part of my anatomy. But this relationship was destined to fizzle out as well.

Breakfast

Like me, Allan had always wanted to visit the towns along the Great Barrier Reef and was also a keen sailor, so when the opportunity arose for him to do some casual work at a resort on Dunk Island he jumped at the chance. He'd come to like the island some time beforehand, when an actor friend from his drama school days had a part in *Age of Consent,* a movie with James Mason and a very young Helen Mirren being filmed on Dunk. Allan had helped to sail a yacht to the island, onto which James Mason had been invited. Now Allan had the chance to live on the island himself and it fulfilled a dream.

It was only a short-term contract and soon he was back in broadcasting, this time at the ABC. Through Allan I got wind of the possibility of sharing a house with him and two others in Townsville's top suburb of Pallarenda, overlooking the beach. The other two were a hairdresser and a flamboyant character who was the cocktail pianist at Lowth's Hotel, for which he had to wear a purple velvet jacket. With the move, Townsville went up in my estimations: this was a glorious area about five miles out of town, with many of the houses rented or owned by people working at the newly formed James Cook University. And it was special, at least to me, to live in a typical Queensland house on stilts.

When Allan left 4AY I took up his slot on the breakfast show. Usually, breakfast is the most important programme, as it gets the greatest number of listeners and as a consequence a higher number of ads. I took a bit of time to get into my stride but one day it suddenly clicked: I stopped trying to be that mythical 'golden voice'. The show started to get good ratings and I was given a raise to $60 a week.

I was hopeless at getting up, though: I set three alarms, two of which were in saucepans to make them even louder. I was meant to be at the studio by 5am to switch on the transmitter and play test music, followed by half an hour of country and western. I was rarely there before 5.30am and more often than not it was just in time for when Murray read the news at 6am and the first ads would be played. I managed to get away with it – until the farmers complained about their lack of country music.

Eventually I came to enjoy my routine of driving to work as dawn broke, with the waves rolling in and the occasional wallaby hopping by, and realised how presenting the breakfast show suited me. I liked how it gave me a kick-start to the day – talking to Mike Read many years later at Classic FM, he said he liked doing the breakfast show for the same reason. I know my production work, once I came off air, was all the more energised and creative because of it.

Townsville, 1969

Living where I was, I could swim in the sea in the afternoons, though this had to be in an enclosure to protect from 'stingers' – the deadly sea wasp, a type of jellyfish whose venom attacks the nervous system and can kill you within five minutes. More deaths were caused by this small creature than by sharks.

Allan was presenting the breakfast show at the ABC, and like me he came off air at 8.30am. The studios were close to each other, so we would meet for breakfast – not at a café, but on Allan's friend Sid's yacht which was anchored in the harbour. A rowing boat was tied up at the quay and once we were on board Allan would cook us a fry-up. The yacht was more *African Queen* than Roman Abramovich, but that made it all the more special.

If two men can ever have a bond without sex, then this was it. Our relationship reminded me of two films that had recently come out where there was a similar bond: *Midnight Cowboy* and *Butch Cassidy and the Sundance Kid*. I suppose we saw ourselves as cowboys of the airwaves, with Townsville in our hands.

Visitors

It was soon after I moved to Pallarenda that my father came out for a second tour of *My Fair Lady*, opening in Melbourne in March 1970. He stopped off in Townsville for a few days, partly to see me but also to link up with John McCallum, who was producing the show. Apart from being the husband of Googie Withers, John was a renowned actor in his own right, as well as creator of the successful TV programme *Skippy*. He was now in Townsville filming another series he'd developed called *Barrier Reef*, about a group of marine biologists on board a sailing ship.

Across the waves

My father stayed with me, and for the first time in our lives we hit it off. For once I felt he was proud of me – he even listened to my breakfast show. I took him to Magnetic Island and we had a couple of al fresco meals where we spoke as equals, lovely long conversations without him trying to put me down. We were never to have the same rapport again.

In April the royal family sailed into Townsville on the *Britannia*. This was the famous 'walkabout' tour of 1970, and I'd been chosen to share the commentary for the Cavalcade of Progress, a history of Townsville from its founding in 1864, with my opposite number at 4TO. Once the parade ended the royals went walkabout, and as the nineteen-year-old Princess Anne walked under the commentary box I shouted, 'Hooray!' which made her look up. 'Are you the announcer chappie?' she asked. When I replied in the affirmative she said, 'It must be hot up there!' I said it was but that I had a good view and then she was gone. I rather fancied Princess Anne in those days and had visions of her maybe marrying a commoner like me. The next day I scoured the newspapers, feeling sure this momentous incident would have been reported, but there was not even a mention.

In July my mother and my six-year-old brother Justin, who'd come to Australia with my father, came to stay with me at Pallarenda. We had a wonderful two weeks and, with it being July, the weather was at its North Queensland best. Something my brother still remembers is the day I took him for a walk along the beach and it was littered with baby sharks that had been washed ashore – we never did find out why. I took them both to all my favourite haunts, including the ghost gold mining town of Ravenswood, 80 miles south of Townsville, the last 20 miles of

Townsville, 1969

which is all dirt track. On my first visit I'd seen tumbleweeds, and goats roaming through the town, which gave it the feel of the Wild West. Its heyday was in the 1900s when it had a population of 5,000 and forty-eight hotels, but it was now virtually deserted.

We went onto Dunk Island, with Justin spending the day collecting coconuts, and we then virtually repeated the trip I'd done with Archie a year earlier. From Cairns we flew to Cooktown, another gold mining town that had seen a dramatic population decline. Most of its old buildings had been destroyed either by fire or cyclone, but I do remember the fascinating James Cook Museum housed in a stunning nineteenth-century former convent, which had been opened by the Queen that April.

It was lovely to see my mother. We were extremely close and she and I shared a fascination with travel, something that didn't seem to rub off on my brothers. I also felt I could talk to her about anything, though this would lead to problems later in her life when she would divulge personal information to all and sundry, leading Simon and I to stop being so confessional with her. Her visit to me coincided with my father preparing for the opening of *My Fair Lady* in Brisbane, and she and Justin flew back in time for the first night.

Back on the prowl

Determined to find love, I tried Lowth's again and picked up with a girl called Barbara who had a son. Her first husband had been in the army and they'd been based in Singapore, and she was still grieving for her father who had recently drowned in a parachuting accident. She said she fancied me because of my

Me, Justin, Pat and two of
my flatmates outside our
house on stilts in Pallarenda

Ravenswood

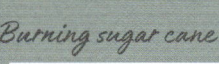

Burning sugar cane

Justin on our visit to Magnetic Island,
close to my plot of land

turned-up nose. My car was now a Fiat, which had the advantage of the front seats reclining right back to form an improvised bed, which we made full use of on our encounters in a hidden cul-de-sac by the beach. But after an intense three weeks she, too, suddenly gave up on me, and it was back to square one.

I'd been at 4AY for a year and it was time for my annual two-week holiday. I decided to hitch-hike my way to Sydney via Moree, look up some old friends, and then end up in Brisbane with my parents. I was lucky to get a lift for a good stretch of the journey but with a maniac who was intent on driving round corners as fast as he could. When we reached the outskirts of Rockhampton he stopped the car in a bush area and told me to get out. A grassy area under a tree was to be my bed for the night while he slept in the car, which he locked. This was the Australian winter and although in the north it was extremely pleasant during the day, and warm enough for shorts, at night the temperature plummeted. By the time I was allowed back in the car I was freezing. He dropped me off at a point where I could get a lift to Goondiwindi right on the border with New South Wales, and then it was on to Moree, where I joined Bob in his flat for a few nights before continuing my trip to Sydney. I had a lovely evening with Allan's parents, and saw the Australian production of *Hair* with the sister of a fellow DJ at 4AY, then continued my hitch-hiking north, ending up in Brisbane.

My parents had a flat in New Farm close to the city, and I stayed with them. I was really looking forward to seeing my father again following the really close time we'd had in Townsville earlier in the year. But he was back to his usual cold and distant self, and I was so disappointed. I was also running out of time for getting back to Townsville for my breakfast show: hitch-hiking would take too long and I didn't have enough money for the plane, but my mother insisted I ask Robin for the airfare. Asking my father for anything was something I dreaded, but he reluctantly gave it to me. It was such an awkward conversation that I decided never to ask for anything from him again.

The Maraka Queen

I was now doing the breakfast show six days a week with a long shift on the Saturday, from 6am to 11am. In October 1970 I broadcast my Saturday breakfast show from Ingham during their annual Maraka Festival, which culminated with a Mardis Gras. I was put up in a hotel in the centre of town for two nights.

It was my task to interview the Maraka Queen, a very attractive brunette called Rosalind, and there was an instant mutual attraction. This led to drinks on my balcony with the scent of burning sugar cane on the air and the singed flecks of the leaves landing in our beer. By the afternoon we were in bed together; by dawn she'd slipped out using a back route to avoid passing through reception. I had the feeling she'd done this before.

A couple of weeks later she got in touch to say she'd won a night in Cairns and asked if I would like to join her. We had a romantic dinner followed by a night of passion. On the leisurely drive back she rested on my shoulder the whole time, and we said a tender goodbye. But I never saw her again. By this time I was feeling exhausted by my breakfast routine and maybe I hadn't satisfied her sexual appetite, but a pattern was emerging with my patchy conquests.

Townsville, 1969

Restlessness

Whereas I'd had my fair share of one-night stands in both London and Sydney where I felt I was in the driving seat, here it seemed the tables had been reversed (not that I'm complaining about being used for sex!). But I think the problem was that I was looking for love, and any Townsville girls who wanted love wouldn't want to sleep with anyone until they were married. Maybe my mistake was getting too keen too quickly, as I felt I had done with Frances in Plymouth, and I was scaring away girls who were happy to have a casual encounter by seeming too serious. But it was hard to find a middle ground between a casual relationship and something more lasting.

Cairns, five hours drive away, was my usual weekend getaway. I'd grown friendly with a couple of girls from the town and I usually stayed with them. One was a teacher and the other the rep for Avis Rent a Car, and although I liked them both I really had designs on the teacher. But it never came to anything, despite a weekend in Ravenswood compering their annual Halloween ball when we all stayed at the Imperial Hotel. The Avis lady came with an Englishman who was a pilot for Bush Airways, and I'm sure he was as disappointed as I was when it became obvious we were all destined for separate rooms.

The six-days-a-week breakfast routine was beginning to take its toll and I hankered for something different. I'd started to lose interest in the production side and a new DJ with the unfortunate name of Steve Pead had become the boss's favourite. I was envious that Allan had managed to find work on Dunk, so when I went camping on the island one weekend with him and his girlfriend I seized the opportunity and asked the boss for a job. He said they had a position for a 'yard man' (Aussie speak for odd-job man, particularly outside). Even though I knew this would be a most unsuitable job for me I accepted. The manager, Bob Stewart, also thought I was a most unlikely yard man; it was only later that I realised he was also looking for young men who would mix with the guests and in some cases act as a gigolo.

Townsville, 1969

Dunk Island, 1971

Mr Schmid was amazed when I resigned from 4AY, particularly when I told him where I was going, but I was on a high. I sold my car and used the money to pay off the outstanding loan on the Magnetic land, and at the beginning of January 1971 I flew from Townsville on a tiny eight-seater aircraft to the small landing strip on Dunk, with a wonderful view of the Great Barrier Reef from the air along the way.

The resort was overlooking the beach, with low-rise wooden huts dotted around under the palm trees. I was assigned a hut to live in and we dined communally in another, where we ate much better than the guests. We had fresh milk, pork, and fruit salad made with papaya and pineapples grown on the island. The guests, meanwhile, were offered nothing local – their supplies came from the mainland, including tinned fruit salad. When I queried this I was told it was too much trouble to use the fresh fruit from the island.

Yet Dunk was the most sophisticated place I'd encountered since leaving Sydney. The people working there were well-travelled Australians and a smattering of Brits, mostly couples, looking for a bit of adventure. January was the off season, with relatively few guests, so the ratio of staff to guests was about one to one. The staff could use the same pool and the same bar, and there were no name badges.

There was a tropical downpour like clockwork everyday at 4pm which lasted about an hour. There's nothing better than that fresh feeling you get after there's been heavy rain and it certainly eased the oppressive heat of the day.

Duties

My job was to drive the tractor to pick up the supplies from the daily ferry, take pigswill up to the farm and collect the fresh milk, clean the bars and outside toilets, and cart all the rubbish to the dump. My first duty every morning was to fish out the mating cane toads from the swimming pool using a net before the guests were up and about. One of my favourite tasks was lighting the flares along the beach after the afternoon rains. It was a twelve-hour day and each night after dinner I'd crawl into bed exhausted.

Driving the tractor was one thing, but it also had a trailer that I was expected to reverse onto the jetty. I could never do it and so carried everything instead. I had similar problems when taking rubbish to the dump, but at least I didn't do what my predecessor had done: he'd reversed so close that the whole trailer had gone into the rubbish tip, with the tractor hanging on for dear life.

I wasn't really suited to the work, it must be said. On one of my first mornings, when washing the bar floor, I dipped the mop into what I thought was washing-up liquid but turned out to be cooking oil – it would have made Mr Bean proud. But I did make a good job of using the steam cleaner for the paths and to clean

Dunk Island, 1971

the outside public toilets. The urinals were a popular habitat for the elephant beetle, the largest beetle in the world at 4 inches long. They would climb into the urinal trough at night and emit a hissing sound when disturbed. As with the toads in the pool, it was my job to move the beetles on before the toilet started to be used. With about thirty beetles making their threatening sound it was initially quite frightening, but it soon became a challenge. They were never harmed but moved to open ground, where no doubt they lay in wait for their next nocturnal toilet visit.

On the third day, my boss, Bob, cornered me and asked why I hadn't been to the bar, and this was when I realised it was part of my job too. I gradually got used to the routine and loved the exchange with the guests, although my gigolo duties were not required. I probably wouldn't have had the stamina in any case, although I did have a liaison with one of my fellow workers, a mature lady who worked in the kitchen. It was left to two of my male co-workers to service any lady guests.

Dunk was owned by Avis Rent a Car and written off as a tax loss, but was put to good use entertaining visiting VIPs. You couldn't get bigger than Henry Ford II, the grandson of the founder of the Ford Motor Company, and the CEO at that time. As one of Ford's biggest clients, Avis wanted to put on a good show, and Bob called us all together to announce the forthcoming special guest and organise the total repainting of the resort. Luckily I wasn't called on to do this task – which is just as well, as it's something else I would say I'm hopeless at.

Henry Ford arrived with an entourage that included his second wife and an assortment of assistants and their ladies. They all got drunk one night and ended up in the pool, with Henry making

Dunk Island from Mission Beach

The beach huts of the resort

love, but not to his wife. I couldn't resist saying a pointed good morning to him the next day over breakfast.

While I was on Dunk I made a visit to Bedarra, the island alongside, which was even more beautiful, and I made my first trip to the Barrier Reef itself. After Lord Howe Island ten years earlier I was disappointed, as the coral didn't seem as colourful, but it was still a thrilling experience.

I would have loved to have stayed on at the resort, particularly as the film star Gina Lollobrigida was the next VIP to arrive, but my blundering was becoming embarrassing and I thought it best to resign before I was sacked. After a month in paradise I hitchhiked back to Townsville, where one of my former flatmates was soon to drive to Sydney and I agreed to join him. I'd heard through the grapevine that there was a newsreading job going at the 4BH radio station in Brisbane, so I applied on the off-chance and thought no more about it.

Sydney, 1971

Back in Narrabeen, I was working out what to do next when my friend Norman from the *Fairstair* and his new wife, Joyce, came to the rescue and offered me accommodation at their place in Collaroy. They'd just had a son, Justin, and were grateful for the rent. Now I just had to find a job.

In the *Sydney Morning Herald* I noticed Grahame's Bookshop, located in the centre of the city on Hunter Street, was looking for an assistant. I'd hardly read a book in my life, but decided to apply. When asked about my education I said it was up to O-level standard, which seemed to impress the interviewer no end – luckily he didn't ask how many. So I got the job, which was just as well because I was down to my last $10.

My only experience of selling books was on the bookstall at the Mermaid Theatre, which I had taken on as an extra job for three nights a week at £1 a night. This was in a totally different league, and for the first two weeks I felt totally lost. I kept messing up people's phone orders, and got a right telling-off from the manager, Ron Cleaver. But his assistant, Pauline Catt, an attractive married lady of about forty, soon made me feel better. She took a fancy to me and we often had kisses in the store room. She was an incredible flirt, though, and eventually moved on to a good-looking new recruit with rippling muscles but no brain, who reminded me of Barbie's counterpart, Ken.

I quickly became friendly with a Dane called Frederik Christiansen who arrived a couple of months after me in April. He was five years my senior, and like me he'd emigrated to Australia some years before. He was probably the only person there who knew what he was doing, as he'd been in the book trade in Copenhagen where to sell books you were expected to serve an apprenticeship. He was also well read.

With Frederik's guidance I soon got into my stride and realised I liked the whole process of selling. Well, who wouldn't like selling books? I also discovered books for myself, and became particularly fond of George Orwell and Christopher Isherwood. I was fascinated to see which books sold and would get annoyed when people asked for something that we didn't have in stock. The bestselling book of 1971 was *Love Positions*, basically porn in the guise of education – not so much a book as a series of illustrations. Of course I had to have a copy for research purposes. I used to love the furtive glances towards the shelf and the hesitant way men would ask for it. I can't remember any couples coming in to buy it.

Getting my act together

I was enjoying my time living at Norman's place, but following a marital argument Joyce asked me to leave. I asked my old school friend Allan, now married to Carolyn, if I could stay with them for a while. They had a cosy unit in Double Bay and, although I could see it was only just big enough for them, I overstayed my welcome until it was suggested nicely that maybe I could find somewhere else. Allan told me about a place his parents had lived in temporarily and so I moved in there, but it was awful: the worst sort of boarding house, with terrible food, run by a dragon of a lady. But it was the best thing for me – it gave me a kick up the bum and I went once again to the trusty *Sydney Morning Herald*, this time looking for a flatshare. I found one in Double Bay with an attractive couple, Jenny and Leighton, and Norman, a Brit, who worked for the civil service. Norman was very pedantic and didn't really get on with Leighton, who was artistic and laid-back. All I really remember about Jenny is the noise she made when she made love to Leighton.

I was getting really frustrated about the lack of a relationship and thought maybe my woeful fashion sense, made worse by my time in Townsville, was part of the reason. So for the first time in my life I spent any spare money on clothes, and strutted around like a peacock in expectation.

A departure – and an arrival

Frederik decided that after three years in Australia it was about time he went back to Denmark, leaving a heartbroken girlfriend behind. We all went to Circular Quay to see him off that August, but I kept in touch and he's become one of my greatest friends. I'm sure that if Frederik had stayed he would have got the promotion that came to me instead: head of paperbacks. Grahame's had the highest turnover of Pan and Fontana in Australia, and although these shelves were stocked regularly by

Sydney, 1971

the reps it was my job to oversee everything and to become the buyer for the Penguin and Pelican books, which also had a large section. It was a position I relished, and I got a great thrill seeing books that I'd ordered going through the till.

It took some time for Frederik's replacement to arrive, but when she did I fell for her straight away. She had a 1940s look about her, both in clothes and hairstyle, and I liked what she had to say. Her name was Anne.

I'd now moved to Balmain, where Norman from Double Bay had bought his own place and took me with him as a lodger, where I slept in the sitting room. I thought it would be a friendly gesture to take Anne for a drink after her first day at work and we talked for ages. Actually I talked for ages. But she seemed fascinated with my tales of the outback and North Queensland. She was twenty-one and had recently been working at another bookshop, Dymocks, and unlike me certainly knew about books. She'd also been to Sydney University but hadn't quite finished her degree, as she had problems with her mother at home and wanted her independence. Working at the bookshop gave her just enough money to rent a bedsit in Glebe. Much as this first encounter had been successful I decided to tread carefully as I didn't want to fall into the trap of being too keen too quickly. After several weeks I eventually plucked up courage to ask her round for spaghetti bolognese. The evening went extremely well and I should have kissed her then, but still held back.

The weeks continued to tick by, and it was Anne who finally took the initiative when she kissed me while we were watching *Death in Venice* at the cinema. I must have appeared ungrateful, as I really wanted to watch the film and thought the kissing could wait. It was later at her place in Glebe where she'd prepared strawberries that we declared our love for each other.

She must have found it galling to have this uneducated Englishman acting as her boss, but when you're in love you will accept anything. Anne said later that she thought I sounded and looked like a cultured Australian (was there such a thing in the seventies?) and that the clothes had made an impact. And because I was so industrious she assumed I was an established family man and working hard to be a good provider.

All was going well: I was enjoying myself with Anne and loving the job and the thrill of buying and selling, which reminded me of my time in Tangier exporting pouffes. But then suddenly a telegram arrived from 4BH in Brisbane, offering me a job as a presenter and newsreader at $70 a week. Anne was very pleased for me, and we decided she'd soon follow me to Brisbane and we'd find a place to live together. It was what I had always dreamt of – to work on a capital city radio station – and it was really an offer I couldn't refuse.

Sydney, 1971

Brisbane, 1971

I arrived in Brisbane on a Sunday night. I was starving but when I asked a passer-by if he knew a place where I could get something to eat he replied, 'Nowhere's open after nine, mate.' By area, Brisbane was the largest of Australia's state capitals and the biggest city in the world at the time, but to most Australians it was just a 'big country town.' To me, it looked like one enormous suburb.

With its 'Super Oldies' format 4BH had until recently been Brisbane's number-one station, but its crown was beginning to slip. It was part of the Macquarie Network, which meant its news bulletins were broadcast throughout Queensland. I was to read the news between 4pm and 7pm, ending with a half-hour bulletin, then present a show between 9pm and midnight. I was also to broadcast on Saturday afternoons.

Russ Walkington, whom I'd worked with at 4AY, was on breakfast: his catchphrase was, 'These are the Russ hours on 4BH.' A talk-show format then took over until the afternoon when John Fleming, with a splendid handlebar moustache, presented *Drive*, followed by Jimmy White, who had the persona of a cheeky chappie. The station manager was George Lovejoy, who'd made his name as a rugby commentator and was nicknamed 'Mr

Football'. Ben Beckinsale was the programme director who produced creative jingles, with a voice to match – and, unusually for management, was a genuinely nice guy. He was having a relationship with Denise, one of the weekend presenters, who was equally friendly. My boss was John Taylor, the studio manager and news director, and although I didn't warm to him I suspect it was he who'd taken me on because of my 'news' voice. In the newsroom I worked alongside the journalist Ken Guy. His was a name I was familiar with as he'd had a stint at the ABC, where he'd read the news statewide. He later became the first newsreader on LBC in London when it opened in 1973.

Home life

Anne was soon to join me in Brisbane, but first I had to find us somewhere to live. I was shown a magnificent flat in New Farm, the suburb where my parents had lived the year before, and snapped it up immediately. It was close to the city and overlooked the river and the Story Bridge, Brisbane's two most famous landmarks. The flat was in an attractive period building that even had its own boat shed. There were two bedrooms and, as I couldn't afford the rent on my own, I asked Dennis Lister, a teacher friend from Townsville now living in the city, to join me.

Anne came up from Sydney about six weeks later and we set up home. At first she tried to complete her degree in Brisbane, but the university authorities wouldn't allow her, so instead she got a well-paid job with the civil service. For a while the rent was split three ways, but I think Dennis felt like a gooseberry so he decided to leave. We didn't have the flat to ourselves for long, though, as

Brisbane, 1971

Jack Grant, whom I'd known at 4AY, came to Brisbane in straitened circumstances following a stroke whilst on air. I invited him to join us. I'd always looked up to and got on well with Jack, but hadn't really spent much time with him socially in Townsville. Now I had a chance to get to know him better, and at some point he told me he was gay. At the time it was a brave confession – homosexuality wasn't decriminalised in Queensland until 1990.

Anne worked at night at the Venice restaurant around the corner from the station on Adelaide Street. I would have my meal there between newsreading and going back on air, so the arrangement worked rather well, although it must have been tiring for Anne. She'd make me toast and tea in the mornings before she headed off to work, and I'd listen to the ABC's current affairs programme before going back to sleep.

Late Saturday afternoon and Sundays was our time together, where we'd play squash and catch a film. I've always loved rivers and on a whim bought a rubber dinghy to use on the Brisbane River. We had our own jetty to launch it from, after all. We hadn't taken the current into account, though, and were quickly swept downstream. It would have been impossible to row back, so we sheepishly had to take it out of the water and carry it with us all the way to New Farm, which by this time was 2 miles away.

Work

I was put on breakfast when Russ was away, which was nerve-racking and hectic. The commercials were all on cartridge and had to be individually fired. In commercial radio a few seconds' dead air not only sounds terrible, but is lost revenue as well, and

*Our building
in New Farm*

Down by the river

Anne, riverside

Story Bridge

A picture of me at 4BH, from the National Archives of Australia, taken for a campaign showcasing successful migrants

A cartoon presented to me as a leaving gift

Seeing Allan in Townsville before heading off on my travels, October 1972

The house in Pallarenda in Townsville, after Cyclone Althea

I must have lost them a fair bit of money during my stint. George Lovejoy was understanding, however, and gave me some good broadcasting advice. I got to see how cut-throat commercial radio can be when you are competing with more than half a dozen other stations. Unlike the situation in the UK, Australian stations could change format overnight and this happened at 4BH when 'Super Oldies' gave way to middle-of-the-road. Luckily I had a suitably mellow voice, but others struggled. The new format was 'enhanced' with a package of pre-recorded jingles from the US with the generic title of *Have a Happy Day*. It was totally naff.

On Christmas Eve 1971 I read the news that Cyclone Althea, with winds of up to 134 miles per hour, had hit Townsville and totally destroyed Magnetic Island. Obviously it wouldn't affect my plot of land, but I wondered about my good friend Allan, who was still living at Pallarenda. He'd gone off to his job at the ABC early in the morning, and being the eternal optimist he expected Althea to veer away from the coast. It didn't, and when he got back it was to find the house wrecked with its roof blown off. He had to borrow an army tent, erecting it under the ruined house, and lived rough until he moved in with my old Townsville flatmate Murray, who was by then also working at the ABC.

I'd made up my mind once I got the Brisbane job that I'd give it a year and then start travelling; I was getting itchy feet and I was also conscious that commercial radio would be starting up in England in 1973. Much to Anne's disappointment the travelling was something I wanted to do on my own: I wanted to use it as a chance to challenge myself. It was strange timing, really, when I'd finally found the kind of relationship I'd been looking for all this time. Maybe it had something to do with my

Brisbane, 1971

relentless moving around with my parents and often being left to my own devices. I thought the best thing to do would be for Anne and I to end our relationship. Anne accepted, albeit reluctantly, and we went our separate ways.

Farewell to Australia

Anne went back to Sydney a few days before me. I'd planned to spend a week in the city before taking the bus to Townsville, from where I would start my travels. I thought this could be the last time I'd be in the city, and there were several people to whom I wanted to say goodbye. I stayed in Double Bay with Jenny and Leighton, and was browsing in the local newsagents when, there in front of me, was Anne. She knew I was staying somewhere on Anderson Street, and had come to find me. I had to admit I was pleased and I belatedly realised how much she meant to me. We decided to correspond whilst I was on my trip, with a view to her joining me in England once she'd completed her degree. I'm sure she had an idea that I was likely be sowing a few more wild oats along the way, but was prepared to put up with this providing none of my liaisons became serious.

I had several stop-offs planned already. A journalist friend from 4TO in Townsville, Dennis Simmons, was working in New Guinea as an assistant manager at a radio station, and I planned to end my trip in Copenhagen, where I'd stay with Frederik.

Hong Kong was also on the itinerary. Before I left I'd been given a list of contacts at Radio Hong Kong by a print journalist called Barry Whelan, who'd worked in the colony. I hoped to do the same, and he also suggested I stay at the YMCA, which was reasonably priced and well situated. To secure a reservation I had to send a telegram from overseas, as they accepted only guests from outside the territory.

But first it was back to Townsville to stay with Allan and Murray whilst I finalised my travel arrangements. There was a Qantas travel office in town, and I managed to get the most amazing deal. I think the man running it didn't get much business – certainly nothing like the trip I was planning – and perhaps he was overly generous. I bought a ticket valid for a year from Townsville to London via New Guinea (including internal flights), then onto Hong Kong, Bangkok, Delhi, Cairo, Istanbul, and Copenhagen.

Murray had once worked in the post office, and he told me how you could send coconut postcards. All you had to do was pick a coconut off the ground, write on the nut's shell and then the post office would stamp it for you. This was how I sent my final Australian message to Anne.

Brisbane, 1971

Hong Kong, 1972

In October 1972 I left Australia and began a slow journey back to England. My plane stopped off in Cairns before flying on to Port Moresby and then to the highlands of New Guinea. The airport at Goroka was tiny, more like a landing strip, with groups of bare-breasted women sitting nearby on the grass. They looked magnificent, as did the men with their war paint and spears.

I stayed with Dennis, my friend from Townsville, who was working at the local radio station. With New Guinea's independence only three years away, it was Dennis's task to train local staff to take over once the Australians left. After a week at his bungalow in the wonderful climate of the hills, I flew to the beautiful 'garden city' of Lae on the coast, where the style of dress was noticeably more westernised and the influence of missionaries was in evidence. I took a boat trip along the coast to Madang, sleeping and eating on deck with the crew, and after a couple of days there I did the journey in reverse and flew from Lae to Port Moresby to pick up my flight to Hong Kong.

As my plane flew into Kai Tak, the airport serving one of the most densely populated areas on earth, the rooftops seemed to be within touching distance and I wondered how any pilot could land safely. If we managed to avoid the buildings, there was still a strong possibility of overshooting the runway and ending up in the waters of Victoria Harbour.

As advised by Barry in Brisbane, I'd sent a telegram before I left to book myself in for five nights at the Hong Kong YMCA in the centre of Kowloon. It had a magnificent view of the harbour from the roof garden café and just as good a position as the prestigious Peninsula Hotel next door, at a fraction of the price.

Radio Hong Kong

On my first full day in Hong Kong I took myself to Radio Hong Kong on Broadcast Drive. This enclave in the Kowloon Tong district housed all the broadcasting stations in the territory. In the riots of 1967 during the Cultural Revolution, the media had been particularly targeted, culminating in a commercial radio talk-show host being set alight in his car. It was decided to move both TV stations, commercial radio and Radio Hong Kong into one area, so they could be sealed off in case of emergency.

I presented my list of names at reception, and was told that the first person had died and the second was just about to leave and become director of broadcasting in the Seychelles (I was gatecrashing his farewell party). The third name on the list was Geoffrey Weeks, and he'd just taken over as head of English radio. I couldn't believe my luck when he said they were holding auditions on Monday. (It was only later I found out that auditions were held every Monday because of the high turnover of staff.)

Audition day came and I was handed over to the assistant head of presentation, an Australian called Ken Scott, who'd previously

Hong Kong, 1972

worked at the ABC in Australia. I seemed to be sailing through until Ken asked me to talk for a minute about the main street of Brisbane. Commentary had never been my strong point, and to be honest Queen Street didn't have much to offer. I ummed and ahhed, but I somehow got through it. I was offered a one-month rolling contract, which was perfect for me – it would make it easy to leave when the time came. I set myself four months.

Geoffrey warned that accommodation was incredibly expensive and suggested I find somewhere to stay before making a decision to accept the position. After a quick wander round, I found myself a room at Haiphong Mansions in Tsim Sha Tsui, not far from the YMCA. Mansion it certainly wasn't – it was a fire trap with rusty water coming out of the bath taps – but it had a series of relatively cheap en-suite rooms with an inclusive amah (maid) service. I accepted both the room and the job.

Before I was let loose on the airwaves, I was to trail Sue Earl, one of the announcers. Radio Hong Kong operated a revolving shift system, which gave me quite a bit of time off. Day one was the evening shift from 6pm to 1am. The second day was 11am to 6pm, and on the third day I would start at 6am and finish at 1pm. I would have the following day off and wouldn't have to be back till 6pm the next day to start the rotation all over again.

The morning shift started with a classical programme called *Sleepers, Awake!,* taken from the Bach cantata of the same name. This was my first experience of presenting classical music and I loved it. Some of the pronunciations were a bit tricky, but there was a very good card index with a phonetic system that was easy to understand. The early shift finished with an hour's programme of my own choice of music. There was plenty of newsreading, presentation of classical concerts and general continuity. I couldn't have asked for a more well-rounded experience.

Sue put me through my training, including how to talk up to the 'pips' for the 1pm news. My predecessor had left under a cloud because he had become rather blasé about this task. On one occasion he left himself thirty seconds before the pips were due to come in from the Royal Observatory, but instead of silence what the audience heard was, 'Let the buggers wait.' He'd left the microphone on by mistake.

Central casting

Over the next few weeks I gradually met a fascinating cast of characters, either at work or in the Radio Hong Kong Club, a tiny bar in the basement that buzzed with gossip. Geoffrey Weeks was a renowned amateur actor and had landed a starring role in Bruce Lee's final film *Enter the Dragon*, where he played the M-type character of Braithwaite. Head of light music was Ray Cordeiro, a former warden at Stanley Prison, who'd been in broadcasting since the late 1940s. When I arrived he'd just started presenting his own programme called *All the Way with Ray*. He had a genial style on air. He's still presenting the same programme at the age of ninety-three, and in 2000 was voted the world's most durable DJ. Ralph Pixton had been a policeman in Britain before becoming a tea planter in India, where he'd met Geoffrey Kendal and his troupe of travelling actors (the inspiration for the film *Shakespeare Wallah*). With his commanding presence and booming voice, he was asked to join them. He ended up in Hong Kong in 1963 and applied for a job at the station. When asked if

Hong Kong, 1972

he had any relevant experience, he boomed, 'I am an act-or!' He presented the morning programme on the AM channel and was president of the Radio Hong Kong Club, where he was always giving the bartender, Mr Wong, a hard time: 'Do NOT wash the beer glasses with *soap*!' I was rather frightened of him.

One night after my shift I noticed a familiar face in the bar. It was Wilfrid Brambell of *Steptoe and Son* fame, who'd come to visit Ralph. He was a regular visitor and they would both hold forth in the club. Physically they looked like Laurel and Hardy, and to outsiders they were lads about town, but in reality they were lovers. (Despite Hong Kong being a British colony, homosexuality was not decriminalised until 1991.)

Houses of ill repute

At Haiphong Mansions I met a gorgeous blonde called Eva, who had a plummy English accent. We got chatting and I asked what she was doing in Hong Kong and she replied, 'Actually, I'm whoring at the moment.' I muttered something in embarrassment, but once I got over the shock we became good friends. She would come into my room and talk about her clients. She took her job seriously and must have been earning a tidy sum. She said, 'I have to "come" once a day and I don't mind who it's with, even a panting, fat Chinese punter.' But if Eva was a high-class call girl, Haiphong Mansions seemed a poor base.

Back at the club I got chatting to an American, Bob Williams, who presented an evening easy-listening programme. He was a Korean War veteran who'd lost a leg in action. I told him about Haiphong Mansions and he suggested I move to where he was

Ray Cordeiro

Bob Williams

At the desk at Radio Hong Kong

The view across
Victoria Harbour
from the YMCA's
rooftop café

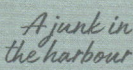

A junk in
the harbour

Trams on
Hong Kong
Island

(Pictures taken
by Allan Porter)

staying, Palatine House. He said they even gave discounts for 'artistes'. It was indeed cheaper and the room was bigger, although I thought it odd that they had mirrors on the ceiling. I soon found out this was a proper brothel, with a nightly parade of available girls of all nationalities in the bar.

Colonial life

In 1972 no one thought that China would want to reclaim Hong Kong in 1997. Even after Nixon's visit earlier that year China was still very much a closed shop, and as Hong Kong was China's window on the world it suited both parties to keep the status quo. Although Hong Kong Island and the Kowloon Peninsula had been ceded to the UK in perpetuity following the two Opium Wars, the New Territories was on a 99-year lease due to expire on the 1st of July 1997. But it seemed that no one wanted to think about this issue, least of all the UK government. In Britain's last important colony, life continued as it had done since the war. The Hong Kong Club didn't allow Chinese members or women. Colonial administrators thought they had a job for life. And the Legislative Assembly passed laws, rubber-stamped by the Governor. Many of the old buildings were still there and in use: the Kowloon and Canton Railway, the General Post Office, Hong Kong and Shanghai Bank, the Hong Kong Club and, my favourite, the Repulse Bay Hotel which did a splendid afternoon tea. But the most amazing sight of all was the Hong Kong Cricket Club, which had its pitch right in the centre of town, rather like having Lord's in the middle of Piccadilly. The sun may have been setting on the rest of the Empire, but not in Hong Kong.

Hong Kong, 1972

I spent Christmas 1972 with Gregory Leung, the only Chinese announcer to work for the English service. His mother had a large flat on Hong Kong Island, where I shared turkey and all the trimmings with Gregory's extended family. For New Year I'd been invited by Claire, one of the new announcers, to join her and her family at the Hong Kong Club, a bastion of colonial prestige housed in a grand Victorian edifice in the centre of Hong Kong Island. Claire was the daughter of a high-ranking government official and, as we sang 'Auld Lang Syne' from the balcony I felt rather out of place. I'd bought an ill-fitting jacket from the Temple Street Market, and since leaving Dunk Island my hair had gone rather wild. I didn't have much money, but as I'd been treated to the evening by her parents I thought the least I could do was pay for a taxi to take us back to our respective homes. I struggled financially for the rest of the month.

Claire had promised to take me to the Foreign Correspondent's Club, but her contract wasn't renewed after she pronounced the name of the composer Borodin wrong: she'd said BoROdin and there'd been a letter of complaint to the *South China Morning Post*. Being somewhat deflated, her enthusiasm for showing me the more exclusive parts of Hong Kong evaporated.

The tiny Portuguese territory of Macau was 40 miles to the west of Hong Kong, accessible by ferry. This was my first taste of anything Portuguese, and I fell for its colonial buildings, its food and its laid-back lifestyle. Most of my visits were to soak up the history, but I also had an obsession with roulette, something Macau was well known for. (You could bet on the horses in Hong Kong, but not gamble at a casino.) One night I took the equivalent of £30 to the Lisboa Hotel, with the aim of lasting the night at the roulette table. Looking back I can't believe I did this – £30 in today's money is worth £370. But I didn't regret a moment: I started gambling at 10pm and made the money last until 6am the following morning. I had just enough left to buy myself an Irish coffee before catching the ferry back to Hong Kong.

Looking to the future

In early January 1973 Allan Porter from Townsville joined the presentation staff at Radio Hong Kong. After I'd persuaded the brothel owners that Allan was another 'artiste', we shared my room at Palatine House. In the end he would stay for two years and became adept at dubbing kung fu films, but I was always looking ahead to my radio future in Britain.

One day I was summoned to see the director of broadcasting, Donald Brooks. Many working at Radio Hong Kong had never met him, let alone been invited into his office. He was leaving shortly to set up Radio Orwell, one of the first commercial stations to launch in Britain. He wanted to pick my brains because I had experience of working in commercial radio, and as I left of course I took the opportunity to ask for a job at Orwell. In the event the station didn't open until the end of 1975, by which time I had found employment elsewhere.

A much better lead was the British Forces Broadcasting Service (BFBS), of which I'd previously been unaware. Radio Hong Kong had an agreement to broadcast programmes made by BFBS in London which were of an extremely high standard. One of my colleagues was a major's wife whose real name was Spottiswood, but she gave herself the wonderful stage name of Roma Berlyn.

Hong Kong, 1972

She told me about the organisation and the stations they had around the world, and this seemed to be my ideal job, combining radio and travel. I decided to apply on my return to England.

Following a programme of personal selections where I'd played an hour of José Feliciano, I had a phone call from a Chinese lady saying how much she'd enjoyed the show. I was going to say thank you and put the phone down, but the presenter who was taking over from me, an Australian called Geoffrey Powell, egged me on to arrange a meeting. I met Betti, a sophisticated divorcee in her mid thirties, at a restaurant, where we chatted amiably. After the meal I asked her back to my room, but I wasn't sure whether to try something or not. In the end she took the initiative and unzipped my trousers. When I asked her out again she said, 'Didn't you realise it was a one-night stand?'

But I persevered. Eartha Kitt, who was playing at the Mandarin Oriental, had phoned the radio station asking for help with some song lyrics. I was tasked with the job and as a reward I was given two tickets to see her show. I asked Betti, and she agreed.

We began seeing each other. Betti introduced me to the sort of Hong Kong only a local would know. She knew how to do the 'Shanghai squeeze', a technique Wallis Simpson had learnt whilst living in Shanghai with her first husband. Was it worth giving up the throne for? Maybe it was.

Betti didn't want commitment, which suited us both. She'd been abused by her first husband, and now she wanted to be in control and was looking for short-term relationships. Foreigners such as me, passing through the colony, suited perfectly because they always had an onward ticket. When my four months were up we had a fond farewell before I caught my flight to Bangkok.

Across the waves

Homeward bound, 1973

When I arrived in Bangkok I went to stay with Boonsom, a short, roly-poly Thai man who spoke fluent English, picked up while living in the UK. I'd met him in Hong Kong when he was on a visit there with his girlfriend. When I'd told him that Bangkok was the next destination on my trip he'd insisted I stay with him.

My first impression of the city was of an overgrown shanty town with the worst air pollution I'd ever experienced, but there was an exotic feel to the place that wasn't evident in Hong Kong. It was the time of the Vietnam War and, as Thailand was the closest to the action you could get without actually being in the war zone, many of the war correspondents were based there.

On my first night, Boonsom and his girlfriend took me out to an open-air restaurant where I ate the best food I'd ever tasted. Thai cuisine has since become ubiquitous in the UK, but in 1973 it was little known outside Thailand. Boonsom tested my chilli tolerance by pouring more and more of the hot stuff onto my plate, and kept asking me if I wanted a girl for the night, even suggesting I take the waitress home. If Tangier was a gay paradise, then Thailand appeared to be the heterosexual equivalent: perhaps I was being naive, but all the girls seemed so friendly.

Boonsom was keen for me to smarten up my appearance, suggesting I get a haircut and explaining that it wasn't etiquette to wear shorts. The haircut I welcomed, and it turned out to be an experience in itself: a man cut my hair, then a female assistant cleaned my ears and gave me a manicure. The long trousers were less tolerable, but none of the Thai men wore shorts, despite it being the hottest time of year.

I was introduced to the delights of Patpong, Bangkok's red-light district. Now incredibly seedy, forty years ago it had the air of the Folies Bergères, with classy clubs and sophisticated sex shows where couples could go without embarrassment. Admittedly it did have girls demonstrating creative methods of smoking and launching ping-pong balls, but it was all done with such grace and good humour. It was all part of the Bangkok experience, in the same way that a visit to Bugis Street in Singapore was considered a must.

Very much an Anglophile, Boonsom listened to a radio station with an English announcer. As I was looking for work, I somehow tracked the source of the voice to a young man broadcasting from a shed as a solo operation. It quickly became clear that the shed wasn't big enough for two – he was just scraping a living, and most of his money seemed to be spent at the VD clinic.

Two weeks into the stay, Boonsom decided on a whim that we would take a trip to Cambodia, so we all piled into his Citroën and at the border we talked to the guards into letting us through. My French was still pretty good, so I got a reasonable sense of what was happening. Although there was a supposed truce in Vietnam, this didn't apply to Cambodia and in April 1973 the country was 80 per cent occupied by the Khmer Rouge. Gunfire could actually be heard in the distance. We took the ferry to Koh Kong, an island popular with Cambodians as a holiday destination and one of the few areas in the country still at peace. Our visit coincided with that of a group of university students from Phnom Penh University who were camping nearby. I struck up quite a friendship with one of the male students and, as our trip also coincided with the local school fair, I became friendly with a teacher too. They both sent me pictures of my visit and for some time I kept up a correspondence with the student, but I fear they would have both been killed during Pol Pot's Year Zero.

My next stop was India, and the first thing I noticed at Delhi airport was a sign saying 'We welcome all people, except missionaries.' I had no accommodation organised, so I thought the YMCA would be a good bet. 'It's full,' my taxi driver told me. I took him at his word and even more naively asked him to suggest somewhere else. By default I struck lucky: I was taken to a guest house where everyone ate vegetarian food with the family. The taxi driver had insisted on coming in with me because he wanted to sell me some marijuana, but he was also interested in my shirt. Anne had sent me a new shirt for my forthcoming birthday while I was in Bangkok, so I could afford to sell the shirt I had on, which I did for £1.

I made the mistake of going into town on my first day in Western clothes including some smart shoes, so I was an easy target for fraudsters, particularly as I didn't know where I was going. Some 'friendly' boys got talking with the usual tactic of 'Where you from?' They suddenly looked down and said I had paint on my shoes. But they were willing to clean it off at a price, and by some miracle they just happened to have shoe-cleaning

Homeward bound, 1973

kit with them (along with a suspicious-looking jar that no doubt had the paint in it). The next day I got round all these problems by putting my newly gained £1 to good use. I bought an Indian pyjama outfit along with some sandals and I wasn't hassled again.

I took the Taj Express to the Taj Mahal, before travelling third class to Varanasi on the way to Nepal. I survived the journey with copious amounts of *chai* served at each station in clay cups and on arrival I found a very clean government rest house. The next day from the viewing platform I sat for hours watching bodies burning on their pyres before they were thrown into the Ganges. What the dogs didn't eat, the fish would. Strangely though, I found the whole spectacle a rather moving spiritual experience.

Kathmandu was like a series of dolls' houses – elaborate, wooden-framed buildings with low ceilings, befitting of a race where the average height for a male is five foot four. The old town had a medieval air, with little sanitation or electricity, but I loved it. It had been one of the hippie capitals, so there were numerous cafés serving food to suit all tastes. Whereas in India I'd heeded all warnings and been vigilant about what I ate, here my guard slipped totally, and I drank my first lassi with crushed ice and even had an ice cream. Marijuana was still legal and a friend asked me to join him in a 'pleasure room'. I was confronted by mood music and bodies on the floor staring into space. 'Hey, man, what you having?' asked a waiter in kaftan and beads. I was given a menu and decided on the hash cake: it wasn't long before I was one of those bodies staring into space, saying, 'Hey, man.'

The visibility wasn't good enough to see Mount Everest, so I decided to head for Pokhara and the Annapurna range. I found a place to stay by the lake that cost 4 rupees a night (there were

Teacher and children at the local school in Koh Kong, Cambodia

Lunchtime, Koh Kong, Cambodia

The Annapurna Range

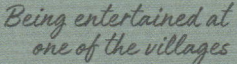

Vaudanda, Nepal

Being entertained at one of the villages

22 rupees to the pound). The toilet was just a hole in the ground, but they boasted that they served only *boileo* water. This was important because even before I left Hong Kong, hepatitis A was seen to be the main scourge for travellers.

People went to Pokhara to trek and officially you needed a trekking permit which was only available in Katmandhu. I certainly wasn't going back so I gathered up some like-minded travellers who didn't have trekking permits either and just went into the hills. The highest point was Poon Hill and as dawn broke the sight was breathtaking. The whole Annapurna range was in front of us and, even though the Annapurna base camp was two days away, I felt I could touch the mountains. It was a great way to celebrate my twenty-sixth birthday.

I had no plan of where to stay on my next stop, Cairo, but I rather liked the look of a man at the airport who wore a chauffeur's uniform with a cap that said 'Gresham's'. The hotel was in a run-down 1930s building but it was quite central and only £1 a night. It had a dusty, faded grandeur and breakfast was served by tall Sudanese waiters wearing kaftans. The people staying there were my type, including an American DJ who expressed a feeling about India that I shared: 'If there's a God hanging about somewhere, he's in India.'

Apart from seeing the pyramids, my main memory of Cairo was chatting to a trader in the souk. He was doing a good job trying to sell me ambergris, which he said could be stirred into tea and used as an aphrodisiac. When I said I couldn't afford the £5, he came up with an unusual solution. He said he'd give it to me providing I promised to send him some long johns from Marks & Spencer. I kept my part of the bargain, and he later sent me a postcard simply saying, 'Thanks for the long johns – Mohammed.'

At Gresham's I met a couple of South Americans who like me were off to Istanbul, so we decided to share a place once we got there. We found a room in the old city for $1 a night between the three of us, with a charge of an extra dollar if we wanted hot water. I was running out of money, but still managed to do the usual tourist things such as the Grand Bazaar and the Blue Mosque, before sending a telegram to Frederik in Copenhagen to let him know my planned arrival date.

Thank goodness Frederik was at the airport with his girlfriend Anita because I was literally down to my last dollar. I did have a fallback position, though: I'd asked for my Australian tax rebate to go straight into my UK account, and once my parents sent this over I was solvent again. Frederik had a flat close to the centre of the city which meant it was easy to explore. I loved the Tivoli Gardens and its live music, the city's canals and what was reputed to be the first and longest pedestrian street in the world, Strøget. By this time Frederik was the manager of a lovely little bookshop that had a small cafe attached, which I thought was a very civilised way of selling books. He eventually became managing director of a popular bookshop chain in Denmark.

The only blot on my time there was that I was getting terrible wind in my stomach, as if it were being tied in knots. I thought maybe it was the food, but it wasn't constant and I kept forgetting about it. My adventure was almost over and, although I travelled by myself, I probably couldn't have done it without the moral support of Anne. We were writing to each other throughout the trip, but I found out later that she'd never received a long letter I sent from Nepal – and that silence had almost split us up.

Homeward bound, 1973

England 1973

I arrived back in the UK in June 1973 and was elated to see my family again. Although my parents and youngest brother had been out to Australia, I hadn't seen my brother Simon for more than five years. When I left he hadn't seemed to be a particularly happy boy and we weren't that close, but now he was a long-haired youth of nineteen and we had an instant rapport.

My biggest priority was to find a job. I auditioned for the BBC World Service and I passed, but they could offer only occasional shifts, so I decided to look for more full-time work. My next port of call was the British Forces Broadcasting Service, where I was hoping for another audition, but instead a lot of form-filling was involved. I also sent audition tapes to LBC and Capital Radio in London, the first two commercial stations to go on air.

Culture shock

While waiting for results, I wandered around London and it seemed a sad reflection of what it had been like when I left in 1968. Then there had been a feeling of optimism and excitement, and London had felt like the cultural capital of the world. Now the Swinging Sixties were long over, and there was a seedy and depressing atmosphere pervading the city, rather like a party that had gone on too long with just a few desperate stragglers. Smoking pot was no longer cool but had become just another bad habit. Carnaby Street, decked out in psychedelic colours that had been the cutting edge of fashion when I left, just looked five years out of date. My friend Lyn was still trying to sell Moroccan goods but the market had been saturated and he had most of the bead necklaces we'd bought as a job lot from Tangier five years before. Since the Beatles had broken up it felt like innovation had gone out of the music scene. And then there was decimalisation: I couldn't get over how expensive everything was, particularly small items, which seemed to have doubled in price.

Hepatitis

The tawdriness of London was clearly getting me down: my mother remarked that I'd gone from a period of extreme elation to the depths of depression in less than a month. I also had discomfort in my stomach and incredible lethargy, but the doctor put it down to the stress of coming back to the UK and my uncertain job situation, and prescribed indigestion tablets.

It was only when I turned yellow a couple of weeks later that hepatitis A was diagnosed. I'd had no suspicions: the disease has a six-week incubation period, so at least it hadn't spoiled my trip. In Nepal I'd overheard two American girls talking about hep A, saying that if you got it your pee would go black and poo would be white. From my own experience that was an exaggeration, but certainly the former does go darker and the latter lighter, although

England, 1973

not to the extent that I felt either was a cause for alarm. I was immediately put into quarantine on the top floor in my father's study, and fed a strict fat-free diet, with no alcohol for six months. The diagnosis gave me a great sense of relief and with a proper diet I soon felt a lot better. But as I was still infectious I wasn't allowed out of the house for a month.

Finding my way to BFBS

Once I was clear of infection, I resumed my search for work. Capital Radio got in touch to say they liked my tape and called me in for interview. I met the programme director, Michael Bukht, to whom I took an instant dislike. He had a confrontational style, asking strange questions and generally making me feel ill at ease. He struck me as arrogant and charmless, but little did I realise he would become my boss twenty years later at Classic FM. I had a live audition in the presence of Dave Cash, who'd been a successful DJ on the pirate ship Radio London with his programme with Kenny Everett called *Kenny and Cash*. I thought I did pretty well and Dave seemed keen, but in the end I didn't make the final line-up.

The next commercial station on air was Radio Clyde in Glasgow. They were impressed with my audition tape and the bosses wanted to meet me in London. The interview seemed to go well and I was so certain of getting the job that I used it to chivvy things along with BFBS, saying that I was 'being considered for a job with Radio Clyde'. In the end Radio Clyde got cold feet, I think mainly because I'd never been to Scotland, but by then the long-awaited interview with BFBS had been set up. It was with a

In training at BFBS, November 1973

BFBS trainees, left to right: Sarah Bawden, Rick Lunt, me, Richard Gwynn, Richard Clegg and Nicole Raymond

selection board chaired by the director of the organisation, an enigmatic character called Ian Woolf who'd been with the Special Operations Executive during the war, where he'd been parachuted into Burma behind enemy lines. It was there that he saw, through his window, a Japanese poster wanting him dead or alive. Woolf spoke fluent Italian, which had been put to good use when interrogating Italian prisoners of war. I felt I was going through a similar interrogation when he deliberately goaded me into losing my cool just so he could see whether I was calm in a crisis.

Despite my five years of radio experience, they wanted me to join their first-ever training scheme. Although I baulked at this at the time, the all-round experience the scheme gave me proved invaluable. I had a month in London, where I joined my fellow trainees in learning the ways of BFBS. There were six of us, including Sarah Bawden, who was sent to Singapore where she married a Captain Kennedy. As Sarah Kennedy she later made her name on the television programme *Game for a Laugh* and for many years was a star on Radio 2. Patrick Lunt was posted to Cologne and after some years in Germany he also joined Radio 2 as a newsreader and continuity announcer, where he met his wife, Jan Leeming. Richard Gwynn was sent to Malta, whilst Nicole Raymond and Richard Clegg served their time in Cyprus.

When they asked where I would like to be stationed, I was given a choice of Singapore, Cyprus, Malta, Gibraltar or Germany. I chose Cyprus – so they sent me to Gibraltar.

Gibraltar, 1973

I flew from RAF Brize Norton on a cold November day in 1973. With Gibraltar being a naval base, the commanding officer was a rear admiral and on board was the admiral's wife. When we landed I heard the RAF sergeant say, 'Would you like to lead off?' and assumed he meant me. What I had failed to hear was the last word of the sentence, 'ma'am'. So instead of the admiral's wife leading off, I went marching ahead.

I was met by the programme organiser, ebullient ginger-haired Alan Clough, who immediately put me at ease. The station controller was a New Zealander, James Nation, who chain-smoked and had a ruddy complexion from too much red wine. He introduced me to my 'training officer' Roger Hudson, a former BBC World Service announcer. Much as Roger was a terrible bully he taught me a lot, especially in the techniques of interviewing, which eventually became what I enjoyed most. But as I was already experienced in presentation I was given shifts straight away, in particular on breakfast. The lovely camp librarian Tony Fawcett was charged with showing me around and explaining the day-to-day workings. He had the most infectious laugh and was generally known as 'mother'.

I was housed on Bomb House Lane in the Royal Engineers' Officers' Mess, a characterful old building with a rope from the upstairs bathroom window serving as a fire escape. There were two permanent staff: a Gibraltarian caretaker called Felix and a chef who saved his best meals for regimental dinners. The rest of the time the chef appeared to be limited to cheese omelette and chips, which put me in a bit of a spot. Although my doctor in London had told me my liver had fully recovered and that I could resume a normal diet, this wasn't the case. After my mess lunches I felt quite ill, and soon realised I couldn't eat cheese or eggs – and haven't been able to since. Cream, salad dressing and strong coffee were all things my liver couldn't cope with, and at formal mess nights a few sips of port would make me queasy.

The border

Across the border, Franco was still in power, and since 1969 it had been forbidden to cross the frontier into Spain either on foot or by car – though strangely there was a return flight to Madrid once a week. Gibraltar was a mere 2½ square miles with a population of 30,000, but I think the closure of the border had brought Gibraltarians closer together. Clubs flourished and it no longer felt like a ghost town at weekends. On the downside, you kept bumping into the same people but the locals got round this by simply saying 'Bye' as they passed.

The Spaniards who used to come across the border to work as cleaners and waiters were replaced by Moroccans. Fruit and vegetables were imported from Tangier, and parts of Gibraltar took on a Moorish air – Moroccan workers had to live in the territory, unlike their Spanish predecessors. There was a daily ferry to Tangier, and for £5 you could fly on the local airline GIBAIR, which became known affectionately as 'YOGIBAIR' following some graffiti that was daubed on the plane one night.

I decided to visit Tangier again, curious to see if it had changed since 1967. I stayed at the Venezuelan Consulate, cheap and central, where I slept on a rattan bed. The only issues were that the water supply was erratic to the point of non-existence and Señor and Señorita Consul General were forever shouting at each other. The city was still a gay haven, but the French and Spanish who'd hung on after independence were largely gone. French street names remained, French cuisine was still available at knock-down prices, and there was still a French air to the place, partly influenced by the king who was a great Francophile. All in all, I felt Tangier had retained its raffish and faded air.

On-air gaffes

Tangier was involved in my first telling-off. I ought to explain that the resident battalion in Gibraltar at the time was the 3rd Battalion of the Queen's Light Infantry, known as 'Three Queens'. I'd bought a pouffe in the souk for old times' sake and mentioned this on-air, but then went on to say 'Talking of pouffes, Three Queens are having an open day on Saturday.'

Management was not amused, but I did get a laugh from the boss when talking about the dredger in the harbour, which looked like a mechanical dinosaur and made such a noise that it was audible in the studio. After one particularly loud sucking sound I said, 'There's the dredger, eating another tourist.'

Gibraltar, 1973

There was one Sunday when I wished the dredger would swallow me whole. I was on continuity that day, and it was my responsibility to play the omnibus edition of *The Archers*. I'd somehow erased the tape by mistake, but as we still had the previous week's episodes in the library I played these instead. It overran by fifteen minutes and listeners must have been fed up with the theme tune at the beginning and end of each episode but at least they got their beloved *Archers*.

Anne joins me

Anne was flying over from Australia in March and after meeting her in London we were to fly back to Gibraltar. But I hadn't managed to find anywhere for us to live: nowhere decent wanted to take me on as a single guy, and they wouldn't take my word that I had a girlfriend to share with. They wanted to see her in the flesh first. Anne booked some cheap accommodation for herself, which led to some awkward trysts with me in the officers' mess, including one morning when the fire officer came round inspecting all the rooms. He was accompanied by the Officer Commanding Major Ballard and, while Anne was trying to hide in the wardrobe and I still hadn't answered the knock on the door, I heard the major say, 'Oh, he's on shift work, so we'd better not disturb him.'

With Anne by my side I was considered a safer bet by landlords. We found a two-bedroom flat in Governor's Street, parallel to Main Street in the centre of town. It was on the top floor and had two magnificent balconies, one facing Algeciras and the other Morocco. We also had access to the roof to hang out washing.

Across the waves

If we'd been married we'd have been eligible for a married quarter, but at least as a bachelor the MOD would reimburse me £16 of the £20-a-week rent. The radio station was a couple of miles away in South Barrack House, an historic eighteenth-century building that had been built for the then garrison, so getting my own transport was essential. I followed the lead of my BFBS colleagues and bought a 50cc Honda moped, enabling me to get to work in ten minutes and use it for trips to Caleta beach. There was no legal requirement to wear crash helmets, which gave a great sense of freedom when hurtling around the Rock.

Driving around it was one thing, but I never thought I'd actually climb the Rock. I was 'volunteered' to do so in order to widen my radio expertise. With a tape recorder strapped to me, I was taken up a 50-foot segment by an army sergeant. Going up was not so bad, but I was terrified of the abseil back to solid ground. It didn't help matters when I captured the sergeant on tape saying, 'Most accidents happen on the way down.'

Though I was loving my life in the Mediterranean away from the gloom of the UK – and the three-day week – Anne was struggling to find her feet. She'd completed her degree in Sydney and really wanted to be a journalist, but there weren't too many opportunities at the *Gibraltar Chronicle*, the four-page daily newspaper known by the locals as the 'two-minute silence'.

In two years Anne had a tally of thirteen jobs, including training as a nurse, working in a bookshop, and acting as a tour guide to Morocco. Most work involved waitressing, which had its upsides particularly during the six-week bread strike of 1974. Gibraltar's bakers had gone out in sympathy with their counterparts in Britain demanding more money. Home baking took over – but then yeast ran out. Anne was serving some submariners from a visiting nuclear submarine who said they could let her have some bread. The next day we approached the said submarine and, as sub-machine guns were trained on us, several loaves of the precious cargo were handed over.

Ten months in, Anne felt I was dragging my feet about getting married and out of frustration left Gibraltar for a change of scene. She travelled through Spain and France, and eventually ended up in London, staying with my parents. I was on my way to join her there for a couple of weeks when my boss asked if I could extend my stay in the UK to attend a BBC training course. During my five weeks in London Anne and I decided to get married, which we did on the 8th of March 1975. Although I'd been hesitant, I actually loved being married. We were entitled to a married quarter, but we were attached to our flat and living in the town, so I officially became an MAU – Married Accompanied Unaccommodated – and my rent allowance went up to £19.

Honing my technique

The BBC training course I attended in London did wonders for my self-confidence and helped to improve my interview technique. At first you're so worried about your next question that you can forget to listen – and that's fatal. I was taught to avoid the cliché first and last questions of 'What's the purpose of your visit?' and 'What are your plans for the future?' I practised my questions on children first, and saw that once I'd gained their trust they would come up with some real gems, which led me to try the same approach with adults. And I learnt never to interview

The Rock

Interviewing one of the
petty officers on board
HMS Charybdis, 1974

Interviewing
children at
St George's
School, 1974

Just married,
left to right: my
father, Anne, me
and my mother

across a desk, particularly with senior officers: it was important to get them out of their comfort zone and to take charge.

Towards the end of my stint in Gibraltar I was let loose on *Family Favourites*. It was the first time I'd broadcast in the UK since my days on Radio Caroline.

Moorish travels

During our time in the colony, Anne and I attended Spanish lessons and, although I've got a good ear, I'm extremely lazy and never did any homework. Anne, on the other hand, was pretty fluent by the time we travelled to Spain in October 1974. We took a circuitous route, via Tangier and ferry to Algeciras, then buses and trains to Granada, a city I fell in love with: you can't beat the Alhambra palace with its backdrop of the Sierra Nevada. We then went by the train to Madrid, and took advantage of the once-weekly flight from the capital back to Gibraltar.

In November that year we spent a month in Morocco travelling by bus and train. On one occasion we had a lift in a truck from an oasis outside Tata to Goulimine, where we were given barely cooked camel meat, washed down with mint tea.

We had our first holiday as a married couple in August of 1975 where we visited Cadiz, Jerez and Seville. In Seville we saw our first and only bullfight – admittedly cruel, but incredibly exciting and so much part of the fabric of Spain. But what I really remember is being in Lisbon during Portugal's revolution which had started in April the previous year, bringing an end to fifty years of fascism and terminating Portugal's role as a colonial power. There was a palpable sense of freedom, with students roaming the streets handing out carnations and the mournful sound of fado wafting through the air. Rather ingeniously, Anne found a loophole in Franco's blockade – she worked out we could catch a ferry from Lisbon straight back to Gibraltar.

Farewell

Much as we enjoyed Gibraltar we were beginning to feel a bit claustrophobic, so we were glad when we had news of a posting to BFBS Cologne in November 1975. This was the flagship of the network and, as one of the main reasons for joining the organisation was to have the opportunity to travel, we were glad to have the chance to explore another part of Europe. As we left for the airport Gibraltar was bathed in golden sunshine, but soon we'd find ourselves in the midst of a German winter.

Gibraltar, 1973

Cologne, 1975

Neither Anne nor I knew any German, except my father had once taught me how to count up to ten, which impressed Anne no end. On our first night in Germany the only item on the menu we recognised was Wiener schnitzel, so we ordered that.

We were assigned married quarters in the bottom half of a grand house in Eckdorfer Strasse, within walking distance of the station. BFBS had moved from Hamburg to Cologne in 1954 and was based in a large villa in the leafy suburb of Marienburg, where it broadcast throughout northern Germany. Our official audience, about 200,000, was made up of the British Army on the Rhine (BAOR) and associated RAF stations, but unofficially BFBS Cologne had 6 million German listeners.

BFBS tried to be all things to all people and had a whiff of the old BBC Light Programme, which in no way reflected its audience, the bulk of which was made up of squaddies. The staff comprised a motley collection of failed actors, alcoholics, manic depressives and a lone spinster who would treat us and the audience like misbehaving schoolchildren. But in the melee there was talent. The undoubted star was Richard Astbury, known as 'Asters' to his fans, who came on air at 9am. He was famous for flirting with women callers, and for his *double entendres*. To a comment such as, 'My husband has just had an extension,' Richard would reply, 'Oh, really, tell me how long it is.' In the mid 1970s, at the height of the Irish 'Troubles' British soldiers based in Germany were being sent to augment the garrison in Northern Ireland. With the soldier's wives left behind, Richard's programme had the command's full backing, as it was seen to uphold the army maxim that if the wives were kept happy the men would be happy too. His show would often go on the road and wives would turn up in their hundreds, just to get a glimpse of their idol.

I was rather overawed by the size of the audience and the standard of broadcasting. Apart from Richard there was another innovative broadcaster, Peter McDonagh, an Oxford graduate and fluent German speaker, who had a Saturday show called *The Great North Rhine West Phailure* (a pun on the German region of Westphalia) that had become an institution. He was posted to Malta fairly soon after I arrived, and I had the unenviable task of taking over the programme.

Andrew Pastouna presented *Family Favourites*. He drove a Rolls-Royce and was outrageously camp: once on the show he mentioned to Jean Challis, the presenter at the BBC end, that he'd had a riotous evening with friends the night before and was a little worse for wear. 'Think of your youth,' Jean said. 'Oh, he'll be all right!' replied Andrew.

Our other famous character was Bill Mitchell, known to thousands of service children as 'Uncle Bill', with his *Big Wood Stories*. He wrote and performed these live every day at 5pm, often wearing full scout uniform. His large office was taken over by an electric train that would visit all the places described in the

Cologne, 1975

Big Wood Stories. These revolved round a cast of animals including Owl, Badger, Nightjar and Water Rat who all had their own distinctive voices. This he was brilliant at, but as a regular presenter he was from another era: off-air he had an 'estuary' accent that would turn into hammy received pronunciation once the red light was on, with every syllable enunciated. He sounded false and it was felt the audience couldn't relate to him. But for me he was very much part of the family and it was quirky characters such as Bill that made working at BFBS so enjoyable, before the organisation turned more corporate in the 1980s.

Apart from my Saturday slot I was initially sent all over Germany to interview various forces personnel for the nightly news programme. At first this seemed a very inefficient way of doing things because I could spend all day travelling for a three-minute interview, but as Cologne was so far away from any of our broadcast areas there was really no better way of gathering the information. I did at least get to know the terrain, and came to admire the efficiency of the German trains.

I was also given various continuity shifts and tasked with broadcasting an hourly country and western programme called *Blazing Saddles*. Apart from modern jazz, this was my least favourite form of music – particularly after being forced to listen to innumerable Slim Dusty records in Moree, where 'Pub with No Beer' had been the most popular request. But when I decided to move away from the mournfulness of the likes of Jim Reeves and Tammy Wynette, and lean more towards country rock, I really got into it. The record companies sent all the latest releases, and it was great fun building a programme that also included interviews with passing stars. Germany was the world's third-biggest market

Richard Astbury in the studio

Lunchtime darts session at the BFBS Bar Left to right: 'Asters', Peter McDonagh and engineer Jürgen Bock

'Uncle Bill' Mitchell in scout uniform in his office with his beloved train set

for records, after the US and Japan, so exposure on BFBS could make a huge difference to a record's success.

The sound of BFBS Cologne was very old-fashioned at times, with links such as 'We now pause for some local announcements' and the station as a whole lacked cohesion. Some very good programmes made in London were sent out to us, however, and we could delve into the BBC transcription disc archive. But I always felt rather embarrassed when playing *Dad's Army*. It was thirty years since the end of World War II after all, and I wondered what our vast German audience thought of it.

Scotty Mac

One night I was introduced to a freelance Australian broadcaster called Rod Christopher. I did a double-take: I'd listened to Rod when I was working in Sydney in 1968. He was one of the DJs on 2UW. When he told me Rod was only a pseudonym because his real name was Scott McKinlay, I realised that was another name I was familiar with. He'd been one of my predecessors at 4BH in Brisbane, where he was known as 'Scotty Mac, back to back'. He worked full-time for the German World Service, Deutsche Welle, hence the need to change his name for BFBS. He and his German girlfriend Roswitha were our constant companions and we would often go away together to the Dutch town of Maastricht, where the weekend would invariably end with us eating Indonesian *rijsttafel*.

Cologne was ideally situated for us to visit the Benelux countries, but we also explored more of Germany and in time the little VW I bought travelled through much of Europe and the UK.

Across the waves

Anne and I took German lessons at the Volkschochschule. As usual I enjoyed the class but was hopeless at the homework. Anne was good at both and within no time she became fluent (as she had with Spanish before) and in less than a year was offered a job at the British Council, where German was required.

Radio Roulette

The trainee scheme injected some new blood, and brought the average age of the presentation staff down. Rick Lunt was already in situ, Sarah Kennedy was posted from Singapore, and we were joined by two new female trainees, Liz Shaw and Gillie Butcher. Between us we pushed for a station with a more commercial sound. I was given the task of revamping the evenings, no easy feat as I still had to include *The Archers* and *BBC Sportsdesk*. The programme was called 6.25 (I can't remember why it started at such an odd time) and finished at 8.30pm.

One night I couldn't sleep and spent hours devising a quiz that would attract an audience. It was called *Radio Roulette*, and would run for forty-five minutes from 7pm to 7.45pm. The idea was simple: taking advantage of the top fifty we had in the studio already, a listener would be asked to pick a number. They would hear the record from the chart number they selected and would either get a forfeit, booby prize, a regular prize or the star prize. The inspiration came from *Take Your Pick*, the television quiz show hosted by Michael Miles; I even introduced the Yes-No game as one of the options. It was an instant success and had the same ratings as the breakfast show, helped by the fact that BFBS Television was yet to start.

Cologne, 1975

The twenty minutes before *Sports Desk* was a combination of music and interviews, and the same between 8pm and 8.30pm along with an exchange and mart which Liz Shaw cleverly called *Schnell Sell*. Because of our huge unofficial German audience, record companies fell over themselves to bring in pop stars and where possible these would be incorporated live. Having initially been frightened by any sort of interview in Gibraltar, I now relished live interviews the most and in particular timing it so that I'd hit the live feed from the BBC. A favourite interviewee was Twiggy, who'd brought out a record. She was delightful and still had that girl-next-door charm. Once the interview was over I got her to introduce *The Archers* in her cockney accent, which led our head of presentation, Derek Hale, to choke on his dinner whilst listening at home. Tony Banks and Mike Rutherford of Genesis were regular guests, and it was a pleasure to chat to Peter Noone of Herman's Hermits, who was launching a solo career from his base in France. It did feel odd, though, talking to the Belgian singer Plastic Bertrand and calling him 'Plastic'. Occasionally I'd be flown to Hamburg to interview some of the bigger names, including the Bee Gees at the launch of *Saturday Night Fever*. I was probably fifth in line to chat to the trio and was worried they'd be so exhausted that their answers would be monosyllabic, but as soon as they realised I was English they opened up, more with relief than anything else.

At that time in Germany, pop radio was as dire as it had been in Britain before the pirates. For young Germans, BFBS was the only station in the north worth listening to (in southern Germany the American Forces Network had the monopoly). Applications for the trainee scheme were in such numbers that A-levels were made mandatory for the next intake, and soon a degree was the minimum requirement. One newcomer was Mike Allen, whose first duty was providing studio backup in case anything went wrong during an outside broadcast. On a forces' station there's nothing more important than Remembrance Sunday, but about halfway through the two-minute silence Mike panicked and apologised for loss of transmission, then went straight into a record. By the time he'd realised what he'd done the 'silence' was over. It wasn't the sort of occasion where you could say, 'For those who missed it earlier, here is the two-minute silence again.'

Family Favourites

Following Andrew Pastouna's posting to Brunei I replaced him on *Sounds Like Sunday*. My first link was reading out a letter that started 'Dear Sir or Madam' and I added, 'Now that Andrew has left there's no need to write that any more'. People in the know got a laugh, but I was told off. The programme included *Family Favourites,* which was required listening in many parts of Britain at Sunday lunchtime. It was great exposure for me, as Cologne was included every week. If anything the satellite link was too good and there was a memo circulating at the BBC suggesting that pops and crackles might have to be reintroduced to make it sound more authentic. These were the days of vinyl and it was hard to get everything in sync. We both had copies of the same tune, but in order to make sure the Cologne end finished at the same time as the BBC there was a device on my turntable that could make the disc go slower or faster. No wonder we had complaints about Matt Monro sounding drunk.

Cologne, 1975

It's good 'ere, innit

At the beginning of 1977 I was promoted, and tasked with setting up a department to make commercials and advertise local events. I devised a huge chart in which these promotions could be properly scheduled. Not all were made into mini-productions, as I thought some would be more effective read live. I also pinched an idea from listening to 2UW in Sydney in 1968, where they recorded visiting personalities announcing their name followed by, 'It's just great in '68 to listen to the New2UW.' Consulting some squaddies for a suitable catchphrase, they suggested, 'It's good 'ere, innit'. So we had, 'Hello, this is Victor Borge on BFBS – it's good 'ere, innit' in Victor's unmistakeable Danish accent, packaged with suitable music front and back to kick off a commercial break. I thought the gimmick would give the station a bit more of an identity and would have our audience mimicking the various personalities. I had the backing of senior programme director Ken Doherty, but the station controller, Pat Pachebat, didn't like it and I was told to stop. But soon I had broader horizons, when I was offered what was considered to be the plum posting of BFBS – that of Berlin representative.

Berlin, 1978

For me, the attraction of BFBS was that there was no time to be complacent or bored. Like chess pieces on a giant map of the world, our moves were in the hands of our director, Ian Woolf. Richard Astbury had been posted to Berlin about a year after I arrived in Cologne. There was no doubt that Richard was a talented broadcaster, but Ian Woolf could see his management potential too. So 'Asters' was being sent to Malta as station controller, and I was to be his replacement in Berlin.

This was seen as a highly prized position within BFBS, where diplomatic skills were required alongside the usual duties of a broadcaster. As Berlin representative I was answerable to Pat Pachebat in Cologne, but the day-to-day running of the station was left to me, with a team of freelancers to manage and my own budget and secretary. I would also still be on-air with a programme between 4pm and 7pm, including a link-up with Cologne that was broadcast throughout northern Germany.

Leaving Anne behind to fly on to Berlin a couple of weeks later, I loaded up the VW and drove through what was known as the 'Berlin Corridor', a route through East Germany with Soviet checkpoints. It was April 1978, just a couple of weeks before my thirty-first birthday and seventeen years after the Berlin Wall had gone up. Since the end of the war, Berlin had been divided into four sectors: Russian, American, French and British. The Russians had the largest slice and arguably the best bit, encompassing the State Opera, Pergamon Museum and Unter den Linden, the main thoroughfare. But Britain had the pick of West Berlin, including the ruined shell of the Reichstag, the Kurfürstendamm with its famous department store KaDeWe, and the iconic Café Kranzler. The British Berlin Infantry Brigade was housed in one of the city's best-known landmarks, the Olympiastadion built for Hitler's 1936 Olympic Games. I'd visited a month earlier, when Richard had given me a helicopter tour, followed by swift introductions to people I should know. Richard is a brilliant mimic, so I felt I got to know a lot of the characters before I met them, and had to stifle a laugh whenever one of their traits came to the fore. The general officer commanding (GOC) in charge of the British sector was Major General Robert Richardson, an imposing Scot who'd been in command since the beginning of the year. He'd had a hard act to follow: his predecessor, Major General Sir Roy Redgrave, nephew of actor Sir Michael Redgrave, was a flamboyant character who spoke fluent German and became a darling of the German public. His language skills would have been useful when visiting Rudolf Hess in Spandau prison. Sir Roy was later to have an indirect impact on my life.

BFBS Berlin was in Summit House in Theodor-Heuss-Platz, a large city square in the Westend district of Berlin. It was in the same building as the NAAFI, and as we were on the top floor it had a light and airy aspect with a large studio. Jackie Scheuner, a young English lady, was my secretary. Jackie was married to a

In the studio, left to right: Jackie, me, Wolfgang and Annie.

Listening to a caller on 'Radio Roulette'

The studio as seen from the control room

German, and a fluent German speaker, an absolute must for the job. Jackie and a brilliant German engineer, Wolfgang Melchart, made up the permanent staff, but there was also a trainee, Tony Orsten, and Annie Atkinson, the wife of a Welsh Guards captain, who acted as the freelance interviewer. It was really exciting to be in the epicentre of the Cold War, but all the new names and places were a little overwhelming. It was my first true management role and the first time I had to deal directly with senior officers. Annie and her husband, Julian, really made me feel at home and I relied heavily on Tony, who was mature beyond his years.

We were given a big house with garden in Tapiauer Allee in Charlottenburg. The station was just ten minutes away by car, yet within walking distance of the Grunewald, a forest on the east side of the river Havel, and at more than 7,000 acres the largest green area in Berlin. The city has a marvellous climate and is renowned for its pure air. Since the age of twenty-six I had suffered very badly with perennial rhinitis and for the first time I was free of the condition. The summers were hot and although the winters could be very cold there was usually a clear blue sky.

As part of the military, we had the benefit of the seemingly bottomless pockets of the Berlin Budget, an allowance paid by the Germans to sustain an Allied military presence in the city. One of the perks was having the choice of a babysitting service or a cleaner, known as a 'hausfrau', and as we had no children we chose the latter. Another perk for the Allies in West Berlin was the Families Ration Issue Service (FRIS). These were emergency rations, held in a bunker in case of nuclear war. They were kept for six weeks, then sold off at reduced rates, and this is where we got most of our meat. It was even delivered to the door.

Although we lived the high life with an almost colonial existence (a UK broadsheet at the time compared it to the British Raj), there was a constant threat from the Soviet Union. This was the height of the Cold War with Brezhnev consolidating hard-line policies that would lead to the invasion of Afghanistan the following year. If the Soviets did invade Berlin, there wasn't much the Allies could do about it except hold the line.

To keep the British troops on their toes there was the charade of Exercise Rocking Horse, a drill for Soviet invasion. Invariably occurring in the middle of the night, we'd know the exercise was under way because of the commotion outside. Having the drill in daylight would mean major disruption with tanks on the streets, which no doubt would increase fear among the city-dwellers.

A more immediate threat was the Baader-Meinhoff Gang, a far-left terrorist organisation with a history of bombings, kidnappings and assassinations. Late one night I had a call from the British Security Service to say that the gang was planning an attack on a radio station in the city and I should ensure BFBS was secure and couldn't be taken over out-of-hours. I approached the studio with a pounding heart, but it turned out to be a false alarm.

On the air

I continued with *Radio Roulette*, which remained as popular as ever. I even had members of the Royal Military Police phoning in from Checkpoint Charlie, and I'd ask what they'd seen that day. This information must have been a gift to the Stasi, who were constantly monitoring movements, although they must have found the silliness of the game's forfeits rather bewildering. To

Berlin, 1978

give a flavour of West Berlin I ran live reports from different parts of the city, including one from a mixed sauna where the reporter was completely naked. This was possible only through the ingenuity of Wolfgang, who had cleverly devised a portable outside-broadcast kit. It was so successful that a German station in Berlin pinched the idea for one of its programmes.

I introduced what became known as the *Pop Panel*, a kind of *Juke Box Jury* where members of the military reviewed the new releases and gave them points. I would then track their progress in the top fifty and at the end of a certain period there would be a *Pop Panel* trophy. I even managed to get the commanding officers of all three battalions to take part. Needless to say they didn't win, but it was great for squaddies listening to hear their commanding officer make a fool of himself. Lieutenant Colonel Patrick Stone, commanding officer of the 2nd battalion of the Royal Anglian (known as the 'Poachers') made particular use of the station. He knew his soldiers would ignore routine orders so anything of importance would be routed through me.

Networking army style

Entertaining was considered an essential part of the job – I even got an allowance for it. We'd give a large dinner party at least once a week, for which we'd stock up on cheeses from the Economat, the French equivalent of the NAAFI. Anne would be the first to admit she wasn't a natural cook but she rose to the occasion, even when our gas supply was cut off and she had to boil potatoes in a kettle. There were weeks where we were out every night on an endless round of cocktail parties, reciprocal

Outside broadcast at RAF Gatow

Charity badminton tournament, with me seated between Piers Wedgwood (left) and General Richardson (right)

1st Battalion Grenadier Guards Officers' Mess Pop Panel — they voted a hit for everything they hated, and won the trophy!

invitations and regimental dinners. It was through this social intercourse that the machine of the brigade was oiled, and a quick word in someone's ear was often far more effective than a barrage of memos.

I got on particularly well with Brigadier Thomas McMicking, a former commanding officer of the Black Watch and General Richardson's number two. He saw BFBS as not only a useful tool of command but also very cost-effective. His patronage made my life much easier: through him I managed to get extra studio equipment and a station car. McMicking's right-hand man was the brigade major Mike Jackson, an ambitious officer. He had a certain charisma and I wasn't surprised when, twenty-five years later, he was appointed head of the army. Brigadier McMicking and Colonel Stone were useful allies because BFBS as an organisation was always under threat, but I knew they would fight our corner in high-level meetings.

The secret of my job was to be accepted by all ranks and one of my proudest possessions is a 'gold' disc given to me by the corporals' mess of the 2nd Royal Anglian Regiment, inscribed: 'To Mr BFBS Berlin, Nick Bailey, who played a million.'

The lonely prisoner

Spandau prison was in the British Sector, but all four Allies took it in turns to look after the prison's sole occupant, Nazi war criminal Rudolf Hess. He'd been alone there since 1966, when Albert Speer and Baldur von Schirach were released. Hess's only companion was the warden, Eugene K. Bird. With the exception of the commandants of each power, no one was allowed to see him, but when he became ill, which was quite often, he was transported to the British Military Hospital. There he would have a 24-hour guard but would come into contact with other people, including a male nurse who sometimes did volunteer work at BFBS. He became friendly with Hess and, whenever there was a hospital visit, they would greet each other like long-lost friends.

'Corridor' commuting

Three military trains ran through Soviet-occupied territory, each with an armed guard, as a means for the Western allies to exercise their right of access to West Berlin. As train enthusiasts, Anne and I travelled on all three, going to stay at the French Officers' Club in Strasbourg, and visiting Frederik in Denmark, via Bremen.

The British military train ran to Brunswick, a journey of about four hours. Families based in Berlin could enjoy a shopping trip in Brunswick during the turnaround period. At the border, East German guards with dogs would search the train for illegal goods and, in particular, East Germans trying to escape to the West.

The highlight of the return journey was the afternoon tea with a soft-boiled egg, and everyone was distraught when the egg was discontinued. As an April Fools' joke we said it had been reinstated and even gave the date of the new 'Boiled Egg Train'. We were delighted when the *Daily Express* correspondent Clive Freeman turned up at the appointed time to run a story.

Fun as travelling by train was, it was easier to traverse the 'corridor' by car. This never lost its excitement but I regret not buying a Russian soldier's belt, offered at a checkpoint in return for 10 marks. I was worried about being apprehended either by

Berlin, 1978

the Soviet authorities for bribery or the British for fraternising with the Soviets. At least the soldier could keep his trousers up.

As part of the military we were allowed into East Berlin at any time providing we had the right papers. We crossed at Checkpoint Charlie and as soon as we saw the sign 'You Are Leaving the American Sector' we knew we were in the East. Serving officers had to go in full dress uniform, but of course that didn't apply to BFBS staff. We took advantage whenever we could, treating ourselves to slap-up meals and the opera, which was heavily subsidised and cost very little. Before leaving we'd exchange West German marks for East German currency at the rate of four to one, meaning everything we bought in the East was a quarter of the actual price. Although currency exchange was officially illegal, West Berlin banks turned a blind eye and if you had a meal in East Berlin there was no way of tracing it. It was the first and only time I've been able to afford proper caviar. It was tempting to buy goods too, but cars could be searched. We did take the risk with some antique maps, however, and managed to get away with it.

Sex, spies and cassette tapes

In West Berlin everyone lived life as if there were no tomorrow, knowing the bubble could burst at any time. Whereas in Cologne I had found the Germans rather formal, in Berlin there was the decadent and daring atmosphere of the 1920s Weimar Republic. There were live sex shows and even a club that allowed you in for free provided you took off all your clothes. There was also the added frisson of intrigue, like living in a John le Carré novel. The Russian military had the same right to enter the West as we did the East and it was easy to recognise the supposed 'unmarked' cars with their blacked-out windows. The Russians had their public face for such occasions as the Queen's Birthday Parade when the top brass were invited. I remember talking to a Foreign Office official at the garden party following the event where he pointed out the Soviet spies.

In the East of the city it was a different story. The Stasi spied on everybody and encouraged neighbours to spy on neighbours. On one of our trips to East Berlin we had coffee at the Television Tower close to Alexanderplatz and got talking to an East German lady. From the tower there was a panoramic view of West Berlin, and she expressed her regret that she'd never be able to cross the border, despite some of her family being in the West. Many tried but paid with their lives. By the time the Berlin Wall came down almost 140 had died trying to cross. I remember being at a cocktail party chatting with General Richardson when his aide-de-camp, Captain Piers, came over and whispered, 'There's been another escape, sir.' All in a day's work for the GOC.

Captain Piers was Lord Wedgwood of pottery fame, and he became a good friend. One time the general made an unscheduled visit to BFBS. He was accompanied by Piers, who had reported for duty that morning with two black eyes and his a face swollen out of all proportion. His explanation to the general was that he'd slipped in the shower, but he later admitted to me he'd got drunk at a mess night and had been dancing on a table when he fell.

The East Germans could do their best to stop escapes, but they couldn't stop the BFBS broadcasts being heard across the border, even if it was officially illegal to listen. One of our most ardent fans was a young East Berlin woman called Heidi, whom I didn't meet until well after the Wall came down. She would phone my secretary Jackie from a telephone box to have a chat and put in a request. The calls were monitored by both the Stasi and the British. As it was a different call box each time the Stasi couldn't trace her, but British intelligence told us to stop accepting the calls – they were worried she was an East German agent. Heidi later told me that she used to record our programmes and bury the cassettes in her garden; no wonder her Stasi file ran into several volumes. Jackie and Heidi remain the best of friends.

One of my favourite interviewees was an American called Angus Thuermer. I'd been tipped off that he had a story to tell about his time as a reporter for Associated Press in wartime Germany prior to Pearl Harbor. Thuermer was known for getting the only interview with P. G. Wodehouse when the author was being held as an enemy alien whilst living in Nazi-occupied France. That interview, published on Boxing Day 1940, received a great deal of publicity in the US, so much so that a group of influential Americans persuaded the German authorities to release Wodehouse. At the same time the German Foreign Office saw a chance to curry favour with the US authorities by persuading the famous author to broadcast to America. Unaware he was being used as a pawn in a wider campaign to keep the United States out of the war, Wodehouse agreed. But when the broadcasts were heard in Britain he was denounced as a traitor.

I met Thuermer at the Berlin Press Club over a long lunch, and we instantly hit it off. He was soon to be leaving Berlin and I got the impression he was keen to tell his story. Once in the studio, he talked for two hours. It was riveting stuff and, as there was really nothing I felt I could cut out, I decided to turn it into a ten-

With Anne, 1979

At the Berlin Tattoo, 1979

*Meeting our covert listener
Heidi for the first time,
thirty-five years later*

part series. It was only when the British Foreign Office wanted copies of the tapes that I realised Thuermer's true identity: he'd been the CIA chief in Berlin.

The media couple

Anne got a job at the *Berlin Bulletin*, the forces' weekly magazine, and eventually became editor. It was a powerful position and between us we had the monopoly on the media.

I had no problem getting interviews and as BFBS was in such a good location most would come in live. It was a chance for me to chat to some of my Sixties pop heroes, including Peter Sarstedt and Spencer Davis, but also new names such as Bryan Ferry, Robert Palmer and, most memorably, Iggy Pop, who had moved to Berlin with David Bowie the year before. Iggy came in live and appeared friendly in the pre-chat but once on-air he threatened to punch me. He didn't seem to like my questions about his relationship with Bowie, but off-air he reverted to being quite pleasant. I had to wonder whether he had been high on heroin or perhaps it was all part of his anarchic act? Either way I regret having sold my *Lust for Life* album some years later for £100.

Apart from my BFBS job I made a small fortune from voice-overs. I don't think it was felt that my voice was so wonderful, more that I was the *only* English voice. The fees paid for a seven-week holiday to the Far East and Australia where I met Anne's family for the first time. I got so many offers that in the end I had to pass some over to the BBC correspondent in Berlin, Mark Brayne. Our paths were to cross again in Hong Kong, when he became the Peking (now Beijing) correspondent.

Across the waves

The most important military event for the British was the Berlin Tattoo, which was held every two years. Every GOC would try to outdo the previous incumbent with the help of Major Michael Parker, who ran the Royal Tournament for twenty-seven years, and went on to mastermind the Queen's 1977 Silver Jubilee celebrations. Parker was a ruthless director: one unit had spent a year making the model of a ship for some kind of tableau, but at the first rehearsal it was scrapped. Luckily, I got on very well with Michael and would later interview him on Classic FM about the Queen Mother's hundredth birthday celebrations.

I was to do the English commentary for two performances each night which meant I was involved at every stage of proceedings. Michael had decided that this time he'd use elephants and employed Billy Smart's circus to provide them. He even persuaded the Brigadier to ride an elephant along the Kurfürstendamm.

Between performances the commentary team was treated to a sumptuous meal, but I noticed the electrician who was in the box with us had to fend for himself. I complained to the organisers and he soon joined us for a meal as well. I was repaid some months later when he asked if I wanted to do a dubbing at a film studio. It was a porn movie. I took the money and groaned.

Farewell to Berlin

At the end of two and a half years I had an overwhelming feeling of wanderlust, not helped by seeing a vacancy for a broadcast officer in what used to be the Gilbert and Ellice Islands in the middle of the Pacific Ocean. I had been fascinated about this island group ever since reading *A Pattern of Islands* by Sir Arthur

Berlin, 1978

Grimble, which had been one of my O-level set books. When I applied for the job I was sent documents outlining what life on the islands would be like, including a warning that the only fresh foods available were fish and coconuts, and that some foreigners had suffered psychological problems. This only made Anne and me more keen to go. In the end I received a letter saying that they had filled the post by other means – I think the job had gone, quite rightly, to one of the islanders.

But the travel seed had been sown, and I wrote to Ian Woolf to say I wanted to leave. I told him I was prepared to stay with the organisation if I could have a year's leave without pay. It put Ian Woolf in an awkward position, but he did all he could to accommodate my demands. The deal he offered me was to go to Hong Kong to set up the English service, after which I would be able to travel for twelve months, with the guarantee of a job at the end of it. But there was no absolute certainty that this would happen. The previous Commander British Forces Hong Kong, Roy Redgrave, had insisted that the garrison should have an English radio station to run alongside the Gurkha service that was already in operation; however, since Redgrave's departure, the new command was lukewarm about the idea. But Anne and I decided to go to Hong Kong anyway (taking a free ride on an RAF aircraft), and do a bit of travelling, and hoped to have an answer one way or the other by the beginning of 1981.

Across the waves

Return to Hong Kong, 1980

We flew to Hong Kong in early December 1980, on the day that John Lennon was murdered. The news shook us to the core and our reaction was similar to when Kennedy was assassinated – total disbelief. I had repeated my trick of sending a telegram to the YMCA to secure accommodation for the first few days and was relieved to find the roof garden was exactly the same, with its magnificent view of the harbour and Hong Kong Island. The city seemed very much as I'd left it in 1973, although the Kowloon and Canton Railway terminus had gone, with only its clock tower remaining, and the cricket club was no longer in the centre of town. My posting still hadn't been approved but James Nation, my boss in Gibraltar and now station controller in Hong Kong, was confident that it would be within a month. So Anne and I took the opportunity to explore the region, including Thailand, Penang and Burma, where we spent Christmas Day at the faded and crumbling Strand Hotel in Rangoon.

My post was finally approved, and on our return to Hong Kong we were assigned married quarters in Sek Kong, in the area known as the New Territories. The Brigade of Gurkhas, where the radio station was located, had its headquarters in Sek Kong and, as our married quarters were a couple of miles away, I bought a little Honda Civic, which seemed to be the car of choice for many of the locals. I shared an office with my counterpart, Gurkha Major Kishore Gurung, who after a career as a soldier exchanged his kukri for a set of headphones. The Gurkhas had been in the territory since the closure of Singapore in 1971. Their main duty was to stem the flow of illegal immigrants, which had reached epidemic proportions. Gurkha Major Gurung was an ebullient character who had the same hail-fellow-well-met demeanour as Richard Astbury both on- and off-air. Station controller James had already introduced a bilingual breakfast show aimed at improving the Gurkhas' English, and this was my first on-air task. Kishore made sure the music kept flowing, with a mix of both Nepali and Hindi music from India. I'd adored Nepal when in the country in the early 1970s, and here I was happily surrounded by the Gurkhas, their music and the aroma of Nepalese curry.

There was already a small team in place in anticipation of the new English service. Vaughan Savidge, who would go on to read the news on BBC Radio 3 and 4, had travelled the world with his diplomatic father but since his parents' divorce had settled in Hong Kong, where his mother worked for the government information service. Valerie Whitehead was the wife of a Gurkha captain and had bundles of energy. And John Culkin, a Richard Gere lookalike, was a newsreader on one of the television channels. Anne found him so good-looking that she blushed every time she spoke to him.

The aim was to launch a fully fledged station within a couple of months. I would do breakfast 7am to 10am, Vaughan would present in the afternoons 4pm to 7pm, while John would have a show at weekends. The hours in between would be filled with taped shows from London and our own locally recorded music programmes, which would be automated with the help of a machine called Cetec. This would play pre-recorded voice tracks, segue into scheduled music and run sequences of pre-recorded programming. Without the budget for more staff this was thought to be better than dead air – but was it? It kept going wrong, often broadcasting out of sequence, which once led an exasperated senior officer to phone James and ask him to pull his finger out.

Valerie put me forward as the juvenile lead in a play being staged by SKADS, the Sek Kong Amateur Dramatic Society. The play was *The Chiltern Hundreds* by William Douglas-Home. She thought this would be a good way for me to introduce myself to the military. It was directed by Hamish McNinch, an enthusiastic captain from the Royal Electrical and Mechanical Engineers, with a cast of military thespians including a sergeant's wife who was to play my love interest. The first night coincided with the launch of the station and during the play's five-day run I was also presenting the breakfast show. It was the first and only time I've acted in a play, and despite being exhausted I had great fun. Not only did the Commander British Forces come to the first night but the Governor, Sir Murray MacLehose, came too.

Station launch

The English Service of BFBS Hong Kong got under way with a brand-new service from the BBC called GNS (General News Service). The news was sent through on telex and was known as 'rip and read'. It was wonderful when it worked, but often the

Return to Hong Kong, 1980

printer would get stuck – not much help when I was on-air with a minute to go to the news. Vaughan and I muddled through, but I doubt we had many listeners in those first few weeks. The British Forces had been used to listening to Radio Hong Kong, or Radio Television Hong Kong as it was now known. RTHK even broadcast some of the BFBS programmes made in London including the *Top Twenty* presented by Tommy Vance. To gain the command's confidence I needed to build an audience and quickly.

As well as being the home of the Gurkhas, Sek Kong was the base for the Army Air Corps and the helicopter squadron of the RAF, but I was conscious that the bulk of our English audience was elsewhere and it was important to give them a sense of inclusion. The infantry battalion was at Stanley Barracks, at the southern end of Hong Kong Island, the navy was based at HMS Tamar in the centre of Hong Kong, and there were barracks in Kowloon and other parts of the New Territories. We had the use of an office in the HMS Tamar building where we could record interviews with a portable tape machine, but what we needed was an operational studio in the centre of town that would complement the one in Sek Kong.

A growing audience

The military was starting to realise our value and more money was forthcoming. We poached a broadcaster from commercial radio, Steve Britton, who was an instant hit. I rejigged the presentation team, which enabled me to come off-air and focus on my work as programme director. I would take advantage of the helicopter service from Sek Kong, which had daily return

On stage in 'The Chiltern Hundreds'

With James Nation and the dreaded Cetec machine

Hitching a lift in the Army Air Corps chopper, on my commute to Tamar

flights to Tamar and also Stanley, getting me to the centre of Hong Kong in ten minutes. Here I would line up a series of interviews for later broadcast, but also have meetings with military hierarchy whom I hoped would help me in my cause of getting us a permanent studio in Tamar.

My main researchers were Joy, an army wife, and Wenche, the Norwegian wife of Bryn, the squadron leader in charge of the helicopter squadron. I also had a series of RAF wives who acted as interviewers, including Alison, who later worked in radio in the UK. Another army wife, Kate, was in the library and Roger Dentith, an ex-naval officer, was also added to the broadcasting team. I hired Hamish, my director in the play, to present a sports programme and introduced *Instant Nepali* as a daily two-minute language lesson. I also produced a series called *The Battle for Hong Kong* recounting the eighteen days it took the Japanese to capture the city in 1941. This was told through interviews with survivors and Oliver Lindsay, the author of a book called *The Lasting Honour*. Each episode ended with popular music of the time.

It seemed these initiatives were starting to have an impact. The more popular the station got, the more clout I had in expanding into the Tamar building. What certainly helped our cause was being on the front page of the *TV and Entertainment Times* with an article explaining how we worked and why we were gaining so many listeners. I was friendly with the military's head of public relations, and through him I gained the permanent use of the office we already used, as well as another office next door that could be turned into a studio. With budgets approved work started straight away, but it wasn't until I left at the end 1983 that it became operational.

Sally

Although we'd been trying for children in Berlin it wasn't until now that Anne became pregnant. Before the birth, we travelled as much as we could, our first priority being China, which was letting in foreign tourists for the first time. No independent travel was allowed, so we booked a tour that took us to Peking and Shanghai. The skyline of the latter hadn't changed since the Communists had taken over in 1949 and Peking – or Beijing as it is now known – was all bicycles and Mao suits. My youngest daughter Lucy now works in Shanghai, teaching at an international school, and she says I would find the place unrecognisable.

We also visited Brunei, where there was a BFBS station for the Gurkha battalion employed by the Sultan. We stayed with Dave Raven, the BFBS rep, and his wife, Suellen.

From there we went on to Malaysia's Kota Kinabalu, where I climbed Mount Kinabalu, the highest mountain in South-East Asia. It was a hard slog getting to the first hut and I was overtaken by a team of Malaysians. The next day we set out at 2am and not one of them made it, either because of the cold or the altitude. I was the only one who reached the top and, whereas the day before my legs had been like lead, I now felt I was floating on air. Our final stop was Kuching in Sarawak, which still had a whiff of the White Rajahs and the most magnificent anthropological museum.

We were at a party on New Year's Eve when Anne's waters broke but Sally didn't arrive until almost a week later on the 6th of January 1982. She was born at the British Military Hospital, and I was there to witness the magnificent spectacle of our daughter coming into the world.

Return to Hong Kong, 1980

This Is Your Life

Fairly soon after Sally's birth, my mother got in touch to say my father was to be the subject of the TV show *This Is Your Life* with Eamonn Andrews, and the television company wanted to fly me over to the UK. They also wanted to film a short clip of Anne and myself with Sally, who by then was six weeks old.

A whole group of us gathered at the White House Hotel for the event. Most were from different parts of the UK, but Bunty Turner, who'd been Eliza to my father's Professor Higgins, had come from Australia. When approached by Eamonn my father was genuinely surprised and delighted. The programme included video clips from Peter Ustinov, Mary Martin and Petula Clark. I was last to come on as the 'big surprise' finale.

Expat life

With a child in tow I'd abandoned the idea of taking a year's leave without pay, and in any case I was enjoying the job and lifestyle. All the flats had maid's quarters and most couples with children took advantage of hiring a Filipina.

There were 80,000 Filipinas in Hong Kong, most sending money back to the Philippines to support their families. They offered help around the house and acted as an ever-ready baby sitter. As I'd grown up with au pair girls I had no qualms about these arrangements, but some mothers, including Anne, were understandably worried that their roles might be threatened. But we were lucky with Melly, who became a friend to us all and looked after Sally without ever seeming to take over.

Across the waves

On the balcony
in Sek Kong, with
Anne and Sally,
aged six weeks

On the air

Being presented with a
kukri as a farewell gift
by Gurkha Major
Kishore Gurung

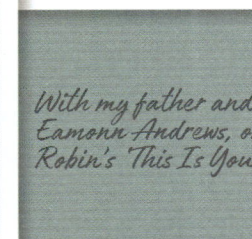

With my father and
Eamonn Andrews, on
Robin's 'This Is Your Life'

Another important aspect of expat life was the Club. We'd had the Officers' Club in Berlin with its heated outdoor pool, but also had access to its French equivalent, Pavillon du Lac, which had the most wonderful restaurant at amazing prices. In Hong Kong we joined the United Services Recreation Club (USRC), an oasis in the middle of Kowloon with a pool for both children and adults. I also took advantage of the army's training facilities by completing both a sailing and a rock-climbing course.

Thatcher

The reality of the Falklands War didn't hit me until I heard Vaughan lead the news one morning with the sinking of HMS *Sheffield*. And then we heard of the death of Lieutenant Colonel H. Jones at the Battle for Goose Green. As soon as war was declared I volunteered to work for any forthcoming BFBS station on the islands, but was told there was already a long list of volunteers and that I was more useful where I was.

The military love a war, particularly a battle as clean-cut as this one, and recruiting always goes up during times of crisis. It's what they're trained for, and this applies to both officers and other ranks. One Gurkha battalion had already been sent to the islands, and the army was preparing to send another when the surrender was declared. A young Gurkha captain told me that he'd missed his chance because there had been a 'nasty outbreak of peace'.

There's no doubt the Falklands War helped Mrs Thatcher win the 1983 UK election, but when she had come to Hong Kong the previous October following the conflict she was overconfident. The Chinese may have wanted Hong Kong back in any case, but she didn't help matters with her bullish attitude and insisting that the treaties, which were obviously unfair in the first place, should continue. I was at her press conference and was determined to ask a question about the future of the British forces in the territory after 1997. Her reply was shorter than my question, but the fact I had actually asked the question upset the Commander British Forces Major General John Chapple, who was quoted as saying that the press conference had gone well 'except for Nick Bailey.' (He later became chief of the general staff and our paths crossed at Classic FM twenty years later, when he helped to organise the visit of the Duke of Edinburgh. He remembered the incident and we both laughed.) Despite Thatcher's undiplomatic stance we all still expected the Chinese to opt to maintain the status quo. Work was even under way to house another battalion at Kohima Barracks that was to include a small studio. But following Thatcher's talks with China any hope of Hong Kong continuing as a colony evaporated, and two years later the Sino-British Joint Declaration was signed. This laid down the principle of 'one country, two systems', ensuring that Hong Kong's capitalist way of life would be preserved for a period of fifty years.

Typhoon Ellen

Hong Kong, with its scattered islands, peaks and harbours, was a difficult territory for sound waves, but our chief engineer Roger Dunn did a sterling job with our various transmitters. He had a simple theory: go high, and you'll get good coverage. There were some big hills in the New Territories, of which he took full advantage.

Return to Hong Kong, 1980

On the night of 9th of September 1983, Hong Kong had a direct hit from Typhoon Ellen. Nine people were killed with more than a hundred seriously hurt,while 2,000 lost their homes. I decided to broadcast through the night, with regular weather updates as the storm raged. Next morning when I emerged there was complete devastation, but I was satisfied that I'd done my duty. But then I saw that our antennae had been cut in half, so no one would have heard a thing.

Merger

In 1982 BFBS director Ian Woolf retired from the service at the age of sixty. It would have been awkward if he'd stayed, as he'd resisted vigorously a proposed merger between BFBS and the Services Kinema Corporation. As the name suggests SKC ran the cinemas for the forces, but they also sold television sets. It was a rather seedy and run-down organisation and we didn't want to be part of it, but in 1983 the merger was pushed through and we became a quango with the new title of the Services Sound and Vision Corporation, or SSVC (Anne had mischievously suggested WANK, Wireless And Now Kino, which seemed much more appropriate). Woolf was given no official recognition for his brilliant efforts in expanding BFBS and introducing television: apparently he'd upset too many people in Whitehall. We were no longer a family, but part of a big corporation, and I worried about becoming a corporate drone.

We came back from a holiday in Sri Lanka to discover I was to be promoted to Network Editor Speech in London. Much as I was pleased to be promoted I was sad to leave Hong Kong. Apart from the fact that I would miss the camaraderie with the Gurkhas in the office, by leaving now I would not be there for the next stage of BFBS Hong Kong's expansion – the Tamar studio was just about to become operational.

The policy of moving personnel every few years was part of the deal I had signed up for, though. I went to London with an open mind, but soon realised I hated the job. There was no live broadcasting and I didn't really want to be back in England. We bought a flat in Maida Vale, within walking distance of work, which at least got us onto the UK property ladder. I'd managed to sell my plot of land on Magnetic Island to James Nation in Hong Kong, and because of the weak Australian dollar at the time I realised £6000, a handy sum to add to the £30,000 I'd already managed to save, to put down as a deposit.

I didn't want to be trapped on the BFBS corporate ladder, but I didn't fancy commercial radio in the UK either. With Anne's blessing I started to negotiate with my previous employers in Hong Kong, RTHK, with a view to getting an expatriate contract. This was no easy feat and it was soon evident that if I wanted to follow that route I would have to go out there initially as a freelance. As these secret negotiations were going on I was asked to face the selection board for the post of station controller Gibraltar. I reluctantly went for the interview and got the job. By this time Anne was pregnant with our second child and, though we could have taken the easy option and gone back to the Med, we persevered and just before my thirty-eighth birthday I flew out to Hong Kong, leaving a pregnant Anne behind with Sally, with a view to them joining me once I was on expatriate terms.

Return to Hong Kong, 1980

Hong Kong third time around

On the plane to Hong Kong I was on a high, in both senses of the word. I had missed the buzz and excitement of the place, and after so many years abroad I had to admit I'd been finding it hard to adapt to life in the UK. I could easily see myself becoming a permanent expatriate.

I felt I'd had a lucky escape from the corporate ladder of BFBS: good as the money was, I realised that any future with them would just mean working my way up the ranks, and the higher I went, the further away from broadcasting I would become. Whilst acting manager at BFBS London I had intercepted a telex to the station controller in Gibraltar, saying that admiral so-and-so would be visiting and could they make sure he was given the red-carpet treatment. I realised then that being a glorified tour organiser for visiting VIPs could easily be my fate. But what really brought it home was talking to one of my successors in Berlin, Patrick Eade. After the merger with the Services Kinema Corporation, the BFBS boss in Berlin had 'control' of the cinemas. But the programme of films being shown was in fact predetermined, and Patrick had to concern himself with sales of Maltesers and popcorn.

It had been arranged for me to stay with one of the announcers, Keith Jay, at his government flat on Broadcast Drive, within walking distance of RTHK. When I first worked at the station in 1972 (it was known as Radio Hong Kong then), the building had recently been purpose-built, modelled on the BBC's multi-departmental structure. It was still a vast organisation, but now the premises were somewhat fraying at the edges.

There were six channels. Radios 1 and 2 were the main Chinese channels. Radio 3, which I worked for, was the English speech, information and entertainment channel. Radio 4 played classical music with both English and Cantonese presentation. Radio 5 was dedicated to Chinese opera, while Radio 6 relayed BBC World Service. (This has recently been stopped during the day, to the consternation of advocates of free speech.) Later, Radio 7 was added, broadcasting bilingual traffic reports, with Cantonese announcers. The English presentation of this service was under the control of the boss of Radio 3, Tony Baynes, who encouraged his presenters to be more forceful in their tone when traffic was particularly heavy. This led one keen recruit to say, 'If you're travelling along Nathan Road this morning, beware that the traffic is bloody heavy.'

My natural milieu

I was given the afternoon show from 3pm to 6pm and I was in my element. I could play what I liked and also line up interviews. It was twelve years since I'd last broadcast at RTHK, but some of my old colleagues were still there. I actually said as much in my first link, when I said things hadn't changed and referred to Ray

Cordeiro still being on air with *All the Way with Ray*. Ralph Pixton had officially retired, but was still broadcasting with RTHK in a freelance capacity. Whereas before I'd been intimidated by his imperious demeanour, I now warmed to him. He was still brilliant on air, but seemed to have hit hard times, with drink and debt problems. I often sat with him in the RTHK lobby trying to shake him out of his melancholy, and I did sometimes manage to make him laugh.

One feature I introduced was talking to tourists. I would go out in the morning, Alan Whicker style, and wait outside the Star Ferry terminal with a tape recorder to intercept likely-looking people of all nationalities. After a quick edit at the studio I would broadcast the results, even if the interviewee's opinions of Hong Kong were not always favourable.

I also had access to the library at the *South China Morning Post*, where I plundered the archives for a 'hits-and-headlines' feature which later led to a series called *Scrapbook Hong Kong*. There was one letter to the paper that I remember well. It was dated 1967 and was from the former King of Cambodia and then head of state, Norodom Sihanouk, who was waxing lyrical about his beautiful country and asking Hong Kong people to visit. This would have been three years before Cambodia was dragged into the Vietnam War, when no one could have foreseen the subsequent horrors of Pol Pot and the Khmer Rouge.

Occasionally there would be outside broadcasts, including the opening of the Island line of the MTR, or Mass Transit Railway, Hong Kong's underground network. Despite the technical difficulties of being underground, I managed to broadcast the programme and even got the station announcements to say it was being broadcast on RTHK. A regular outside broadcast was the Sedan Chair Race, held every October to raise awareness of the Matilda Hospital on the Peak. The idea for the race, first held in 1976, came from the fact that a sedan chair or rickshaw was the only way to get to the hospital when it opened in 1907. The race was a team event where all participants wore fancy dress, with a course starting at the hospital and then running along Mount Kellett Road via Homestead Road and back, a distance of just over 2 kilometres. I was sad to read that the 2017 race was to be the last, following a decline in donations. In forty two years it had raised HK$70 million for more than 140 local charities, and certainly put the Matilda on the map.

Anne and Sally

Although work was going well there was no sign of an expatriate contract, even though there were two staff vacancies. As RTHK was part of Hong Kong's civil service, the job had to be advertised first in the local press, just in case a local could be hired. It was a bit of a charade, really. I had hoped everything would be settled within three months but this seemed increasingly unlikely. In the meantime Anne in London was starting to have complications with her pregnancy, and we both felt that she and Sally should join me regardless of my status. We couldn't all stay with Keith, so I went flat-hunting and found a place in Causeway Bay close to where the Noonday Gun, of 'Mad Dogs and Englishmen' fame, was (and still is) fired every day. The flat was only 550 square feet and it had to fit a family of three with one on the way. It had a bedroom, a dining room and a sitting room, and as with all

Chinese flats a tiny kitchen with no hot water and a two-burner gas hob. What sold it to me was the location (it was like being in the middle of Piccadilly) and its excellent light, which was rare for a flat in the centre of town. This was only because the building in front had been demolished, and no doubt another would soon be built, but the flat was nicely furnished and I could see its potential.

I took leave without pay and flew to the UK to help prepare for our return and to sort out the letting of our flat in Maida Vale. In retrospect I should have gone back earlier and combined it with attending the funeral of Nanny, who'd recently died at the age of ninety-two. At least I was there to help scatter Nanny's ashes with my mother and my brother Simon.

Causeway Bay

Living in our tiny flat in the Chee On Building was one of the happiest periods of my life with Anne. We both enjoyed the edginess of freelance life, and soon made the flat our own with additional furniture from IKEA. We enjoyed the convenience of the nearby shops and markets, and Sally was soon enrolled in a local playschool.

We got to know the neighbours living on our floor, including an illegal dentist who would often leave his door open to let in more air. The sound of drilling and glimpses of gaping mouths were as commonplace to us as the clatter of the mah-jong tiles from our other neighbours playing the game late into the night. The flats weren't built for entertaining, but it was such good value to eat out, and a middle-aged couple next door sometimes took us to their favourite local restaurant. Experiences such as this gave us an interesting glimpse of life in the Chinese community.

As a freelance, I did not have the benefit of the civil service's medical cover, so Anne would have to give birth in a private hospital. We chose the Matilda on the Peak, which was a glorious location and easy to get to by taxi from where we lived. The baby was due at the end of December, but we managed to squeeze in Christmas at the Excelsior hotel (opposite our flat). As Sally had been a natural birth, Anne was hoping for the same this time but after a long labour a caesarean was performed instead. Our latest addition, a baby girl, was born on New Year's Eve 1985. We decided to call her Lucy in honour of my Nanny, who'd died six months earlier. (Ironically, Nanny had always hated her name.) Nowadays after a caesarean the mother comes home almost straight away, but Anne was in hospital for a week, which meant I looked after Sally and we had a wonderful time exploring Hong Kong together and eating at the local Chinese restaurant, where Sally even got used to the local black tea. For her fourth birthday I bought her a fancy dress costume and took a cake to the hospital to celebrate with Anne and Lucy.

The cost of living generally was very cheap, with the big exception of accommodation. Our rent ate a good third of my wage, but I got a helpful financial boost thanks to one of the announcers at work, Len Tracey. He was married to a copywriter working for TVB Pearl, one of the local TV stations. She was looking for a continuity announcer, and Len suggested me. The job involved recording all the announcements for the day during a half-hour session. It was very lucrative and led to quite a few television commercials too.

Hong Kong third time around

Open Line

Warren Rooke, the director of news, asked if I'd like to host *Open Line* from 8.30am to 10am. Considered to be Radio 3's most important programme, it was very politically charged. Even though I felt slightly out of my depth, I accepted the challenge.

Off-air it led to numerous invitations to the upper echelons of society and was a crash course in the way Hong Kong ticked. The programme also had its humorous side, and one call I particularly remember was a local Cantonese complaining that his Chinese copy of *Penthouse* had been heavily censored, with nine pages taken out. We asked the director of information, Peter Tsao, to respond to the complaint. It emerged that there was one person employed by the Hong Kong government whose sole job was to go through all publications looking for pornographic material, and in this issue he had decided there were too many girls playing with themselves. Peter said it was a terrible job and as this individual had been doing it for years it was time for him to move on. I replied by saying that it was surely a subjective view and that if his job were advertised there would be plenty of takers.

After one incident, I was given a complete bollocking by Warren. It followed the visit of Tim Renton, the MP with special responsibility for Hong Kong. It was 1985, the year after the Joint Declaration had been signed, and people were looking for some clarification. Like many MPs, Renton spouted a lot of waffle and said nothing of import. Following a spate of calls complaining about his visit I played the 'Party Political Speech' by Peter Sellers and dedicated it to Tim Renton. I got a dressing-down for my disrespectful attitude towards a visiting politician. Luckily Keith

Jay, acting head of Radio 3 while Tony Baynes was on leave, backed me up and no more was said.

With *Open Line* came another programme, *In My Opinion*, a political half-hour discussion broadcast live on a Friday night. I consider myself a journalist *manqué*, so this was right up my street. There would be three guests with me as chairman, and we'd discuss the burning issues of the day, invariably centred on Hong Kong's impending handover to China. My favourite edition included the urbane financial secretary Piers Jacobs and the journalist Claire Hollingworth, who in her seventies was as feisty as ever. The doyenne of correspondents, Claire had been the first journalist to report the outbreak of the World War II. She had made Hong Kong her home, and died there in 2017 at the age of one hundred and five. Her daily ritual was to dine at the Foreign Correspondents' Club, but she didn't turn up one day and was later found dead at her flat in Central.

RTHK was always looking for presenters, and I suggested to Keith that he may be interested in my friend Scott from Brisbane. Scott, Roswitha and their two sons were planning to relocate to Germany, and I thought a few months in Hong Kong might be fun before they flew on to Europe. A deal was agreed with a view to Scott doing a show straight after *Open Line*. I found them a flat in Wan Chai, which had become famous as the red-light district during the Vietnam War, and which was where the film *The World of Suzie Wong* was set. It was rather seedy, with the bars having seen better days, but it was central and walking distance from where we were living. They loved the experience, despite seeing a rat climbing their curtains one day. Their elder son Justin enrolled in the local German school and Scott was a success on-air.

Hong Kong third time around

Change at the top

At the beginning of 1986 our director of broadcasting, Stuart Wilkinson, came to the end of his tenure. As the last expatriate director, he was to be replaced by Cheung Man Yee, a dynamic Hong Kong Chinese woman who'd spent fourteen years working her way up to become the first local director of broadcasting. She was roughly the same age as me, attractive and charming, but ruthless at the same time.

One of her first tasks was to take me off *Open Line*, but she did it in such a nice way I didn't mind. In any case, I could see there was a hidden agenda: Man Yee wanted to clear away what she saw as 'dead wood', but being unable to sack people her only choice was to reshuffle. She moved Chris Hilton from television onto *Open Line* (which he saw as a demotion) and Warren Rooke as head of news was demoted, to be replaced by Terry Nealon. Terry was a hard-drinking Scottish journalist with a quick temper, but he had a zeal that was infectious and he was ideal for the job.

I was given a two-hour talk show called *After Eleven* which would have four guests of my choosing. I was actually more comfortable doing this, as I felt I was better at feature interviewing. My researcher was a work colleague from my first time in Hong Kong, Gerry José, who was brilliant at booking guests.

Most interviewees were live and some of my favourites included Prince Charles and Ronald Reagan (albeit in the guise of impressionist Rory Bremner), the actor Harold Sakata (who played Oddjob in *Goldfinger*), the King of Tonga, Edmund Hilary and Tenzing Norgay, just before he died. I also interviewed tennis legends Jimmy Connors and Fred Perry, and photographer Robert

Freeman, who lived on one of Hong Kong's outlying islands. He was behind the album covers for *With the Beatles*, *Beatles for Sale*, *Help!* And *Rubber Soul*.

One of the most interesting live interviews I ever did was with Peter Ustinov, who talked about how he had been waiting to interview Indira Ghandi in October 1984 at the moment she was assassinated. Her last act had been to ask one of her servants to exchange the tea set that was being taken to Ustinov for fancier china. A few seconds later two of her Sikh bodyguards opened fire and she was fatally wounded.

Expatriate terms

Things were gradually beginning to move on the expatriate contract, with an interview before a selection board followed by a medical. In the end I was offered a contract for two and a half years with a 25 per cent gratuity on my total earnings (in lieu of pension) on completion. The contract was then automatically renewable unless I did something awful like sleeping with the governor's daughter. Each contract was followed by five months' leave, a relic of empire, when the only way to get to and from the colony would have been by ship. We were given a business-class ticket back to our country of origin, which most of us exchanged for a round-the-world economy-class ticket. I had to take two months of the leave, but could accrue the rest up to a maximum of twelve months. The package came with a government flat at a low rent with free maintenance and school fees heavily subsidised. With a very low tax threshold of 15 per cent, it was easy to understand why everyone kept renewing their contracts.

Hong Kong third time around

Mid-Levels

Causeway Bay was cosy and fun for three, but with the arrival of Lucy we were really squashed: the only space available to change nappies was on top of the washing machine. Ideally we wanted to live on Hong Kong Island, and we found the perfect flat in Buxey Lodge on Conduit Road, in what is known as the Mid-Levels, meaning halfway up the Peak. It was a huge place, with three bedrooms, two bathrooms, dining and sitting room, maid's quarters and large balcony overlooking the harbour. The view was protected for the time being because there had been a moratorium on building in the Mid-Levels following a devastating landslide in 1972 that had killed almost seventy people. During a violent downpour a garage had cascaded down a steep cliff, crashed across Conduit Road and into the base of a tower block on the street below, which tilted and then crashed to earth 'like a felled tree' according to one onlooker.

Anne asked Susan, a Filipina who'd done babysitting for us at Causeway Bay, if she'd like to be our live-in help and she said she'd be delighted. But as soon as Susan moved in, I could see that Anne wasn't happy. Almost overnight, Anne's personality changed from happy-go-lucky to anxious and unhappy at what should have been a joyous time. She felt she was being usurped as a mother, but also complained about not having help in the house. When I told her I felt she was being unreasonable, she felt I was being unsympathetic. The arguments were terrible and at one stage Anne suggested she take the children back to London. I certainly didn't want that so I persevered, hoping that the mood would pass, but it didn't. After a couple of months we both suspected it could be a medical issue, but the male doctors we saw were most unhelpful. Eventually a female doctor diagnosed the problem as postnatal depression and gave Anne a course of tablets, but it took almost a year for Anne to get back to herself. We then were able to employ a new maid, Fe, as full-time help, and over the next five years she grew to be a part of the family.

Television

I'd never had an ambition to be on television: I'd always felt too self-conscious and I liked the anonymity of radio. But Man Yee had other ideas: she chose me to do the commentary for the RTHK *Youth Spectacular*, to be performed in front of the Queen and Duke of Edinburgh in October of 1986. Their visit to Hong Kong followed the Queen's meeting in Peking with China's leader Deng Xiaoping. (This was the trip where Prince Philip was infamously heard to say to a group of English students studying Mandarin that he had found Peking boring and that if they stayed too long they would all get 'slitty eyes'.)

The live commentary went reasonably well, but I didn't like the reliance on so many technicians: in radio it's just you and the mic. I couldn't have done too badly because on the strength of this I was asked to co-present the televised inauguration of the new governor, Sir David Wilson in April 1987, with Kit Cumings from the newsroom. Sir David replaced Sir Edward Youde, who had suddenly died of a heart attack whilst on official business in Peking, the first Hong Kong governor to die in office. It was the last time an incoming governor wore the full colonial regalia, complete with plumed hat: Chris Patten, who followed Sir David, would choose to wear a suit instead. But at that moment, with only ten years to go before the handover to China, it was as if this was the last hurrah of the British Empire.

Hong Kong Today

Man Yee was a woman with a grand vision who shook RTHK out of its lethargy. In particular she targeted the newsrooms. For some time, the morning news programme on Radio 3 had just been a regurgitation of what had happened the day before. Local news consisted of pre-recorded reports and to pad out the programme there were news features from BBC World Service. There were hardly any live reports, and it lacked immediacy. With ten years to the handover, Man Yee wanted a programme along the lines of the *Today* programme on BBC Radio 4, but including telephone calls, incorporating features, and, above all being as live as possible. It would be a joint venture between the newsroom and Radio 3, replacing both the morning news and *Open Line*. I was chosen to co-present the programme along with Nick Beacroft, one of the senior journalists. Terry Nealon, the newly appointed head of news, was our editor. We agonised over a title for the programme until Nick suggested what should have been obvious – *Hong Kong Today*. The name immediately stuck.

Apart from presenting, my role was to help set up the mechanics, as I'd also be driving the desk. We had an enormous studio complete with not one but two grand pianos, and a satellite studio in Queensway, not far from Central on Hong Kong Island. This had a video link so we could see the guests whilst interviewing, although they couldn't see us. *Hong Kong Today* ran

With Peter Ustinov just before going on-air

With the King of Tonga – note the two watches, one set to Tongan time, and the other set to local time

Listings 1-7 Apr 1987 $7

&ENTERTAINMENT

TV TIMES

Nick Bailey

Nick Beacroft

A winning combination

'The two Nicks'

between 7am and 10am, with the first half devoted to hard news, and feature interviews after 8.30am, but with the flexibility to 'interrupt' the programme if a major story broke. Terry and his team were in charge of news items, while I was the features editor.

I hosted a financial phone-in on Wednesday with a flamboyant American called Leon Richardson, who would make a name for himself by predicting the financial crash of 1987 on the show. I knew nothing about finance, but it's amazing what you can get away with by asking the right questions. I was so convincing that I was approached by Cathay Pacific to do a business programme for them, which unfortunately I had to turn down because it would have flouted the terms of my contract.

I also devised a programme called *3's a Crowd* which went out on Mondays. I'd select three people who were connected in some way and host a discussion. One I particularly remember, on the subject of the children of famous people, included Annabel Heseltine, daughter of Michael, who talked about the fact that she loved debating with her father, although she invariably lost. Another concerned memories of the Vietnam War with the ITN foreign correspondent Michael Nicholson and the owner of Bottoms Up, the girlie bar in Tsim Sha Tsui that featured in *The Man with the Golden Gun*. It had been a famous watering hole for American GIs on R&R during the war.

We still took the news from BBC World Service at 7am and 8am, but also had our own bulletins on the half hour read by Ralph Pixton, whose booming voice gave the programme gravitas.

Hong Kong Today launched on the 16th of February 1987 and was an instant hit, becoming required listening for the movers and shakers of Hong Kong. We had a large English-speaking

Chinese middle-class audience who tuned in to hear the political interviews first-hand, rather than the second-hand translations of the Cantonese-speaking channels. We became known as 'the two Nicks', adorning the cover of *TV and Entertainment Times.*

There would be up to a dozen live interviews every day, which Nick and I would split between us. Some would be on the phone but as many as possible would either be in the studio in Kowloon or on video link from Hong Kong Island.

I revelled in the cut-and-thrust of a news programme, with Terry giving directions in my headphones: 'Keep him going – haven't been able to get hold of the next guest,' or 'Get rid of him, he's boring.' Interviews always had to be out in time for the 'pips', but I loved the challenge. The large studio gave us the ability to incorporate groups of musicians, as happened with an ensemble from India with all kinds of percussion instruments, and we once had a 'battle of the pianos' with a classical and jazz pianist.

Sometimes we'd be greeted in the morning with a terrible smell: it was invariably a rat that had eaten through the electric wires and been electrocuted. The whole building was infested but once they got hold they were very hard to get rid of.

Nick had to get to work an hour earlier than me to write the main news stories. I was up at 4.30am to get showered in time for my walk down to Central where I would hitch a lift with the newspaper van, reaching RTHK at 5.45am. The broad range of interviewees on *Hong Kong Today* made this possibly the most exciting programme I'd ever done. I felt like a journalist who'd entered via the back door but, although Nick was probably better at getting the soundbite in the political interviews, I felt that I was more than capable of holding my own.

Hong Kong third time around

Buxey Lodge

Although I'd worked in Hong Kong twice before, this was the first time I'd lived on the Island. Our location in the Mid-Levels, with its view of the harbour and the ability either to take a taxi or to walk into town, was perfect for us. We had a large balcony that was big enough to hold a dinner party but, unusually for Hong Kong, Buxey Lodge's biggest asset was its garden with a large lawned area and gazebo. Sally and Lucy had a safe play area, and as there were quite a few children in the block Sally would ring her friends and arrange to meet them in the garden. I say 'safe', but the scrubbier part of the garden had some wild bananas trees, which tend to attract snakes. Thinking back, I wonder if I might have been a little lax: whenever the children reported seeing one I would rush down to have a good look, with no concern for the little ones' welfare. Anne and I even consented to the girls camping out in the garden overnight.

Sally attended Glenealy Primary School, and I remember how proud she was on her first day with school uniform and satchel. Lucy meanwhile was at the playschool housed in the Victoria Hospital, one of the few remaining old buildings in the territory.

Macau

One of the advantages of being in a British colony with a Chinese population was that we had plenty of public holidays, including Chinese New Year, Lantern Festival, Ching Ming (grave-sweeping day), the Dragon Boat Festival, and even Buddha's birthday. These were useful to tack on to my annual leave which amounted

Anne and Sally at the Matilda
Hospital after Lucy's birth,
celebrating Sally's fourth birthday

The view from our flat at Buxey Lodge

Sally and Lucy in the
garden at Buxey Lodge

Taking a ride in a Mini Moke at
the Pousada de Coloane, Macau

to only two weeks a year. Our destination of choice was the Portuguese colony of Macau, 40 miles west, which I'd grown to love on my first stay in Hong Kong.

Macau was a short ferry ride away and relatively cheap. We would hire a Mini Moke from the ferry terminal and drive across the causeway to Coloane, where we'd stay at the Pousada de Coloane. This simple hotel, run by a Portuguese couple, offered nourishing home cooking: *caldo verde*, plenty of locally caught fish, followed by *pudim* (crème caramel), all washed down with *vinho verde*. The hotel overlooked a beach and had a swimming pool surrounded by gardens with plenty of trees for shade. The local village had retained its old-world charm. There was even a junk building yard – never have I found the sound of sawing and smell of sawdust so romantic.

Sally was familiar with Macau from our previous stint in Hong Kong, when we used to stay at the beautiful but fading Bela Vista Hotel on the Macau mainland. The building dated back to the 1870s, when it was erected as the private residence of a British expatriate couple. At some point it was turned into a hotel called the Boa Vista, before becoming a hospital, a school and then reverting back to a hotel in 1936 with the new name of the Bela Vista. (Sally's first trip there had been as a baby in a Moses basket, precariously balanced on a pushchair – as we bounced down the hotel's grand staircase she fell out, but luckily didn't seem to be any the worse for wear.)

It was the sort of hotel where if you adjusted a light in your room, the fitting would come off the wall, but it had a wonderful character, and a stunning view over the Praia Grande (sadly no more). Despite the constant power cuts, breakfast on the hotel's balcony overlooking the South China Sea was one of life's pleasures. Following the handover of Macau to China in 1999 it became the residence of the Portuguese consul general.

As Lucy got older she fell in love with Macau, too, and although she was only five when we last visited it, she's had a fascination with all things Portuguese ever since. So it's ironic that she's now become Mrs Valerio following her marriage to David, whose family come from the Portuguese Azores.

Long leave

By mid 1988 it was time for my contractual leave, and we decided to take two months and let the remaining three accrue. We deliberately engineered it so that the flat in London would be free and by only taking two months we could hang on to the flat in Hong Kong. We converted the business-class tickets into economy, enabling us to fly to Kenya for a safari in the Masai Mara followed by a beach holiday in Mombasa. It was a private safari designed for families of four providing the children were more than two years old and under twelve, so perfect for us. There was even an allowance for hiring a car.

It was a wonderful holiday staying at boutique-type lodges and, except for a lion kill, we seemed to have the savannah to ourselves. Following the safari we travelled first class on the overnight sleeper to Mombasa. Dinner on the train was served by waiters in white gloves, with old-fashioned British food including crumble and custard, and whilst eating a full English breakfast the next morning we were followed by giraffes in the same way that dolphins follow a boat. (Sadly, five years after our trip this same train crashed into a bridge and plunged into a flood-swollen river, killing 140 people.) As for Nairobi itself, we stayed at the Fairview, at that time a famous watering hole for old Africa hands, though it has now become a plush hotel. We wandered freely around Nairobi during the day, although we were advised not to go out at night. When staying in Kenya ten years later, Nairobi had become a complete no-go area.

Apart from some time in France, the rest of our leave was taken up with seeing family.

Peking massacre

It seemed that within no time we were back in Hong Kong. With my incremental pay rises and Anne now teaching English at Hong Kong University, it was possible for us to buy a car, which was useful when taking the kids to ballet, brownies and birthday parties, and of course to get us to the United Services Recreation Club, which was our Mecca during the hot weather.

Although Terry Nealon continued as editor of *Hong Kong Today* my co-host changed. Nick Beacroft was now in charge of the newsroom from lunchtime onwards, culminating in a half-hour bulletin at 6pm; my new sidekick was Kit Cumings. Kit was an ex-Hong Kong policeman and former aide-de-camp to Sir David Trench, the governor at the time of the 1967 riots. He'd left the police force in the early 1970s because corruption had been rife. He'd had to start his new career as a journalist from the bottom, but had now worked his way up to principal programme officer.

Although I was conscious of my lack of education I'd never felt it had held me back, but when the opportunity arose for me to take O-level history I thought it would be a fun exercise. Before going on leave I took an evening course at Island School and passed with an A. This spurred me on to continue with history A-level, which was another nine-month course with a weekly evening lecture and exam practice on Saturday mornings.

I booked a week's leave before the exam in order to study, and I was enjoying a rare late Sunday night watching *The Great Escape* on television when the film was interrupted with news from China of events in Tiananmen Square. The date was the 4th of June 1989. The situation had been tense since students had started to protest in mid April, calling for a free press and more democracy. They even made a 'goddess of democracy' statue out of papier mâché, which they paraded in Tiananmen Square – this was replicated in Hong Kong, as students in the city came out in solidarity. Martial law had been introduced in Peking on the 20th of May, but there seemed to be a stalemate and we all thought it would be settled peacefully. This now was obviously not the case.

I immediately phoned Terry Nealon at his home to say I wanted to cancel my study leave and would be at work the following morning. The reports that came in throughout the night brought worse news, with hundreds being massacred in the square. By the time we went on air at 7am on the Monday the full horror was beginning to emerge. We stayed on-air until 3pm with live reports from Peking and reactions in Hong Kong.

The local population was incredibly jittery. It was five years since the Joint Declaration and its promise of 'one country, two systems'. Did it now count for anything or, in the face of this provocation, might the Chinese march on Hong Kong and seize the territory eight years early? *Hong Kong Today* continued in extended format throughout the week, and was on-air until midday for a further two weeks. Mass protests culminated in a million people (a sixth of the population) marching through Hong Kong and riots broke out in some areas, which were blamed on fifth columnists. For weeks Peking and Hong Kong were the centre of attention for the world's media.

For months many of the local population wore black armbands and even taxis had ribbons of black on their bonnet. I was still wearing my black armband on the day I took my A-level history exam. I'd hardly done any studying and was hoping to wing it on the strength of the lectures alone. Our teacher had been certain there would be a question on the Cultural Revolution, and indeed there was but I didn't understand it. I chose instead to write about the Algerian War, a decision mostly based on having watched *The Day of the Jackal.* I scraped through with a D.

Addition to the family

Since our long leave Anne had been pushing for another baby, saying that she didn't think two children was a complete family. I was all for it but worried about the monetary side. In the long term we were thinking of returning to England, where without the expatriate perks we would take a financial hit. So we decided to go ahead but extend our stay in Hong Kong for the time being, meaning we could save more and have help in the house for the first couple of years if a baby arrived.

Anne fell pregnant and Edward was born on the 10th of May 1990 at the Queen Mary Hospital on Hong Kong Island. We'd been worried beforehand because we'd heard horror stories about

Christmas 1987,
Buxey Lodge

In Victoria Park at a peaceful
demonstration in support of
the students in Peking, 1989,
with the Goddess of Democracy
statue in the background

In Canton (now
Guangzhou) for
Edward's first
birthday, May 1991

the public hospitals, which involved sharing a labour room with other mothers. This was true, although there was a screen and some distance between each woman in labour. In the event, Anne was advised to have a caesarean and wasn't aware of her surroundings. My first memory of Edward was seeing a mass of ginger hair. Having a boy certainly made our family complete.

Edward's birth coincided with me being promoted to head of Radio 3. This came about in rather a strange way. A great friend of mine from my Berlin days, Robert Harland, was the PR man for Coca-Cola in Hong Kong. He phoned one night to ask if I knew of anyone who might like to take over his job, as he was moving to Japan to run the operation there.

I think he was hoping that I would offer myself, but I have an absolute loathing for Coca-Cola and all it stands for, so instead I suggested the head of Radio 3, Tony Baynes, and said that I would speak to him. Under the previous director of broadcasting Tony had been groomed to take over as head of English radio, running both Radio 3 and 4, but for a reason unbeknown to me Man Yee had taken a dislike to him so he was having a tough time. I sensed he was ripe for a move, and he jumped at the chance. But who was to take his job? Under normal circumstances, the position would have gone to Keith Jay, but by this time Keith had resigned. Although it wasn't something that I had been angling for I was offered the post. The extra money would be useful, but I really saw a chance to mould Radio 3 into what I thought it should be: a station for an international audience and not just for colonial types. The expatriate population had just as many Americans, Canadians, Australians and New Zealanders as there were Brits. There was also a significant Indian clique and 80,000 Filipinos.

Head of Radio 3

I accepted the job on condition that I could continue presenting *Hong Kong Today* three days a week, knowing that if I came off-air altogether it would be very hard to get back on again. I set about introducing new shows and bringing in fresh people, and at the end of June 1990 the new schedule was launched, just a month after Edward was born.

Initially I enjoyed being a programme director, as I had been at BFBS. RTHK had good admin and engineering backup, but with the handover looming the Hong Kong government wanted a completely independent station, and planned to turn RTHK into a quango. There would be massive cutbacks and sponsorship would be needed to pay for programmes. Consultants from McKinsey's came and sat in with management, including me, asking the most stupid questions. They were there day after day, and it was a complete waste of time. I had to continually write papers for projects I didn't believe in and would never happen.

Getting the sponsorship deals proved to be difficult. The only success I had was with a programme of French music called the *French Connection*, hosted by French-Canadian Pierre Tremblay. The Alliance Française paid for three months. My counterpart on Radio 4, Richard Tsang, had more success but we quickly realised we would not be able to fund two networks in this way.

Eventually it didn't happen – mainland China didn't want an independent radio station and certainly didn't want RTHK dismantled when it could later serve as its propaganda outlet. Self-censorship had already started to creep in on the two TV channels and even the *South China Morning Post*, owned by Rupert

Murdoch, was doing the same so as not to offend China. Ironically, as a government station RTHK was more independent than any commercial enterprise and in a much better position to give unbiased reporting, so the Chinese shot themselves in the foot by bringing everything to a halt. But everyone at RTHK was grateful that the status quo was maintained.

BBC Radio 5

Soon after taking over Radio 3, I had a phone call from Andy Parfitt at the BBC, who was setting up a new UK network, Radio 5. Their flagship programme was *Morning Edition*, hosted by Jon Briggs and Sarah Ward, and they were looking for a Hong Kong correspondent, alongside other reporters from around the world.

My reports would run for about three minutes and include clips of local news with a combination of the serious and comical. I'd been sent a copy of one of the pilot programmes and Radio 5 did seem a strange format – more like local radio than something that would be broadcast nationally. It would become known as a dumping ground for programmes the rest of the BBC didn't want, with the exception of sport which did come into its own. Nevertheless I loved doing the reports – if nothing else, my mother could hear me on national radio.

Morning Edition lasted about eighteen months before the slot was taken over by Danny Baker. The BBC wanted to scrap the foreign reports, but there was a backlash on Radio 4's *Feedback*, including a reverend who 'particularly missed Nick Bailey from Hong Kong', so for a while I phoned live reports in to Danny Baker. We had no rapport as he didn't listen to a word I said, so soon even that stopped. But the BBC Radio 5 experience got me thinking about work in the UK and a phone call to Andy Parfitt at the end of 1991 suggested I might get a contract at the station.

Vietnamese boat people

Ever since the end of the Vietnam War, Hong Kong had been the first port of call for Vietnamese refugee ships, starting with the Danish freighter *Clara Maersk*, which had almost 3,700 aboard when it arrived on the 4th of May 1975. Although the Hong Kong government declared them 'illegal immigrants', by 1980 100,000 Vietnamese had sought refugee rights in Hong Kong. Most succeeded and were eventually accepted by Western countries, but as possibilities for resettlement to other countries dwindled new arrivals were interned in 'closed camps'. These were criticised for keeping freedom-seeking people behind barbed wire but, despite this and the fact that through the 1980s many Western countries were continuing to lower their migrant quotas, the influx of refugees into Hong Kong continued to increase, peaking at 300 a day in 1990.

By June of that year there were almost 55,000 Vietnamese boat people in the territory, increasing by another 10,000 the following year. Most of the boat people were now classed as 'economic migrants', and in 1989 a policy of forced repatriation was introduced, leading to an international outcry.

I interviewed the Labour politician Gerald Kaufman live on *Hong Kong Today*, who was outraged at the refugees' treatment and the so-called 'concentration camps'. But Hong Kong, being one of the most densely populated areas in the world, simply didn't have space, and forced repatriation continued. On a visit to Macau I came across the refugees' plight first hand and this became part of a report I delivered on BBC Radio 5:

Hong Kong is one of the few countries in the region that still retains a policy of 'first asylum'. On a recent visit to Macau, the Portuguese colony 40 miles to the west of us, I witnessed a rather sad sight from our hotel bedroom. Hotel is really too strong a word. For the past three years we've been staying at a pousada on the remote Macanese island of Coloane. All rooms face the beach. This year we were somewhat unlucky with the weather as our four days coincided with Typhoon Fred. Looking out to sea on our first day with the typhoon threatening I noticed what looked like a fishing vessel very close to the shore. The only other activity on the beach was a portly Western gentlemen playing with his family. Suddenly a whole stream of bedraggled-looking people emerged from the vessel and started to wade ashore. I counted about thirty of them. These obviously weren't fishermen. I rushed down to the beach to find out more and soon realised they were Vietnamese. The Macau marine police were already there, herding the Vietnamese back onto their small craft and out to sea. I just hope for their sakes they got to Hong Kong before the typhoon really took hold.

Ten years later the number of boat people in Hong Kong had dwindled to about 2,000 and subsequently the only concern was to integrate the few remaining into Hong Kong society.

I visited Vietnam in 2005 when I was reporting on behalf of World Vision for Classic FM. I couldn't see the join between the old north and south, and ironically it now appears to be one of the few countries in the world that seems to be at peace.

Seeking other opportunities

With the birth of Edward we'd decided to extend my contract with RTHK until July 1992, with the intention of searching for work in the UK before that. I'd created a rod for my own back by taking on the role of head of Radio 3 and also continuing to broadcast. I'd left BFBS because I was being propelled into upper management and now the same thing was happening here. I was also frustrated by the inner workings of the civil service. Much as there was individual talent at RTHK, there was a lot of dead wood and it was virtually impossible to get rid of people. I even resigned at one point when Man Yee rejected my new schedules, but was persuaded to stay on.

But the real reason for wanting to leave was my age: if I'd been ten years younger I would have stayed until the handover, or if I'd been ten years older RTHK would have taken me to the end of my broadcasting career. But I was coming up to forty-five, and by the handover I would be fifty which would make it very difficult to get another job. It would have been comfortable to stay on, particularly as the girls were enjoying their school and Anne now had a very lucrative job teaching English to Chinese journalists at Reuters. But Anne was also keen to get to England, and from a professional point of view I wanted to pit myself against the best. There was a saying that Hong Kong was a first-class place for second-class people, and I suppose I wanted to prove that wrong.

I flew to London in March 1992 with the sole purpose of looking for work. Ideally I wanted to continue in features and current affairs, so my first port of call was Andy Parfitt at BBC Radio 5. We had lunch but all he could offer me were a few newsreading shifts – and he was about to leave for Radio 1 anyway. (He later became head of the network, and was the one who decided to put Chris Moyles on breakfast.) Michael Harrison at BBC World Service was my next call. I knew Michael from my first stint at RTHK in 1972 and later when he was at BBC staff training. He had also come out to Hong Kong as a consultant for *Hong Kong Today*. But here again he could only offer my name to the head of presentation, and I wanted more than sporadic newsreading shifts. I then contacted Paul Brown whom I'd worked with at BFBS Gibraltar; he was now head of regulation at the Radio Authority, an independent body that issued licences to new commercial stations and monitored broadcasting standards.

Paul told me about a radio station that was being launched later that year which would play non-stop classical music. It was called Classic FM and would be the first national commercial radio station in Britain. It was being set up by Ralph Bernard, the managing director of Great Western Radio, based in Swindon. At my interview Ralph told me they'd got the licence by default: the frequency had originally been offered to the highest bidder, a consortium called Showtime, which would play music from West End shows, but their financial backers pulled out at the last moment. Ralph told me he was trying to tap into what he called the 'Pazza factor', referring to the phenomenal popularity of Pavarotti's 'Nessun Dorma' during Italia '90, which made the singer as much of a household name as the footballer Paul 'Gazza' Gascoigne. Ralph and I had the same views as to how classical music should be presented, and I remember him remarking that what I had to say was music to his ears. I had always loved classical music and had interviewed many classical musicians in

Hong Kong. It struck me how in the main they had no pomposity and yet classical music had such an elitist label.

It seems incredible now, but on the strength of that interview and no promise of anything, I decided to hand in my notice at RTHK with a view to leaving at the end of my contract in the summer. Of all the family, this decision affected Sally the most. She was now ten, and really enjoying in her life in the territory. For years afterwards Sally would yearn for Hong Kong and get homesick whenever the weather was humid. Lucy had developed a great affection for Fe, and of course Anne and I would miss the expatriate lifestyle and our network of friends. On the day we left I remember Anne spending a minute in silence, poignantly looking at the garden at Buxey Lodge, reflecting on the fun times we'd had there with the children, who had all been born in the territory. But with my parents in London it would be a chance for them to enjoy their grandchildren, particularly my mother, whose health was rapidly declining.

The months went by with no sign of any offer from anywhere, and although I could have rescinded my resignation we were determined to leave come what may. With only six weeks to go the call eventually came. It was the day of the Dragon Boat Festival, a public holiday, and I'd just come back from producing our annual outside broadcast. Anna Gregory, head of music at Classic FM, said the programme controller liked my tape but wanted to meet me before making a final decision. I asked his name and when she replied my heart sank. It was Michael Bukht, a man I'd met and taken an immediate dislike to twenty years before, when he'd interviewed me for a job at Capital Radio.

Hong Kong third time around

Classic FM

Michael Bukht hadn't changed – he still had the air of someone who might fly into a rage at any moment, a confrontational style and an unpredictability that made me ill at ease. But perhaps I had changed: twenty years after our first meeting, I could see Michael possessed an infectious energy and drive. Over the years I'd had bosses who were charismatic but often difficult, with an obsessive streak and a vision. I thought of Bernard Miles at the Mermaid Theatre, Ronan O'Rahilly at Radio Caroline, Ian Woolf at BFBS and Cheung Man Yee at RTHK. I had come to realise that it all went with the territory.

   Michael was certainly a complex and unusual character. The son of a Pakistani diplomat and a Welsh mother, he had been brought up in England as a devout Muslim, a faith he would follow throughout his life. As a graduate trainee with the BBC, in his early twenties he was seconded to the Jamaican Broadcasting Corporation as programme controller of both radio and television. While he was in Jamaica he developed a love of reggae, leading him to champion the music in the UK. He made his name in the radio business with the launch of Capital Radio in 1973, where he was the original programme controller. But he became known to a much wider public, in the guise of Michael Barry, when he appeared as the chef on the BBC's *Food and Drink,* at the time the only regular cooking programme on national television.

I soon found out that Michael, along with Ralph Bernard, was a co-founder of Classic FM. Ever since his Capital Radio days, Michael had felt there was a gap in the market for a radio station playing classical music presented in the casual manner of a pop DJ. He was also conscious that the public was absorbing classical music without realising it, through films and TV commercials.

The interview

I was well aware that a live audition or an audition tape would be the key to my getting any job in radio, while my academic qualifications would be of little interest. Even so, with a paltry three O-levels to my name (including history, taken in Hong Kong) I decided it would improve my chances if I 'added' English Literature and Maths, to make it up to five. In the end, Michael only glanced very quickly through my CV, though he did seem impressed that I'd been to a comprehensive school (I later learnt his political leanings were to the left) and that I'd taken history A-level as a mature student.

Because of Michael's impetuousness, I was on tenterhooks the whole time, worrying that any potential deal could be stopped in its tracks simply by me saying the wrong thing. To make conversation at one stage I asked if he'd had many applications for the job. 'Is the Pope a Catholic?' was the offhand reply.

Michael explained that he deliberately didn't want to employ classical music experts, but he did want his presenters to have a working knowledge. Out of the blue he asked me how many symphonies Mahler had written. I answered ten, which was a lucky guess – he wrote nine but had been composing a tenth when he died. I later found out that Michael knew very little about classical music: in that respect he represented a typical Classic FM listener. He knew that the audience would want nuggets of information, but wanted us to avoid trotting out Bach's biography every time a piece by the composer was played.

At one point in the proceedings he looked at me intently and asked if I'd miss running my own radio station as I had been doing in Hong Kong. I replied with a most emphatic no, and explained I'd been trying to get out of management for years.

I felt the best I could hope for was an arts correspondent job, so I was genuinely astounded when he said he had me in mind for the breakfast show. As such I would launch the station when it opened on the 7th of September 1992, quite a gamble as I was a complete unknown. Michael liked taking risks and I was flattered by his faith in me, but he took the wind out of my sails somewhat when he said, 'Stars won't do breakfast!' I remember wondering what Terry Wogan might think of that.

Next was the negotiation of my fee: I gave him a somewhat inflated figure of what I was earning in Hong Kong, to take account of the various perks. As expected he knocked it down slightly and then we shook on a deal.

Start date was the next hurdle: I'd already booked a five-week holiday in Australia, but Michael was insistent that I should start on a certain date which would mean coming back two weeks earlier. When I baulked at this he erupted and said, 'Look sunshine [a favourite form of address] I've already cancelled a holiday to

Greece. Do you want the job or not?' Of course I backed down straight away, but when I did arrive a month or so later it was galling to find that the microphones weren't even in place.

Farewell to Hong Kong

I'd spent ten years in Hong Kong, and despite the issues of being head of Radio 3, it had been a wonderful experience. I'd enjoyed working alongside the newsroom at RTHK, and I knew my new job probably wouldn't have the same buzz. There was no obvious successor to me as the boss, but before leaving I poached a young presenter from BFBS, Petroc Trelawny, to replace me on air.

Man Yee gave me a superb send-off, first with a Chinese lunch attended by the RTHK hierarchy, and then a glitzy party with many members of the Hong Kong government. The governor, Sir David Wilson, wrote me a glowing letter and by coincidence we were leaving Hong Kong on the same day: his replacement was Chris Patten, Hong Kong's final governor. (A few months later I saw Sir David in London when he was buying shampoo from the same hairdresser as me – it was like meeting the Queen in Boots. In Hong Kong he had all the trappings of royalty, living in the Colonial Renaissance style Government House, and being driven in a Rolls-Royce with motorcycle outriders. We had a pleasant chat before he left to catch the tube home.)

The hardest part was saying farewell to Fe, who for more than five years had really become a part of the family. It was also hard to leave our home, Buxey Lodge, although our harbour views had been reduced to mere glimpses since the lifting of the moratorium on building in the Mid-Levels.

Classic FM

To shave two weeks off our Australia trip we cancelled the North Queensland leg and stayed in Sydney, where Anne's mother lived, and saw friends in Brisbane and Warwick before flying back to the UK via Singapore. I had accrued eight months' leave, so until the spring of 1993 I would receive double wages. The extra money would come in handy, to buy a car and help us to resettle into our flat in Maida Vale, which would now have to accommodate a family of five.

First day

There was certainly no time to miss Hong Kong. We arrived in the UK on a Friday towards the end of July and on the following Monday I reported for duty at Classic FM.

The studios were in Camden Town, in the former boiler room of the Gilbey gin factory. Two studios were still under construction – one for on-air and another for production – and the office was open-plan, with Michael holding court in the centre. We were in the basement, with full length windows overlooking the Regent's Canal, although you had to stand to get any view.

Michael immediately called all staff to a meeting in the boardroom. Research had shown that we'd attract most listeners from Radio 4 – those who would like a bit of music when they'd had their fill of news – so the idea was to strike a tone in our speech content that would appeal to the Radio 4 audience. Michael had taken on Margaret Howard, who for years had hosted *Pick of the Week*. She was to present the news programme, *Classic Reports*, between 6pm and 7pm. Susannah Simons, one of Radio 4's *Today* team, was poached to present a lunchtime programme

Celebrating the launch of Classic FM

Having a quick chat with Henry Kelly in the studio

with music and interviews. Adrian Love, ex-Radio 2 and LBC and with whom I'd worked at BFBS, was to do late nights between 10pm and 1am. But the star signing was Henry Kelly, who had made his name with ITV's *Game for a Laugh* in the early 1980s. He was also a serious journalist, having worked for the *Irish Times* reporting on the Troubles, before joining Radio 4 as a reporter on *The World Tonight*. He was the perfect fit: a heavyweight with a light touch. I also met Chris Vezey, who'd previously worked as a producer at both Radio 1 and 2. He was to be Michael's deputy as head of programmes and my producer on the breakfast show.

As Michael described it, Classic FM would be a 'tapestry' format. Following *Classic Reports,* at 7pm there would be an hour's programme dedicated to different subjects each day, including travel, new releases, books and opera. The new release show, *Classic Verdict*, with Rob Cowan and Keith Shadwick was the first to play Gorecki's Symphony No. 3, which went on to become a bestselling recording. *The Evening Concert* was at 8pm.

The breakfast show at weekends was to be hosted by Sarah Lucas, the daughter of Michael Miles, the man who had devised and presented the television quiz show *Take Your Pick*. It had been my favourite show as a child, and had in fact been the inspiration for *Radio Roulette*, the quiz I'd introduced at BFBS Cologne. Sarah and I hit it off straight away.

Michael explained he had all the daytime presenters in place but was missing someone for drive time. The person he'd originally wanted had an agent who'd asked for too much both in money and holidays, and Michael told them, with characteristic eloquence, to 'Fuck off.' But he'd been recommended a presenter from Hong Kong, who had been hired to present between 3pm and 6pm. To my surprise, it turned out to be Petroc Trelawny, who'd signed a contract with RTHK to replace me as presenter of *Hong Kong Today* only a month before. Obviously Classic FM was a better offer: Petroc was only twenty-one, so I wasn't surprised he had jumped at the chance. This meant that two of our top shows would be presented by unknowns from Hong Kong, but as Anne remarked at the time, it was as if Michael picked his presenters as a trainer might choose his thoroughbreds, and in this case it seemed he wanted to introduce a new bloodline.

Smile, segue and shut up

Quentin Howard, our chief engineer, had a novel idea for our test transmissions. He used a recording of birdsong he'd made in his garden for an amateur theatre production. This avoided copyright issues and meant we couldn't be judged in advance on our music policy. It also created an air of intrigue.

Brian Johnston waxed lyrical about the birdsong on *Test Match Special*, and some people tuned in to listen to it for relaxation – a good omen, as 'relax' would become an integral part of our brand.

As the first national commercial station in Britain we had a lot of press interest, helped in part by Radio 3, which had started to dumb down its content in anticipation of our arrival. Whenever there was negative publicity for Radio 3, Classic FM always got a positive mention. Even my father, who wasn't easily influenced, remarked that Classic FM couldn't have had more publicity. In the end we had so much coverage that an ad campaign worth a quarter of a million pounds was cancelled. Michael was like a creative tornado, with a temper to match, but I can't think of anybody else who could have launched Classic FM with the same panache. He drummed into us two mantras: 'Less is more' and 'Smile, segue, and shut up'. He had deliberately employed broadcasters as opposed to music experts – our expertise was more in speech than music. Again, this was a bid to capture the Radio 4 audience so that our links, succinct as they were meant to be, would have sufficient gravitas.

Classic FM was to be the first fully computerised radio station in the country and we all had to master the technology. We were using a system called Selecta, which had been invented in the US for pop stations to avoid repetition. Robin Ray, who'd been acting as music adviser since the beginning, compiled a repertoire of 20,000 selected tracks from a library of 50,000 CDs representing almost 2,000 composers. Apart from preventing repetition, the computer could be tweaked to separate eras, genres and mood – a system that's still used today.

We all found the desk difficult at first, trying to find which fader to bring up when, and too often the CDs wouldn't cue in time. But gradually it began to click and we all gained in confidence. We did numerous dummy programmes and I used a portable typewriter to make notes directly onto my running order. There was no Google to fall back on for research, but we had a full set of Groves' encyclopedias and a small collection of music books, which were housed in a corner of the office with plenty of light. I dubbed this area 'Study Corner' and it soon turned into a kind of staffroom for the presenters.

We all had to have Michael sitting in on our training sessions. His bullying technique may have worked for some people, but it had the reverse effect on me: I froze, having flashbacks of going through my maths homework with my father. Gradually Michael took his foot off the pedal and even started to praise some of my links, which gave me untold confidence.

At least I had no problem with most pronunciations: my time at the Lycée as a child and in the language classes in Gibraltar and Germany had paid off. I was also genuinely interested in classical music and was always keen to learn more.

As Classic FM had no track record, Michael did everything by instinct, something I suspect he did when he launched Capital Radio. There were no committee meetings or focus groups to decide what our first record should be. With about ten days to go he shouted across the office to Anna, our head of music, that we would start with Handel's *Zadok the Priest*, which we all felt was an inspired choice, and our second piece would be Weber's *Invitation to the Dance*. This could have been a personal favourite of his, or maybe he chose it for the title – the intention being to kick things off with a rousing anthem and then invite listeners to the party. What hadn't been decided was what would be said in the opening link.

Station opening

I had practised the first breakfast show so many times that I felt reasonably confident, and I was getting on well with Chris Vezey, who had the knack of bringing out the best in people. Several features had already been introduced before going on-air. I'd suggested a trumpet alarm call for 6.45am and Michael had come up with *Breakfast Baroque* after the 8am news and *Morning March* at 8.30am. But everything would be judged on this first programme, and I still didn't know how to open. I arrived at the studio at 4.30am on a rainy Monday morning and there wasn't a soul around except for the *Daily Telegraph* radio critic, Gillian Reynolds. Gradually people started to turn up – Sarah Shepherd to prepare and read the news, an engineer to make sure we remained on-air and, reassuringly, Chris to hold my hand. But it was only when Nick Higham, media editor of the BBC, arrived with a television crew that I realised how big a story this was. With only half an hour to go, Michael popped into the studio and told me I could say what I liked to launch the station. It was slightly tricky, as the newsreader would end with 'Classic FM, the time is …' and I didn't want to start with a 'double ident' by immediately repeating 'Classic FM.' But I knew the BBC would want a sound bite, which would need to incorporate all the salient points. So I decided to invert the link, saying, 'Good morning and welcome to Britain's first national commercial radio station. This is Classic FM. I'm Nick Bailey and this is George Frederick Handel …'

And that's what the *Today* programme used in their 7am bulletin. The film crew managed to film through the studio's glass partition and capture the opening, which was shown on the BBC evening news. It had been very smooth. The birdsong had finished at 6am, with Sarah reading a faultless bulletin, and following my link Handel had resonated gloriously around Britain. We were off: I could see the office through the glass, where Champagne corks were flying.

The rest of the programme sailed along nicely including a plug for Petroc Trelawny, referring to him as a well-known Cornish pasty; and a link off the back of Holst's 'Jupiter' wondering whether Holst had also taught astronomy in his time at St Paul's Girls' School. This latter comment was picked up by Gillian Reynolds in her piece in the *Telegraph*. I did put on the wrong track towards the end, but immediately corrected myself with confidence and got a thumbs-up from Michael. He didn't mind you making mistakes; it was how you got out of it that mattered.

They say that your first parachute jump is terrifying, but your second is even worse because you know what you have to go through: that's how I felt for the rest of the week.

Gaffes

We made so many mistakes in those early days, but somehow the listeners forgave us. Michael always said that we mustn't assume prior knowledge, and the fact that we were obviously learning as we went along seemed to endear us to an audience that was learning at the same time.

A story attributed to me is that I once back-announced the 'Toreador's Song' as coming from 'Carmen's bidet'. I even earned myself a mention in Colemanballs in an edition of *Private Eye*: 'That was Beethoven's Symphony No. 1, his very first symphony.'

Many mistakes were caused by getting flustered with the equipment or not finding a CD in time. This happened to Henry on the second day when he couldn't find his opener and grabbed the nearest CD instead. It was Wagner's 'Ride of the Valkyries', which I'd played as my final piece just moments before.

Another problem was getting so intent on timings (like hitting the news on time or making sure an ad break was in the right place) that you'd forget what music had just been played. This happened with a piano version of Jesu Joy Man's 'Desiring' performed by Christina Ortiz, which I said was 'Nessum Dorma' sung by Pavarotti. Christina faxed in very indignantly to point out the mistake, so I made something of it the next day, and she immediately sent another fax saying she forgave me and how much she was enjoying our programmes.

Some of our links were a tad crass and some pronunciations were still iffy. We had playback sessions, listening to recordings of our broadcasts with Robin Ray, with whom I got on extremely well. He was the complete opposite to Michael: he had a gentle approach and could admonish you without making you feel small. But Robin was very busy, so soon we had an ex-Radio 3 presenter, Tony Scotland, as our pronunciation adviser. He also had the gentle approach and he made pronunciation fun, but we all struggled with Italian. Our mispronunciations got right up the nose of one of the board members, Nicholas Tresilian. He arranged for us all to have weekly Italian lessons, which went on for six months, and it certainly helped.

Let's rock

There was a weekly meeting at 2pm on a Wednesday afternoon, which was always heralded by Michael shouting, 'Let's rock!' This was a state-of-the-nation address, with Michael saying we had to give something 'plenty of welly' or that so-and-so was either 'the dog's bollocks', or 'not cutting the mustard'.

But it was a democratic process and we could all have our say. It was a shame it was held after lunch, as Henry Kelly would come in a little worse for wear and sometimes start arguing for no apparent reason. Henry was the sort of person that if he liked you he would stick up for you no matter what, but if he didn't he could make life difficult. (I was lucky in that I was in the former category and we got on very well – we both loved cricket, which helped.) But though Henry had the occasional spat with Michael there was a lot of mutual respect.

We'd been on air for only about six months when it was announced that Adrian Love, on holiday at the time, would not be coming back. Michael didn't think he fitted into the format.

I phoned Adrian to commiserate – I'd known and admired him as a broadcaster for many years, and thought he'd been presenting the late show brilliantly, particularly as he'd hosted live musicians every night for the first few months of Classic FM's existence. He said in a way it was a relief: such was the pressure from Michael he felt it had been like holding a daily audition. Michael Mappin, who'd originally been employed as a producer and had presented *The Evening Concert*, was to take over the slot.

The Bukht phone

About a week after we went on-air what became known as the 'Bukht phone' was installed in the studio. It didn't ring for obvious reasons, but instead there was an enormous bulb attached that flashed whenever Michael phoned. It always startled us, made worse by the light bouncing off the glass walls, as if we were being besieged by a posse of paparazzi.

I don't know when Michael slept: he would call us at any time, even through the night, mostly picking us up on bad links, but as we grew in confidence he became more complimentary.

Classic FM

Henry once played a naughty trick on me. I was still on air when he came into the studio to sort out his programme. Suddenly the Bukht phone flashed, but when I picked up the handset there was no one there. It was only then I realised that Henry was using an empty CD case to catch the bright lights in the studio to replicate the phone's flashing bulb.

Classic Romance

The two most popular time slots on a radio station are Saturday and Sunday mornings between 9am and 12am. Michael had hired Paul Gambaccini to present the chart show called the *Classic Countdown* on Saturday. I don't know how much he paid him, but during one of the dummy runs he said, 'Paul, you may be expensive but you sound like a million dollars.'

Paul was a great signing. Equally at ease on Radio 4 as he was on Radio 1, Paul could talk about the chart and its ups and downs in an entertaining and informative way. He was also extremely affable and his name attracted a huge sponsorship from WHSmith. Michael wanted an equally big draw for Sunday morning.

At Capital in the 1970s Michael had engaged the actor Gerald Harper to present *A Sunday Affair*, where he would give away Champagne and roses to couples who wrote in with their romantic stories. It was an extremely successful format which ran for years and Michael wanted to replicate this at Classic FM, changing its name to *Classic Romance*.

He'd wanted Tom Conti to present, but Tom hadn't been available. He then asked Joanna Lumley, but she didn't want to do it. With a week to go to opening he still hadn't found anyone,

The co-founders of Classic FM, Ralph Bernard (left) and Michael Bukht (right)

Left to right: me with my producer Amanda Lewis, and Robert, who proposed to Kate, live on-air, 1994

In fancy dress for a publicity shot, men left to right: me (as Fletcher Christian), Mark Griffiths, Henry Kelly, Jamie Crick and Allan Mann; ladies, clockwise from the top: Margaret Howard, Jane Jones and Susannah Simons

so at the last moment he asked if I could hold the fort until they did. It was the last thing I wanted – presenting breakfast was more than enough – but I agreed. Apart from anything else it put me in the station's good books. I used the breakfast show to ask for romantic memories, and by the end of the week I had more than enough to put a programme together. I actually felt more confident doing this programme than breakfast, partly because it had a set format, but also because I was acting as a stopgap and didn't feel under too much pressure. It was maybe a bit rough around the edges but I enjoyed it. More importantly, Michael and his wife Jenny liked it and were heartened by the response – they'd thought we'd have to invent the letters to get the show started. After that first programme Michael said I had to do it for only a few weeks, as Nigel Havers was lined up to take over at the end of October. But after the second *Classic Romance* aired Michael said he wanted me to do it full-time.

Audience response

At 7.30am every morning it was *Bailey's Breakfast Bonanza*, a competition with big prizes including luxurious trips abroad. There was no email or texting then, so listeners sent in their answers on a postcard. Each day there was a postbag of more than 3,000. For Michael and me it was like Christmas every day and I remember him saying 'How does it feel to be a success?' People also wrote in for *Classic Romance*. There's something so much nicer in receiving a handwritten letter, or indeed a card. When some years later everything went online, some of that magic undoubtedly disappeared.

Across the waves

No one in the industry had expected Classic FM to do well: a national pop station, yes, but classical music? Our managing director was John Spearman, whose background was advertising. He'd been hoping for an audience of 3 million when the first set of figures were released; it had to be at least 2.75 million, or the advertisers had been promised their money back. But the newly introduced RAJAR (Radio Joint Audience Research) figures were released after the first three months of Classic FM being on-air, and showed that we had achieved 4.3 million listeners. This was double Radio 3 and more than the original Radio 5. We were already the fourth-largest station in the country.

A closer look at the figures gave us a clearer picture of our audience. Paul and I had almost a million each on Saturday and Sunday mornings, but weekday breakfast, although decent, was disappointing. Traditionally breakfast is the biggest show on any radio station, but what emerged was that Henry Kelly, on-air between 9am and 12am, had the biggest weekday audience. It seemed that the Radio 4 listeners were sticking with their news programmes – *Today*, *World at One* and *PM* – and switching over to us when they'd had their fill.

The press were behind us with pictures of Henry and myself in most of the papers, and a highly favourable editorial in *The Times*. This gave us more pulling power in attracting advertisers, and some agencies started making ads tailored to our brand. *Classic Romance* picked up the sponsorship of Black Magic, a fading brand of chocolates that for years I had given my Nanny for her birthday until I found out she didn't like them at all. The programme revived the brand's fortunes, and we had no shortage of offers of luxury weekends away for the winning letter.

Classic FM

In a speech following the figures, a jubilant John Spearman lauded all the presenters for their intelligent irreverence. By now we had the correct tone and, thanks to Tony Scotland, our pronunciations were right most of the time.

Pronunciation lunch

To coincide with the Wednesday meetings, Sarah Lucas would come in early to go through her weekend programmes with Tony. A group of us would then go for a bite to eat at what would become known as the 'Pronunciation Lunch'. Sarah, Tony, Petroc and myself would be joined by Madeleine Kasket, a doyenne of the record industry employed by Michael for her contacts. She'd been a member of the team at RCA who had launched 'The Man with the Golden Flute', James Galway, into his recording career, following his departure from the Berlin Philharmonic. She appeared to know every living artist, and a simple call from Madeleine would guarantee whatever interview we wanted.

Our venue was the Goodfare in Camden Town, a greasy spoon serving very cheap food at lightning speed. The lunches were jolly affairs, but the pronunciations went by the board.

The café attracted an interesting clientele. At breakfast every day the chain-smoking author Beryl Bainbridge would sit opposite a man with an effete voice. For a long time I thought this was the art critic Brian Sewell, until I realised it was her Camden neighbour and fellow writer A. N. Wilson. They would have the Full English, and as I was usually at the next table I could overhear their conversation, which ranged from tax to plumbing: not a whiff of literature would pass their lips. Alan

Bennett, who lived around the corner, never actually came in but was often seen wheeling his bike past the café window with a pannier full of groceries. Rumour had it that Bob Dylan once popped in, albeit just to ask for directions to Crouch End.

The pronunciation lunch eventually moved to the Engineer, a gastropub run by Tamsin Olivier, daughter of Sir Laurence, but I remained loyal to the Goodfare, which became a second home. It was where I would prepare my *Classic Romance* programme. I've always felt I do my best thinking in cafés, where I can work anonymously but observe other people. I spent so much time there I gave Anne the telephone number in case of emergency – just as well because, when Anne broke her leg tobogganing on Hampstead Heath, my eldest daughter knew where to reach me.

I still go there – my dentist is in the same street so I treat myself to a full English after I've seen my hygienist. I wasn't there on the day when David Cameron had lunch with Mary Portas, but there's a picture proudly displayed on the wall – surely the Goodfare should have a blue plaque or two?

A Song of Summer

Back in Moree I'd watched a programme that has stayed with me ever since: Ken Russell's *Song of Summer,* about the final six years of the composer Frederick Delius's life, when he was blind and paralysed, and Eric Fenby had lived with the composer as his amanuensis. I'd been a fan of Delius ever since, though I never thought I'd meet anyone associated with the programme. But just after Classic FM opened Ken Russell came in for an interview on *Classic Reports*. Before leaving he left a short note on Michael's

Classic FM

desk that said 'Dear Michael, have you thought of having a film programme? I know something about film myself – Ken Russell.' Ken was soon hired, and I took the opportunity to tell him how much *Song of Summer* had influenced me. He responded with an appreciative grunt.

I got a chance to meet Christopher Gable, the actor who had played Fenby, at a listener's evening in Sheffield, which he hosted in his capacity as artistic director of Northern Ballet Theatre. I told him how his performance had made such a lasting impression on me, and he graciously returned the compliment by saying how much he enjoyed listening to me.

And I also got to meet Humphrey Burton, the man who had commissioned the programme in his capacity as the BBC's Head of Music and Arts. He had also produced Ken Russell's earlier portrayal of Elgar. Humphrey became a regular stand-in presenter on Classic FM, taking over when Henry Kelly went on holiday. But he blotted his copybook when talking about Matthew Bourne's all-male ballet production of *Swan Lake*. It was a paid-for plug that was to be read live, and while ad-libbing around the supplied copy Humphrey said he'd seen the performance and, although he'd been expecting to see 'a load of poofs', he thought they weren't camp at all. Michael immediately sent him a warning letter, and although Humphrey was allowed to complete his stint it was some time before he was asked back.

In the meantime Barry Took became Henry's stand-in. The programme had a regular cooking spot halfway through where Michael revived his 'crafty cook' persona under his Michael Barry pseudonym. On Barry Took's first day Michael popped in as usual just before 10.30am and Barry told him, 'There's a good joke coming up.' Michael replied, 'About time, too – you haven't said anything funny so far!' Barry was one of my heroes – *Round the Horne*, which he co-wrote with Marty Feldman, had been one of my favourite programmes. We became friends, cemented by the fact he and I were both members of Lord's and would watch the cricket together.

Sony Awards

The Sony Radio Awards, which had started in 1983, were the Oscars of the radio industry. With our arrival as a new kid on the block in 1993 a couple of extra categories were introduced – National Station of the Year and Best Breakfast Show: Non-contemporary Music. Because Classic FM had made such an impact, these were obviously designed specifically for us and we won both awards. Michael Aspel read out my name as the winner of the breakfast award, which was given to me by my former BFBS colleague Sarah Kennedy, who had just started presenting the early breakfast show on Radio 2. I ended my acceptance speech with Michael Bukht's mantra 'Smile, segue, and shut up.' Michael Aspel, who had worked with Michael at Capital, said he remembered the very same instructions.

For Classic FM, the awards capped off a stunning six months. According to one of the station's founders, Ralph Bernard, it was the most successful media launch in twenty years. The ratings were far higher than anyone could have hoped for and now we were receiving accolades from our peers in the radio industry. It certainly gave me a lot of confidence, and as Michael said on one of his Bukht phone interruptions, 'Winning awards suits you.'

Classic FM

Proposal on-air

One of the first letters I read out on *Classic Romance* was from Kate Harwood, a young widow. She'd always wanted to go to Verona with her late husband to see an opera production in its famous amphitheatre, but he'd died before that could happen. A male listener, Robert Harvey, was so moved by her story that he wrote a letter to me asking if it could be passed on to Kate. Fast-forward to 1994 and Robert wrote to me again saying that he and Kate had met up, and the romance was going so well that he wanted to make it permanent. He suggested they both came down to Classic FM, where he could propose to her on-air. That's what happened, and luckily Kate accepted. That programme received a Sony Silver at the 1995 awards.

Stormy seas

My time at Classic FM spanned twenty-five years and it would be fair to say it wasn't all plain sailing. As with most people, life had its ups and downs, both at work and on the personal front. My mother died just over a year after Classic FM went on-air and my father's health continued to decline until he died six years later. Also during this time my marriage was put under strain and sadly Anne and I broke up in 2000. But there were happy times, too, particularly the reconnection with Frances and my eldest daughter's marriage, and in more recent times the birth of my two grandchildren, Benjamin and Emilie.

Pat's final illness

By 1993 my mother had largely been confined to her bed with her ongoing bronchial problems. It required a superhuman effort on her part to go to see my father in *Trelawny of the 'Wells'* at the National Theatre in February that year. The previous Christmas, my mother had struggled up the three flights of stairs to our flat in Maida Vale, but now it was an effort to come downstairs at home, even with a stairlift.

In August, with her situation getting worse, she had a few weeks in the Royal Brompton Hospital. I visited her several times and she seemed quite cheerful, particularly on the day she found out that my brother Simon and his partner Diana were expecting a baby. She came home in early September and on the phone she seemed okay, but soon after that she started to have hallucinations caused by not enough oxygen reaching her brain. Though she'd had an oxygen machine in the house for some time, eventually even this wasn't enough. At one stage, she thought she'd been kidnapped by the Palestine Liberation Organization and was sharing a cupboard with Yasser Arafat.

The last time I saw her at home was on her birthday, the 22nd of September 1993, when she turned seventy-two. She was obviously in a bad way, but she had a neighbour helping out and said my visit had really cheered her up. My father was busy rehearsing at the National for David Hare's *The Absence of War*, but my mother said how marvellous he'd been in helping her. She wouldn't have wanted for one moment for him to pull out of the production.

It wasn't long after that she was rushed to hospital. She'd survived so many scares that we all thought she'd pull through again, and the nurses said they would try a procedure that night that might improve the situation.

When we arrived in the morning we were told there was nothing they could do, but even then I thought she'd hang on for some time. We took it in turns to hold a vigil by her bedside and we started to look for a hospice. I was with her during the day and chatted on and off, but I wished I'd said more. As she was going to sleep I said goodbye, which she acknowledged, and then my youngest brother, Justin, came to take over. He phoned a couple of hours later to say Mum was snoring away and having a lovely sleep. But then just before midnight he phoned again to say she wasn't going to last the night. I phoned my father and my other brother, Simon, in Oxford, and then called a taxi.

But I was just too late, as was my father who arrived soon after. In death my mother looked beautiful and totally at peace. The hospital had given her morphine to help her sleep and she'd just drifted away: it was the best thing that could have happened. We both kissed her on the forehead and my father remarked that it was probably the first decent sleep she'd had in years. Simon and Diana arrived about half an hour later. The date was the 2nd of October 1993, and the first night of *The Absence of War* was that evening. How Pat would have loved the irony that in her final act she was upstaging her husband.

The 2nd of October was a Saturday and my father's first night went well. I presented *Classic Romance* on the Sunday, but then took the following week off and stayed in Wandsworth, which coincided with my father's seventy-fourth birthday on the Tuesday. Not that it was much of a celebration: Robin realised by now he couldn't carry on and took a leave of absence from the National. Along with the feelings of grief and guilt, he was physically suffering too. Up until now he'd been at the top of his game; a leading man at the National Theatre, numerous TV appearances, and dozens of voice-overs. Now he started to take on the symptoms of my mother: breathing became difficult and he felt pain in his spine. But most noticeable was his gradual change in personality. By the time of my mother's funeral he was being irascible and rude, but for the time being we put this down to the shock of her death.

Stormy seas

Pat had chosen music for her funeral from what she'd heard me play on Classic FM, including the adagio from Mozart's *Serenade* and Vivaldi's Guitar Concerto, and I delivered the address. Because of the fragile state of my father, there was no wake except for close family. I felt this was a great shame, as it would have been a chance to share stories with her many friends and celebrate a wonderful lady who had lived life to the full, despite being dogged by illness from childhood.

Aftershock

Soon my father felt he could go back to the National, by which time *The Absence of War* was temporarily out of the repertoire, but as a member of the regular company he still wanted to turn up for 'work'. But I started to get calls at Classic FM from both the director of the National Theatre, Richard Eyre, and the executive director, Genista McIntosh (now the Labour politician Baroness McIntosh). They were worried about his behaviour, including the occasion when he attempted to buy the entire contents of the National Theatre bookshop. Luckily the manager suspected something was wrong and said they couldn't take that amount of money from his card, but then my father flew into a rage.

It seemed obvious that this was a recurrence of his manic depression, something he'd managed to keep at bay for twenty years. For the sake of his dignity, I tried to avoid admitting this to the management at the National, but they had already had strong suspicions, especially after Richard received a presumptuous letter suggesting he put on a 'one-man show' featuring my father's life. I suspect his agent, Michael Whitehall (father of the comedian

Jack Whitehall), also knew. Michael phoned one day to say my father had come to dinner the previous night and had been extremely rude. This was becoming a pattern: on a previous occasion he'd been to the house of an actor friend and had told his wife she was a third-rate actress.

Following a trip to Oxford, he went through his lines with John Thaw with a view to returning to *The Absence of War*. It was a disaster. He 'dried' on his first night back, something that had never happened before, no matter how manic he'd been.

He would never appear on stage again. He continued his other work until his agent phoned to say Robin hadn't turned up for a shoot of *Sherlock Holmes* with Jeremy Brett, another sufferer of manic depression. I immediately phoned home and spoke to Barbara, his Italian lodger. She'd been out the night before to some do with Robin, and said he was still in bed. Despite his manic state it was most unusual for him to miss work, so I took a taxi to Wandsworth and found him in his bed and unable to move, but he was able to speak. He insisted on going to a private hospital where he'd been having treatment, and with great difficulty I managed to get him into a taxi. On arrival it was discovered he had pneumonia. He was rushed into intensive care where he almost died, but he eventually pulled through, by which time the manic phase was over.

Axed from breakfast

At the beginning of 1996 I sensed there was something wrong. Apart from the first frenetic few months when Classic FM opened I'd been largely left to my own devices at breakfast, but now my

Stormy seas

producer Jane Jones was coming down on me heavily and I suspected this must have come from Michael Bukht. Just after Christmas I'd slipped on the ice at home whilst putting the rubbish out and broken my left shoulder, which I knew could lead to permanent damage because it was my polio arm. I haven't been able to raise my left arm since. I took a week off and Mike Read, who'd already stood in for Henry Kelly, stood in for me too.

As soon as I came back towards the end of January there was an outside broadcast in Norway, from Grieg's house in Bergen, and I sat in the room where he composed many of his famous works. On my return there was a change of producer, with Tim Lihoreau stepping in. He was full of ideas and enthusiasm, but in March I was called into the boardroom and told that I was coming off breakfast and that Mike Read was taking over. To soften the blow I was told that *Classic Romance* had been awarded Radio Programme of the Year from the Television and Radio Industries Club. I found out later that Michael thought the only way they could improve ratings at breakfast was to have a big name. I was lucky in that I'd just signed a two-year contract, so at least I had work until 1998, but what would happen after that? In the meantime I would still present *Classic Romance* and fill in at other times.

Saturday Soapbox

It seemed odd that I was still presenting the top-rated programme on the station on Sunday and yet relegated to the second eleven during the week. Michael gave me a new programme on Saturday afternoons, which he wanted as a phone-in to discuss the musical

issues of the day. We called it *Saturday Soapbox*. I was assigned
Rob Weinberg as my producer and we had great fun doing it,
with no shortage of calls. Larry Adler was a regular. I also
introduced *Radio Roulette*.

It was a great ratings success and things were going along nicely
until the record company Naxos threatened to sue me and the
station. Naxos was famous for its classical repertoire at knock-
down prices. None of their CDs was more than £5 and they used
mostly Eastern European musicians whom nobody had ever
heard of, and yet the quality was high. The wife of a musician
who'd recorded for Naxos phoned one Saturday to say the
musicians hardly got paid anything and that's why they could sell
so cheaply. But instead of giving Naxos the right to reply I just
carried on. Michael was adamant that I issue an apology the next
week, but I think he was secretly pleased as it stirred things up
and it couldn't have done the ratings any harm.

Classic Countdown

After *Classic Romance*, the second-biggest programme on the
station was Paul Gambaccini's *Classic Countdown*, which went out
on Saturday mornings and counted down the best selling classical
records of the week. But after three years Paul was poached by
BBC Radio 3 to present their morning programme.

This in itself was a big media story, but Michael was a genius at
publicity. He'd already persuaded the entire *Gardeners' Question
Time* team from Radio 4 to defect to Classic FM following a
dispute with their contracts. This time he poached one of the
biggest presenters of his day, Richard Baker, to host the chart

Stormy seas

show. Giant billboards around the country announced: 'Richard Baker joins new wave band.' Richard had fronted the *Last Night of the Proms* on television and for seventeen years had been the host of *Start the Week* on Radio 4. But *Classic Countdown* never really suited Richard: by his own admission he was outside his comfort zone as a classical DJ and felt like a 'dowager in a miniskirt'. At the beginning of 1997 he replaced John Julius Norwich on *The Evening Concert*, and Michael asked me to take over the countdown: 'If they like you on Sunday morning, they'll like you on Saturday morning too,' he said. This meant I was now presenting the two most popular programmes on the station.

The great thing about *Classic Countdown* was that it was self-produced, which meant I had total freedom. I set to work building my weekly show based on the official classical chart. As it was an album chart there were lots of tracks to choose from, and there were plenty of opportunities to introduce new releases.

As soon as word got out that I was the new presenter I had all the record companies inviting me to lunch, including Naxos, at which we joked about the 'suing' episode. Of course they were all trying to push their product, but it was useful input.

One company, BMG, said it had a CD called *Stanze* that was creating quite a stir in their office. It was an album of electric harp music played by Cecilia Chailly, the sister of the conductor Riccardo Chailly, and was written by someone I'd never heard of, Ludovico Einaudi. *Stanze* didn't resonate with me, but Einaudi's next album, *Le Onde*, based on the novel *The Waves* by Virginia Woolf, certainly did. I was the first person to air this on British radio, and it had an immediate impact. Its success led Classic FM to schedule many of the tracks and his follow-up albums *Eden*

Composer
Ludovico
Einaudi

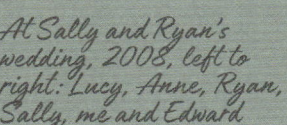

At Sally and Ryan's
wedding, 2008, left to
right: Lucy, Anne, Ryan,
Sally, me and Edward

My grandchildren,
Benjamin (left)
and Emilie (right)

Roc and *I Giorni* were equally successful. I had no idea how to pronounce Einaudi's name so I had a stab with 'eye-now-dee', and that pronunciation stuck, although it took some time to sink in – people would phone the station and say they wanted to hear the 'composer that Nick Bailey likes'. It was only years later when Einaudi made his first appearance in the UK that I realised my mistake: it should be '*ay*-now-dee'. But Einaudi has made his peace with the English pronunciation as I established it.

For years I tried to get him over to the UK, but there were so many excuses, from he didn't want to travel to his English not being good enough. Eventually he did come in the autumn of 2002, and his first concert was a modest affair in a small church hall in the Headingley district of Leeds. I introduced it and it was recorded by Classic FM for broadcast on *The Evening Concert*, a programme I'd just taken over. I also interviewed him. Certainly his English wasn't very good, but he came across as a lovely, unassuming man and over subsequent meetings we became good friends. Just before I left Classic FM he recorded a video to thank me for introducing his music to the UK, and his new record company Decca gave me a framed picture of many of his albums. One album in particular has a sentimental attachment. My eldest daughter, Sally, chose the title track from *I Giorni* for me to walk her down the aisle at her wedding to Ryan in 2008.

The end of an era

Halfway through 1997 Michael collapsed and woke up in hospital, where he was diagnosed with Ménière's disease, an incurable inner-ear complaint triggered by stress. He had an incredible work schedule, alongside his appearances on *Food and Drink*, plus constant pressure from the board to get more listeners. By his own admission it had all become too much, and he had no choice but to resign. For all that he was difficult and a bully I found him to be incredibly fair, and he genuinely looked upon Classic FM as his family. He certainly inspired loyalty and he would back any member of staff in return. By sheer determination he'd launched Classic FM against the odds, and thoroughly deserved his OBE. I'd miss his expressions and quirks – the cracking of walnuts with his bare hands, and his ritual of washing his feet in the gent's on Fridays prior to his visit to the Regent's Park mosque. As a final flourish he hired Kenwood House in Hampstead as the venue for his farewell party, where there were fulsome speeches and genuine tears on the night. Michael certainly went out in style.

New broom

Classic FM's parent company GWR now took control, with the chief executive Ralph Bernard taking a more active part. As an interim measure GWR's group programme director Steve Orchard stepped in as programme controller and set about changing the schedules, with effect from January 1998.

Successful as Michael had been, the listening figures had remained stuck just below the 5 million mark and it was Steve's aim to hit that psychological target. He made many changes and most have remained to this day. Considering his background was rock music, he made some very astute decisions. The radio market was now getting very competitive, and he realised we

Stormy seas

needed to capitalise on our core strength, classical music. Apart from news, speech had to go. Instead of Susannah's interviews between 12am and 2pm it would now be lunchtime requests with Jane Jones. *Classic Reports* would be replaced by a sharper half-hour news programme presented by John Brunning, who like me had been on-air since day one, but in his case as a newsreader. He would also host a new show called *Smooth Classics at Seven* with two hours of relaxing music between 7pm and 9pm. As a cost-cutting measure Richard Baker would go, to be replaced by Nicholas Tresilian, the original chairman of GWR and a classical buff. The former politician David Mellor was brought in, as was Simon Bates to present a film programme. And Paul Gambaccini was brought back to host *Classic Countdown*.

So where did that leave me? Steve wanted me back on breakfast but for only two hours between 6am and 8am. He wanted it as a counter-balance to the *Today* programme, so we named it *Easier Breakfast*. Henry's show would run for four hours between 8am and 12am. My producer for *Classic Romance*, Amanda Lewis, was laid off and I was paid extra to produce the programme myself. Steve's changes were effective: the station's audience figures finally broke through the 5 million barrier for the first time.

New boss

Early in 1998 it was announced that Roger Lewis, former head of music at Radio 1 and currently worldwide president of Decca, would be joining Classic FM as both managing director and programme controller. Roger made no immediate changes, but I was suspicious about his plans for *Classic Romance*, which was now sponsored by Eurostar. He took me for breakfast at Claridge's and asked pointed questions, saying there was no hidden agenda, but I wasn't convinced.

I continued with *Classic Romance* until the end of 1999 when Simon Bates took over. Much as I admire Simon as a broadcaster, he didn't get much response and the programme was kept going with letters I'd received, and it wasn't long before it died completely. Roger, who had produced Simon at Radio 1, had wanted to get Simon on-air at any cost. I don't understand commercial radio's obsession with wanting to change things when you have a successful format. The programme had still been top of the ratings and by Steve Wright's own admission in an interview in the *Radio Times* it was one of the reasons Radio 2 had introduced *Sunday Love Songs*, a programme that is still on-air twenty years later. I was sorry to give up the programme – I loved producing it as much as presenting it because the letters I received were such a wonderful snapshot of social history.

I soon had replacement shows. I presented a once-weekly programme called the *Classic FM Magazine*, which was a radio version of the published magazine, one of the only speech outlets on the station. Then I was asked to present a programme between 2pm and 4pm called *Relaxing Classics at Two*. This was to capitalise on the success of *Smooth Classics at Seven*, but with the potential for a bigger audience. It would be minimalist in presentation and pre-recorded, with about four pieces in a row and then a long back announcement. Each programme took just twenty minutes to record, so I could do the whole week in under two hours. Although it was boring to do, it was an immediate success, with up to 2.5 million listeners a week.

Stormy seas

Death of Robin

Since my mother died, my father's health had steadily gone down hill. A smoker all his life, he'd developed emphysema, which gradually worsened. He'd also been diagnosed with osteoporosis, which had severely affected his spine and he'd lost height.

He continued to work, although not in the theatre. His last television appearance was the miniseries adaptation of Anthony Powell's *A Dance to the Music of Time*. The filming took place in 1997 and he appeared in three episodes. As he said to me, it wasn't a bad swansong. We all came to Wandsworth for his seventy-fifth birthday and afterwards he said to Barbara, his Italian lodger, how proud of us he was. He still went to the cricket and, as he was over seventy five and had been a member of Lord's for more than thirty years, he had the privilege of a reserved seat. The following year he treated the entire family to an evening in the Long Room at Lord's sponsored by Classic FM, where Julian Bream performed. He would occasionally take a river cruise with his friend and fellow actor Peter Sallis, but otherwise he would take it in turns to stay with each member of the family.

His last appearance anywhere was in a play on Radio 3 just a few months before he died. He was booked into St George's in Tooting for a routine hernia operation, but almost immediately picked up an infection and could hardly breathe. After well over a month of intensive care, during which we thought he could die at any time, he spent Christmas of 1998 at the hospital sitting up in bed enjoying a roast dinner with a glass of wine. He continued to get better and had booked himself into Denville Hall, the retirement home for actors, for a period of convalescence.

Then he had a relapse. The last words he spoke to me were about making sure I reserved a seat at Lord's for the following summer's Test series. The next morning I'd just come off-air when I had a call from the hospital saying he was in a coma and didn't have long to live. This time the entire family managed to get there and were with him when he died. He was seventy-nine.

I organised Robin's memorial service at St Paul's, the actors' church in Covent Garden, for a few month later. The most difficult thing was finding a date when all the speakers would be available, but in the end it all fell into place. An address was given by Richard Eyre, from the National Theatre, and Peter Ustinov, who flew in from Switzerland. Other speakers were the actors Peter Sallis and James Grout, and the playwright Simon Gray. In my address I talked about musical memories and introduced the comic poem that Robin had written called 'Poor Fish'. It bemoaned the fact that when it came to music these creatures were invariably left out, notwithstanding Schubert's *The Trout Quintet.* The poem was a very clever piece of writing and showed that my father had far more classical music knowledge than I'd ever thought. I commissioned the composer Paul Ayres to set it to music, and engaged a tenor to sing it. Here are a couple of stanzas:

> *All lizards, and not just iguana,*
> *Like Cavalleria Rusticana,*
> *Reptilian taste, though sometimes patchy,*
> *Includes, of course, I Pagliacci,*
> *But fish that through deep waters dart*
> *Can't comprehend the D'Oyly Carte.*

Stormy seas

The aardvark can, despite the heat,
Follow Solti's awesome beat;
And even irreligious bison
Cope with Kyrie e-lei-son,
But fish that through deep waters crawl
Will never play the Wigmore Hall.

The tenor then sang 'I've Grown Accustomed to Her Face' from *My Fair Lady* and the English folk song 'Foggy, Foggy Dew' which my father had sung for practice before we went to Australia. We left the church to the strains of the organ symphony by Saint-Saens, used as the theme to the film *Babe*, which Robin had recommended to all his grandchildren. After the service we all went to the Garrick Club, where he'd proudly been a member since the 1980s. It was a great send-off – it's just a shame no-one can witness their own memorial. He'd been a difficult father and hard to get to know but I had huge respect for him – a respect that has grown with the passing years.

Marriage break-up

With a small inheritance from my mother's estate, at the beginning of 1995 we had managed to move from the flat in Maida Vale to a house in West Hampstead. Just over a year later I was taken off breakfast and it became a financial struggle, and my subsequent depression put a strain on my marriage. I think Anne realised things weren't working, as she took the initiative to say perhaps we should separate. Bad as things were, I didn't want to do this, and in any case where would I go? It would mean selling the house. For a while we tried to keep things going, but the arguments continued and my depression grew worse. By the time I was put back on breakfast I think the damage had been done: I became distant, and always wanted to do things by myself. This was a trait I'd had since childhood, at its most obvious when I decided to travel back from Australia alone in 1972. Anne found this very hard to live with and sadly, in April 2000, we decided to go our separate ways.

With an inheritance from my father I bought a small studio flat in Hampstead, and I moved in there while Anne and the children stayed in the house in West Hampstead. It was a terrible time for all concerned. After a few months I tried for a reconciliation, but after thinking very carefully Anne really didn't feel it would work and we eventually divorced in 2003. It was a lonely time but I got very close to my son Edward, who would visit every Sunday. We would go swimming and play badminton at the Royal Free Hospital Recreation Club, followed by numerous board games at the flat.

Eighteen months or so after Anne and I separated, I met Marcie who worked at the Hampstead community centre, which was opposite where I lived. She ran a weekly food stall where I would buy flapjacks every Saturday. Her vivacity was an instant attraction, and over the weeks we got talking. Without knowing who I worked for she told me her favourite programme on the radio was *Relaxing Classics at Two*, which she listened to when she was cooking. We were together on and off for seven years and had some fun times, but the age gap of twenty-two years caused problems and eventually we broke up.

Stormy seas

The Evening Concert

In May 2001 *Easier Breakfast* was pushed back to an earlier time slot of 5am to 7am, and Henry's programme ran from 7am to 11am. The earlier time slot would cut my audience by half so I had to swallow my pride, but it was particularly galling given the breakfast show had just been nominated for a Sony. But I was still presenting *Relaxing Classics at Two* and *The Classic FM Magazine*. I'd also been hosting a weekly classical programme for BFBS called *The Bailey Collection* since 1998, and I was presenting an in-flight programme called *Classic Choice* for British Airways.

About a year after these schedule changes I was summoned to see Roger Lewis. He wanted me to take over *The Evening Concert* and to present it live, something that hadn't been done before. It was seen as the meatiest programme on the station and I'd be responsible for my own scripts.

Initially the concerts aired between 9pm and 11pm, but were extended to midnight, which I thought was a mistake. Would I want to be listening to a non-mainstream work at that time of night? I suspect not. Even so, the show got a very healthy audience, even bigger than *Easier Breakfast*.

Malcolm Arnold

One of my favourite films is *The Bridge on the River Kwai,* which won an Academy Award for its composer Sir Malcolm Arnold. Arnold's eightieth birthday was due to fall on the 21st of October 2001, and I suggested that Classic FM should mark the event and Roger Lewis agreed. My producer, Jamie Beesley, and I travelled to Norwich to spend the day with the composer and his carer. It was not going to be an easy task: Sir Malcolm had a reputation for being difficult, having been an alcoholic, a manic depressive, and was now showing signs of dementia. Radio 2 had previously attempted to make a programme, but had given up, following hours of trying to get him to say anything cogent. I knew I'd need a lot of patience, but we were greatly helped by Anthony Day, who'd been Sir Malcolm's carer for eighteen years. I managed to coax out the odd nugget, including the fact that his Academy Award was used as a 'lavatory doorstop', and his reason for not writing the music for *Lawrence of Arabia*: 'Too many camels.' Like many talented people he was a flawed genius, but that's what made him fascinating. Jamie spent weeks editing the hours of tape for two sixty-minute specials, interspersed with his best-known music. It paid off: we won a New York Award.

Duke of Edinburgh

In November 2001 Prince Philip visited the studios, which by now had moved from Camden Town to Oxford Circus. (The Queen had been scheduled to come, too, but pulled out at the last moment.) The Duke's arrival coincided with *Relaxing Classics at Two*, which was normally pre-recorded, but on this occasion I presented it live. He spent about half an hour in the studio with me and was exactly as you'd expect: sharp, brusque and didn't care what he said. I found his approach refreshing, and I think he liked my non-reverential attitude towards him.

Relaxing Classics had one long sequence of music that was used as a theme throughout, considered catchy by many, but it was

Stormy seas

perhaps irritating to some. While the music was playing I asked the Duke if he listened to the programme, to which he replied, 'Yes, when I'm a fugitive from Radio 4, but it's about time you changed that bloody jingle!'

He was later introduced to members of staff, including my producer Jamie. The Duke asked Jamie if he was a presenter and Jamie, who has a strong London accent, replied, 'No, I'm a producer.' 'I'm not surprised, with that voice!' remarked the Duke.

The visit was part of a media blitz by the royal couple, and that night Buckingham Palace was full of the glitterati from radio and television. I was hoping to meet the Queen, and although I hovered in all the right places I never got the royal introduction. Six months later I was at Buckingham Palace again, or at least the gardens, when I hosted the *Golden Jubilee Prom at the Palace* as a live broadcast for British forces worldwide.

A fateful dinner

Every month Roger Lewis treated the main presenters to dinner at the Gay Hussar in Soho. It was mostly a social gathering, but also an opportunity to throw around new ideas in an informal atmosphere. Among the people joining Roger on this occasion were Henry Kelly, Jane Jones, Jamie Crick, Katie Derham, Darren Henley (Roger's deputy) and me.

The evening started off well enough, but as the drink flowed Henry became abusive to Roger. I'd seen this side of Henry's character before at the station meetings. He could be very confrontational with Michael, and it got worse when Steve Orchard took over: on one occasion the meeting ended in a

At home with Sir Malcolm Arnold (left) and his carer Anthony Day (right), 2001

The Duke of Edinburgh visits Classic FM, 2001

At Buckingham Palace for the Golden Jubilee Prom, 2002

shouting match. But this was different – it was almost as if Henry was in self-destruct mode. Roger did his best to hold everything together, but the evening ended awkwardly.

It always amazed me that this aspect of Henry's personality never affected his on-air performance. Next morning he was as professional and witty as ever. But within the week he was called into Roger's office. As he came out he said to me, 'I've been handed a yellow card.' It seemed the writing was on the wall: his contract wasn't renewed the following June, and Simon Bates took over. I suspect Roger had wanted Simon Bates on the show for some time, going back to when Simon took over *Classic Romance*, but Henry's behaviour gave Roger the excuse he needed. It was nothing to do with ratings, as the station had reached an all-time high of 6.8 million listeners a week, a figure never to be surpassed. Henry had been central to Classic's success, and we all missed him when he left in 2002.

A change of boss

In 2004 Roger Lewis suddenly resigned his position as head of Classic FM to join ITV Wales as managing director. This was announced hours after GWR and Capital Radio agreed a merger worth more than £700 million. Roger had been in talks with ITV for several months, but had been unable to announce the move because of the proposed merger. Darren Henley would take over as station manager.

I first met Darren in 1992 when he was a nineteen-year-old student at Hull University studying politics. During that time, he used to come to Classic FM at weekends to read the overnight news, where he would sleep on the sofa in the managing director's office. But his ambitions weren't in presentation – as he said to me once, he wanted to be an editor. He rapidly rose through the ranks and became managing editor in 2000. He had two years as station manager before being appointed managing director in 2006. (He subsequently undertook an independent review of the funding and delivery of music education in England that became known as the Henley Report, and for this he was awarded an OBE in 2013; in 2015 he took over as chief executive of Arts Council England.) Darren was very influential in my career. He had given me *The Classic FM Magazine* programme after I'd told him that my favourite part of radio was interviewing, and subsequently gave me *Relaxing Classics at Two*. It was through Darren that I was chosen to host my first Music Festival at Sea, a role that continues to the present day. But even when he was my boss I still looked upon him as that nineteen-year-old university student with a wicked sense of humour.

Stormy seas

On my travels again

Although Classic FM was firmly rooted in London, there were still plenty of opportunities for me to see new places. In my years with the station I managed to travel all over the world, whether it be for an outside broadcast, hosting a music cruise or trekking for the Classic FM charity. I reported from Vietnam and Senegal for World Vision, attempted to climb Mount Kilimanjaro and even walked through the Channel Tunnel. And as I write this my wanderlust remains undiminished.

Back to Hong Kong

When we left Hong Kong, RTHK had given us return tickets, valid for a year, even though they knew we weren't coming back. Maybe it was cheaper for them to do it that way. I couldn't resist using the ticket even though we would have to pay for the flight back. It was made more attractive by the fact that I'd taken out what was known as absent life membership from the United Services Recreation Club. For a one-off fee, the family could use the club when visiting, but more importantly we could stay there at a very cheap rate.

My initial contract allowed for four weeks' leave and I asked to take three. Chris Vezey was worried on my behalf: my stand-ins on breakfast and the Sunday programme might diminish my audience, or attract a bigger one. I can't remember who did breakfast, but Jane Asher took over *Classic Romance*. I'd been an admirer of hers for years going back to the film *The Greengage Summer* and her later appearances in *Brideshead Revisited*, and of course I'd followed her time as the girlfriend of Paul McCartney. But what really tickled me was hearing her first link, which said, 'Hello this is Jane Asher standing in for Nick Bailey.'

In Hong Kong we caught up with Fe, and Man Yee organised a lunch for me at the Hong Kong Club, asking me to invite who I wanted. Although it was good to visit I think we all felt we'd moved on, except maybe for Sally, who still missed the place.

Though I was no longer broadcasting in the territory, in 1997 I was asked by the Hong Kong Society to host the UK coverage of the handover of Hong Kong to China. The ceremony would be shown on giant screens at Sandown Park. I was also asked to send a report to RTHK. With the lowering of the Union Jack for the final time on Britain's last important colony, it really did seem like the end of the British Empire, an empire that had totally declined in my lifetime. From the partition of India in 1947, the year I was born, to this point was a period of only fifty years.

Le Walk

Fairly soon after I started work at Classic FM, I got a call from one of my old neighbours in Hong Kong, an ex-army man who was now back in the UK and working for SSAFA, the Soldiers,

On my travels again

Sailors, Airmen and Families Association. He wanted me to volunteer for Le Walk, a charity event whereby I would need to walk the full length of the Channel Tunnel. It was set for Saturday the 12th of February 1994, three months before the Channel Tunnel officially opened for train travel on the 6th of May.

I would join more than a hundred others on the 31-mile walk, leaving from Calais at 9am on Saturday and emerging at the other end in Folkestone at 9pm, in time for a live appearance on the BBC evening news. Michael Bukht loved the idea, and decided my breakfast show should be broadcast from Calais the day before. I immediately went into training, walking from the flat in Maida Vale to my father's place in Wandsworth, and on to Richmond. There was a photo shoot for *Radio Times* that showed me in training with the Coldstream Guards.

The broadcast from Calais went well and that night the hotel was packed with all 118 participants, including some of the cast from '*Allo 'Allo!*, the cricketer Graham Gooch, actors Nigel Havers and Jenny Seagrove, and the BBC correspondent Nicholas Witchell.

The route was along the service tunnel with nothing to see except concrete, but it was wonderful to chat for a part of the way with one of my cricketing heroes, Graham Gooch. The tunnel runs for 23 miles under the sea, with a further 8 miles to go on land. Up to the 23-mile mark I'd had no problems, but suddenly I felt like I was walking uphill, even though the elevation wasn't noticeable to the naked eye. Several people had severe blisters and there was one asthma attack, but a doctor was with us along with a team of physiotherapists. I got to the end point about 8pm and was promptly given an aluminium blanket and asked to join

From left to right: back row, Steve Wright, Terry Wogan, Andrew McGregor, James Naughtie and Jane Glover; second row, Russ and Jono (Russ Williams and Jonathan Coleman), me; bottom row, a presenter from the local BBC station and Les Ross from BRMB

Walking through the Channel Tunnel with one of the physiotherapists

About halfway up Mount Kilimanjaro with my two guides

those who'd already arrived in a special seating area, to wait for everyone behind me to catch up. At 9pm we were all to emerge from the tunnel as if bursting out of a cake.

When it was time to make our appearance I could hardly stand: my body had totally seized up. We were all to collect a medal from Richard Branson, and I just about managed to negotiate the two steps of the dais and shake hands before collapsing in the physio tent for a much-needed massage. Anne and the children were waiting, and it was straight into a hot bath on arrival at the hotel. Usually I'd have been on-air the next day for *Classic Romance* but we were running a Valentine's Day special that had been pre-recorded in Vienna the previous weekend, although we pretended it was live. This must have confused the audience: they'd have heard me from Calais on Friday, seen me with the walkers on television on Saturday evening, and then miraculously heard me broadcasting from Vienna on Sunday morning!

Birmingham breakfast

Not long after Le Walk, on the initiative of the Radio Academy, it was decided to have a day where all the breakfast shows from the UK's national radio stations would broadcast from a single venue in Birmingham. The location was the Hyatt Regency which is connected to Symphony Hall. All five national networks from the BBC were there alongside Virgin Radio, Classic FM and the two local stations in the area, BRMB and BBC West Midlands. Following the broadcast we were all interviewed on stage by the radio critic Gillian Reynolds, followed by a group photo that still has pride of place on my wall.

Across the waves

QE2

My uncertain work situation was making me depressed, but there were things to look forward to. As part of an advertising campaign, Cunard had offered *Classic Romance* a fantastic prize of a transatlantic voyage aboard the *QE2* to New York. The deal also meant I could take myself and the entire family, in return for hosting the wind section of the London Mozart Players for a series of concerts on board. We would have a week in New York at our own expense and then Cunard would fly us back.

I'm lucky in that I don't get seasick, but the Atlantic crossing was so rough that the rest of the family each had an injection to tide them over for the journey. Edward, aged six, loved the freedom to explore the ship, while the girls enjoyed the spa. The view of the Statue of Liberty on entering New York harbour is one of the world's great sights, though queuing to go up it was a mistake: the five of us waited for five hours just to get a fleeting glimpse of the view from the top.

Kilimanjaro

One of the advantages of presenting the *Classic FM Magazine* was that I could offer myself as a travel reporter to the programme; and that's exactly what I did when I decided to climb Mount Kilimanjaro, which had always been an ambition. The upmarket adventure travel company Abercrombie & Kent were looking to raise their profile via the magazine, and having the programme's presenter attempting to climb Africa's highest mountain seemed to be a good fit.

On my travels again

I flew to Kilimanjaro in Tanzania, via Nairobi, and after a night in the Mount Meru Game Lodge I started the climb, accompanied by Julian from Abercrombie and Kent and a couple of guides who carried the equipment. To begin with it was a nice leisurely stroll, but it gradually got tougher and tougher and by the time we'd reached the top camp at 15,000 feet, four days later, I found I couldn't go any further because of the high altitude. The final ascent of another 4,000 feet was supposed to be that night, but I knew it would be dangerous to go on.

So I stayed in the tent while Julian completed the climb. The weather was unusual for the time of year: a blizzard raged all through the night, and when Julian returned, having successfully reached the top, he was suffering from frostbite and hallucinations, but at least he had made it. I had no regrets – it was the highest I've ever climbed, and an experience worth every step.

Teaching in Thailand

In late 2002 I had a call from BBC World Service asking whether I was willing to go to Bangkok to teach Thai broadcasters how to introduce classical music in English. I immediately said yes. It was part of a quid pro quo agreement the BBC had with the Thai government. In return for allowing the BBC to house one of its transmitters on their soil, the BBC would provide radio training courses. Usually these were journalistic, but on this occasion they'd been specific in their request. I had been recommended by Michael Harrison, my former colleague from RTHK who was now working for BBC World Service. The reigning monarch of Thailand was King Bhumibol, a renowned jazz and classical musician, as well as a composer and a great supporter of the arts. I suspect this was part of the reason for the proliferation of radio stations broadcasting Western classical music.

The lessons took place in the ministry of foreign affairs and I had a class of five: three classical broadcasters and, for some strange reason, a speech producer and a pop presenter. Maybe they were there to make up the numbers, but the pop presenter in particular excelled and taught the others how to be more relaxed in presentation. Whether it's pop, classical or speech, the same rules apply: being a good broadcaster depends on communication. It was a happy team and, as Thai is my favourite cuisine, I was in culinary heaven at the staff canteen.

World Vision

In 2005 Classic FM began an association with World Vision, a charitable Christian organisation working with children regardless of their faith in almost a hundred countries, aiming to improve their health and education. I was asked to go to Vietnam to report on their work, to coincide with the thirtieth anniversary of the end of the Vietnam War. Before going, I started sponsoring a seven-year-old girl, Kim Anh, and part of the trip would involve meeting her at her school. Vietnam was a country I'd always wanted to travel to and this would be an opportunity to visit parts of the country that most people wouldn't see. My report started in Hanoi at the Hilton hotel (known as the 'Hilton Opera' to differentiate it from the prisoner of war camp named 'the Hanoi Hilton' by the Americans). Four musicians played Dvořák's *American Quartet*, but I don't think they understood the irony. At

On my travels again

Kim Anh's school I was greeted with the French nursery rhyme 'Gentil Alouette' sung in Vietnamese, a legacy of Vietnam having been under French control. And of course I was keen to speak to Kim Anh, a lively girl who said she wanted to be a teacher. My reports won Classic FM another New York Award.

Two years later I was sent to Senegal on a similar assignment. This time we were taking a listener with us, on a trip labelled the 'journey of a lifetime'. This was no luxury holiday, but a chance to see the work of World Vision in remote villages. It also gave me the chance to visit the island of Gorée, 2 miles off the coast of Dakar. Although I'd been to the Slave Museum in Liverpool, standing at the Door of No Return in one of the countries where slaves were taken really brought home the horror of slavery to me. My guide likened it to the Holocaust but, whereas that had lasted twelve years, the slave trade had continued for 300. It was a poignant end to my trip to Senegal.

Music Festivals at Sea

Around this time I was picked to host a 'Music Festival at Sea' on board P&O's *Aurora*, in a joint venture between the company and Classic FM. The festivals had been run since 1984 by Stephannie Williams, built around Richard Baker as presenter. They had become so popular that there were up to seven music cruises a year. Richard was still hosting three a year, but as he approached his eightieth birthday he wanted to pull back slightly.

Stephannie wanted to tap in to the more popular approach of Classic FM and was hoping for a permanent partnership. My task was to interview the artists at the start of the cruise, introduce the

With Kim Anh in
Vietnam, 2005

At the Door of No Return,
Île de Gorée, Senegal, 2007

Classic FM listener Jo on her
'Journey of a Lifetime', on the
Gambian border, Senegal, 2007

concerts and recitals, host a quiz and have a 'desert island discs' session with the captain. I was also required to mingle with the passengers and generally incorporate them as part of the festival. I was very nervous at first, but grew more confident as the days went by. You need only one person in the audience to laugh at a joke – it's amazing what a boost that gives you. My experience on the *QE2* came in very handy, and one of the musicians from that cruise, clarinettist Angela Malmsbury, was also on this one and made me feel at home.

It was the perfect job for me, as it played to my various strengths of presentation and interviewing and yet there was no commuting. My food and accommodation were laid on, and I got paid, while at the same time travelling to sunny destinations in the Mediterranean. Stephannie had persuaded P&O to give up one of its suites for the host to occupy, so I was travelling in style, and it was November, a great time to get away from the UK.

The hoped-for partnership between Classic FM and P&O didn't come off, but I was subsequently hired by Stephannie in 2006 to host a cruise to the West Indies. My daughter Lucy accompanied me for the month-long journey, and we had a wonderful time together. On the strength of that cruise, Stephannie asked me to host another that summer, to the Baltic. I took my eldest daughter Sally, and she's had a love of pickled herrings ever since. One of the highlights was marvelling at the group of islands that greet you as you make the approach to Stockholm, some of them just big enough for a single house.

These cruises became a regular feature of my life for the next ten years, travelling as far away as Istanbul and Cairo, but I almost wasn't invited again following a trip to the Caribbean. I was ad-libbing on stage, trying to fill in time before the next act, when I remembered one of the musicians had said they'd been to Stingray City in Antigua, and had learned that stingrays have two penises. I mentioned this on stage and said in another life I'd like to come back as a stingray. Stephannie was appalled – audiences at these festivals tend to be of a certain age and from Middle England, and she had been sitting next to a rather strait-laced cruise director as I held forth about my hopes for reincarnation.

On my travels again

Frances

In January 2008 I received an email that would change my life. It was from Frances, my first girlfriend from forty years ago in Plymouth. She'd been living in Nottingham, happily married until she and her husband split up in 2006. She now wanted a fresh start in her home county of Cornwall and was moving to Looe to set up a bed-and-breakfast business, and had thought of me because it was in the West Country where we first met. What finally prompted her to get in touch was listening to me on the radio and hearing me play the 'Benedictus' from *The Armed Man* by Karl Jenkins. Frances is a Christian and when she heard this beautiful, moving piece of religious music she felt it was God telling her to contact me.

I was delighted to hear from her and we started corresponding. When we'd last seen each other she had been at teacher-training college in London, but obviously so much had changed since then and it occurred to me that we wouldn't necessarily have much in common. But as it turned out we had a lot of shared interests, in the arts particularly, and similar values. We wrote to each other for six months before meeting up, but when we did we got on straight away and we've been together ever since.

Across the waves

Frances has been a brilliant hostess on many music cruises and in the past two years she's also accompanied me when I've been giving talks on P&O world cruises, meaning she's had two consecutive birthdays in Sydney. She hit it off with my three children, as I have with her four. We permanently cemented our relationship at a lovely wedding on the 6th of August 2016 when we walked down the aisle to the 'Benedictus' from *The Armed Man*. It took place at Riverside Church in Looe with all families present.

Night of the long knives

Just a month after hearing from Frances I was told that I was coming off *The Evening Concert* and being put on overnights. This was thought of as the Siberia of radio, and if I'd had enough money I would have said thanks but no thanks. But the reality was different: I'd just bought a new flat and was helping to finance my children through university. *The Bailey Collection* was about to end at BFBS, and *Classic Choice* on British Airways had already stopped, following the 9/11 attacks. Apart from the cruises, Classic FM would be the only source of work I had.

Our parent company, GCap, was struggling to survive in a rapidly changing market. What was draining resources more than anything was the investment in digital radio. Rather like FM had been in its day, digital was seen as the radio of the future, but because of so many unresolved issues – few cars had digital radios, lack of coverage – the commercial digital stations weren't making any money. It was decided to pull the plug from all GCap's digital stations, but massive savings were still needed elsewhere. Mark Griffiths, who'd presented the overnights for fourteen years,

Frances

Frances and me celebrating our wedding at Looe harbour with our combined families, August 2016

was told one morning he wouldn't be coming back. *Classic Newsnight* was axed and John Brunning would replace me on *The Evening Concert*. Many staff had to re-apply for their posts and in the end a third were made redundant. At least I still had a job.

Trekking for charity

Prior to this upheaval I'd been chosen to trek the Great Wall of China in the early part of 2008 to raise money for the Classic FM Foundation. I'd always thought I was pretty fit, particularly as I'd done the Inca Trail in 2002 raising money for Action Research, but on the first practice walk my knees started to give – and we hadn't even got to the Great Wall.

On paper the wall had looked easy: no altitude, no awkward terrain, and no ups-and-downs. But I hadn't taken into account the watchtowers at over 40 feet high, with numerous steps to the top – and there was one of these every mile or so. We were in the middle of nowhere and driven to a different part of the wall each day and somehow I managed to get through it, and strangely I haven't had any problems since. The accommodation was basic, but despite the conditions the food was absolutely delicious.

Being a sucker for punishment I volunteered for the next Classic FM trek to Machu Picchu in 2009. It was seven years since I'd last done it, but this time I wanted to take Frances. She'd been used to camping and rock climbing, so was more than willing to give it a go. We flew to Cuzco, the old Inca capital, which at more than 11,000 feet is one of the highest cities in the world. We already noticed the effect on our breathing. The trek would take four days, including the infamous Dead Woman's Pass

Great Wall of China, 2008

Machu Picchu, 2009

*Music Festival at Sea
on board the Artemis, 2010*

at almost 14,000 feet. To combat altitude sickness we were advised to drink coca tea, made with the dried leaves of the coca plant, from which cocaine is derived, and is illegal in the United States. Whether it was the tea or sheer will power, we survived, although Frances said that climbing Dead Woman's Pass was harder than childbirth. We arrived at the Sun Gate overlooking Machu Picchu early in the morning of day four, and before us was one of the most outstanding archaeological sites in the world. For me it was just as spectacular the second time around.

The Pumpkin Club

At first the overnights were a real mishmash. Our schedule varied, with six hours Sunday into Monday (midnight to 6am) and then four hours for the rest of the week (2am to 6am), so it was hard for me, and the listeners, to get into any kind of routine. It was difficult to find any enthusiasm, and I was suffering from lack of sleep due to travelling down to Cornwall every weekend.

Frances eventually insisted that I come down only every second weekend, as I was spending most of our time together asleep. With renewed energy I put in more effort and asked listeners for a name for the programme. As the show was always on after midnight, *The Pumpkin Club* was chosen. After a year I started to really enjoy it, particularly as I was given free rein to engage with the audience by text, Twitter, email, Facebook or even letter. The show had a weekly audience of about 400,000 which covered all ages, from revising students to mature insomniacs, and correspondents ranging in age from thirteen to ninety-nine. The programme soon moved to a new time slot of 1am to 6am, which meant I could have fixed features starting with the *All-Nighter* for students between 1am and 2am, followed by the *Cradle Classic* for nursing mums for the next hour. When asking for suggestions for a name for this slot, someone came up with *The Milk Run*, which I thought was very clever but the managing editor, Sam Jackson, decided it was a little too descriptive! At 3am we had *The Classic FM Hall of Fame Three at Three,* which was later incorporated into Anne-Marie Minhall's show at 3pm. Between 4am and 5am there was the *Truckers' Tune* and a chance to have a glorious choral piece after 5am with the *Dawn Chorus.*

I once had a text saying we shouldn't ask truckers to take part as it lowered the tone, which totally missed the point of Classic FM. We were a station for everybody, and often a lifeline for many, including those who'd been bereaved, were depressed, couldn't sleep or were simply lonely. By 4am it was like a breakfast show for commuters wanting an early start. I had a group of milkmen who would regularly get in touch, but these eventually became less frequent – a sign of the times.

We had a large overseas audience, and in many areas it was peak listening, particularly in the US, Canada, Australia, Hong Kong and New Zealand, where Terry Waite was a regular listener whilst writing a book. Unfortunately these listeners were never incorporated in the ratings, but I was fascinated to find out where people were listening. They ranged from Lebanon to Vietnam, from Africa through to New Guinea and even the tiny island group of Kiribati. Once an American commercial pilot was listening as he was in the air, and he sent a picture from his cockpit to prove it. I had many regulars and, although I never met them, they became friends through the ether.

Frances

After four years I cut my presenting down to four days a week, and when Sam Pittis took over in 2016 he continued the same shift pattern. What started off as a programme I didn't want to do became a joy to present, and I was overwhelmed by the warm response I got when I announced I was leaving. Although I left *The Pumpkin Club* in May 2016, I continued to present daytime programmes until the twenty-fifth anniversary of the station on 7th September 2017.

As the first voice of the station, I was asked by Sam to read the news all morning on the birthday itself, for both Tim Lihoreau and John Suchet. My career had begun as a newsreader on Radio Caroline, so I finished where I started: a fitting end to what had been an incredible radio journey.

Thanks

The inspiration to write this book came from my eldest daughter, Sally, who wanted me to record my experiences before I became too old to remember them. I know my other two children, Lucy and Edward, will also be interested, but having introduced them to Alan Partridge many years ago I am sure they will notice that their dad has many similarities, and no doubt there will be endless teasing (a-ha!). If Sally provided the inspiration to start writing, my wife, Frances, gave me the impetus to complete my story with her constant encouragement. Her patience has been boundless, and now that I've finished the book she's looking forward to getting her husband back.

The book in published form certainly wouldn't have been possible without the help of Simon Daley, Creative Director at Otherwise, who spent months working with me, untangling my original manuscript and sorting through all my pictures to bring the book to life.

I'd like to thank many people who helped with vaguely remembered details, missing facts and pictures – but a special mention must go to my brother Simon, the family archivist and keeper of my parents' diaries.

In Australia I'm indebted to Murray Massey, formerly of 4AY; Allan Porter for providing photographs from our time in Townsville and Hong Kong; and to Megan Evans for recollections and photos of travelling on the *Fairstar* as a fellow £10 Pom. My old mate Norman ('Down here for dancing') helped to fill in some of the gaps in the time on board the migrant ship and in our early time at Wiley Park, and Ken Guy provided memories of 4BH Brisbane. In Denmark, my thanks to Frederik Christiansen, my old colleague from Grahame's Bookshop in Sydney. My main contacts for BFBS were Richard Astbury and my former secretary in Berlin, Jackie Scheuner. Richard provided photos from his Cologne days and reminded me of the perks we had in Berlin. Jackie explained the machinations of the Stasi in East Berlin and details of her friendship with an East German listener, Heidi Brauer. The BFBS archivist, Alan Grace, sent me the picture of Uncle Bill, and Chris Russell provided more information on Berlin.

For the chapter on Classic FM my appreciation goes to Michael Bukht's widow, Jenny; co-founder Ralph Bernard; and managing editor Sam Jackson. Also thanks to the former head of programmes Chris Vezey; to Petroc Trelawny for tracking down the first day's line-up; to two of my producers, Jamie Beesley and Rob Weinberg, for some lovely anecdotes; to Bob Jones for his painstaking work photographing my memorabilia; and to Humphrey Burton and the late Richard Baker for allowing me to quote them.

But above all, appreciation goes to my audience from all over the world during the past fifty years, whether it be the millions who tuned in to Classic FM or the few thousand at 2VM Moree. Thank you for listening!